P9-DFL-888

SUZY GERSHMAN

· · · · · · · · · · · · · · · · · ·

BORN TO

SHOP

PARIS

· · · · · · · · · · · · · · · · · ·

The Ultimate Guide for
Travelers Who Love to Shop

8th Edition

IDG Books Worldwide, Inc.
An International Data Group Company
Foster City, CA • Chicago, IL • Indianapolis, IN • New York, NY

For Judy, my sister-in-law, who lived and died in Paris, but has never been more alive to me than when we did this edition.

IDG Books Worldwide, Inc.
An International Data Group Company
919 E. Hillsdale Blvd. Suite 400
Foster City, CA 94404

ISBN 0-02-863141-2
ISSN 1066-2790

Editors: Alice Fellows and Nicole Daro
Production Editor: Jenaffer Brandt
Design by George J. McKeon
Staff Cartographers: John Decamillis and Roberta Stockwell

SPECIAL SALES
For general information on IDG Books Worldwide's books in the U.S., please call our Consumer Customer Service department at 800/762-2974. For reseller information, including discounts and premium sales, please call our Reseller Customer Service department at 800/434-3422.

Manufactured in the United States of America

5 4 3 2 1

CONTENTS

MAP LIST

ABOUT THE AUTHOR

Suzy Gershman is an author and a journalist who has worked in the fiber and fashion industry since 1969 in both New York and Los Angeles. She has held editorial positions at *California Apparel News, Mademoiselle, Gentleman's Quarterly,* and *People* magazine, where she was West Coast style editor. She writes regularly for various magazines, and her new essays on retailing are text for Harvard Business School. She frequently appears on network and local television; she is a contributing editor to *Travel Holiday.*

Mrs. Gershman lives in Connecticut with her husband, author Michael Gershman, and their son, Aaron. Michael Gershman also contributes to the *Born to Shop* pages.

For updates on Suzy's travels, tour information, or Born to Shop Bulletins from over 25 cities, go to www.born-to-shop.com.

TO START WITH

This is a brand-new edition of my Paris guide, not to be confused in any way with *Born to Shop France,* which covers the French countryside, the Riviera, Provence, and the whole ball of wax.

The beauty of this edition is not only that it's devoted solely to Paris but that it's on a different publication cycle than *Born to Shop France.* Because the two guides are revised in alternate years, it gives me an opportunity to revisit my French sources for each one, always ensuring that you get *le dernier cri,* or the last word, on shopping in France.

I spent much more time in Paris working on this revision because I also helped out my friends at Galeries Lafayette with a project. I am also learning how to speak French, and while my efforts are laughable at this stage, I hope this edition reflects my newfound Frenchness.

I owe a big round of thanks to my family at the Hôtel de Crillon; to Nicolas Ruyer, general manager of the Hôtel Concorde-St-Lazare, which is my home away from home when I'm not at the Crillon or the Hôtel Ambassador. (Hey, a girl has to get around.)

Thanks also to Sherry Newman Gabay, my girlfriend since I was 15, who has lived in Paris for 18 years and who went shopping with me. Thanks also to my French family, Gerard and Marie-Jo Bizien; and to Walter and Patricia Wells and Alexander Lobrano, my best American friends in Paris. Pascale-Agnès Renaud, who has been the Paris correspondent for *Born to Shop* since we started the series in 1984, continues to drive me places, teach me things, check my translations for errors, and teach me French. Her mother, Danielle, and her husband,

Thierry Sahler, are also part of the soul of this book; they are waiting for my French to improve, but still help out. In fact, some of the listings in this book come from them.

I thank all of the team and promise them lunch at Toastissimo—on me!

Chapter One

· · · · · · · ·

PARIS *VITE*

PARIS IS BEST

· ·

Ah Paris, *mon amour*—how I love to visit; how I love to shop! But how I loathe making this list. Putting the best of Paris into one list is an impossible task; it seems that every store I walk into is the best store in Paris. Just being in Paris, pressing your nose to the windows of the stores, is a best-of-show experience.

With that in mind, the selections presented here are really for people in an incredible hurry who have no time to stroll and shop leisurely. If you have more time, you owe yourself the luxury of checking out the finds described elsewhere in this book. But if you must hit and run, flashing your credit cards as you beat a hasty retreat, I hope these choices will be rewarding.

The Best Specialty Perfume Shop

SALONS SHISEIDO
*Jardins du Palais Royal, 142 Galerie de Valois,
1er (Métro: Palais-Royal).*

This tiny shop with high ceilings and royal purple decor is the showcase of makeup genius Serge Lutens, who used to create makeup for Christian Dior, but has been with Shiseido for decades now. His perfumes are also divine. Even if you buy nothing, just look

1

Paris

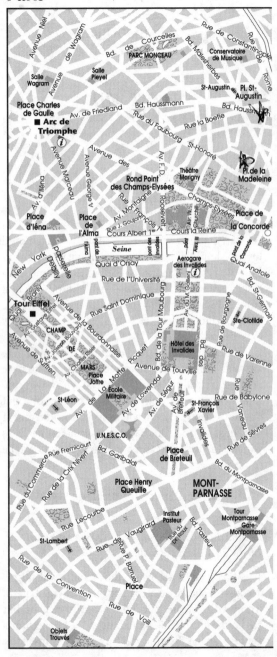

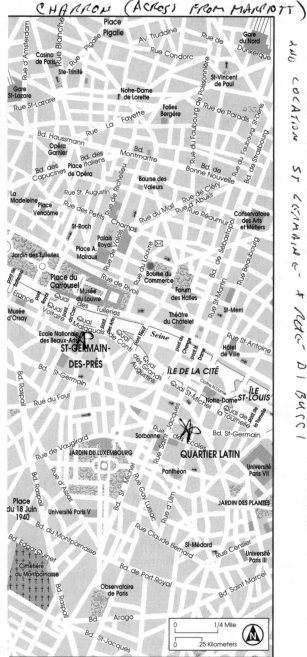

around and breathe deeply. The Jardins du Palais Royal is another terrific shopping experience, so check it out while you're here.

The Best Duty-Free Perfume Shop

CATHERINE
7 rue Castiglione, 1er (Métro: Tuileries or Concorde).

This shop is small, intimate, family run and can get crowded because it's very popular (good news travels). But wait until you apply for a détaxe (value-added tax) refund—Catherine is the only shop I know of that grants the discount up front! Of course, if you don't turn in your paperwork at the airport, you'll be charged the difference, but Catherine makes it much easier on you by effectively giving you the refund up front. Besides all that, they have an excellent selection of scents and specialize in hard-to-find perfumes. They carry makeup and beauty goods by Chanel, Dior, Lancome and Sisley—which is the steal of the century at French prices.

Confused about the whole duty free issue? There's lots more on duty free in these pages, stay tuned.

The Best Mass-Market Perfume Shop

SEPHORA
70 ave. Champs-Elysées, 8e
(Métro: F-D-Roosevelt).

Sephora is a large French chain with several stores in Paris, throughout France, in many European capital cities, and even the United States. In fact, they have just opened a U.S. flagship store at Rockefeller Center in New York. But enough about us. I've chosen this particular branch because it's the French flagship; it's also open on Sundays.

Everything in the large shop is color-coordinated. Fragrances are sold in a specific part of the store, with scads of testers and lots of scent strips. They sell far more than perfume; in fact, you're better off not buying perfume here, since you'll get a better price from a discounter or duty-free shop. What they're good for is bath and beauty products (an enormous selection, including their own line of shampoos and body lotions, makeup, and hair accessories). This is a great place for girls, preteens, and women of all ages. The sample size (15 ml) products for only a few francs make fabulous gifts.

There are books, there's a *parapharmacie,* there's a mix-your-own perfume counter, and there's a computer to teach you everything you need (or want) to know.

The Best Kitsch

It's not hard to find kitsch in Paris—just stroll the tourist traps along the rue de Rivoli or the sixth floor of Galeries Lafayette. Trends bring new themes almost every season. Right now, my favorite is the electric Eiffel Tower, which is very hard to find with the right kind of electrical plug for the U.S. I am wondering if you put one of those little converter things on it if it will work or blow out the lights once I get home.

The Best French Gift Statement

I've got several.

- Lalique belts or stick pins. Exotica is the name of the Lalique line of leather belts with smoky glass buckles. About $200, but you can apply for a détaxe refund. Lalique's stick pins, named Nerita, are also quite chic, and cost a bit less. Lalique, *11 rue Royale, 8e (Métro: Concorde).*
- Anything from Didier Lamarthe. I think the affordable gift of the century is his leather wallet for diskettes, about $50, but his handbags and small leather goods in sublime colors are fabulous, too. I bought a wallet and phone case set to feel very chic and French. Didier Lamarthe, *219 rue St-Honoré, 1er (Métro: Tuileries).*
- If you know don't mind splurging over $100 or so, head to By Terry the tiny makeup atelier of Terry de Gunzberg. Terry mixes color for YSL and has another makeup and beauty line with her sister (Nuxe), and does both custom and off the peg makeup here in her little shop. The custom makeup

is very expensive *(tres cher)* but the little silver palette with the travel selection has two blushes and three eye shadows and a powder and costs about $125 and is *tres chic*. *21 Galerie Vero Dodat, 2e (Métro: Palais Royale).*

- If you know anyone who still smokes, there's this amazing contraption at the Hôtel de Crillon's gift shop. It looks like an enamel thimble, but has a small hole in it. That's where your cigarette tip is meant to poke out. Très chic. Hôtel de Crillon, *10 place de Concorde, 8e (Métro: Concorde).*

The Best Gifts for $10 or Less

- Anything from Sephora, preferably the house brand of bath goodies; many Sephora stores all over town.
- Hot chocolate mix from Angelina, the most famous tea shop in Paris, $5. Angelina, *226 rue de Rivoli, 1er (Métro: Tuileries).*
- A box of Mère Poulard cookies. These indescribably good cookies are imported from Mont St-Michel and sold in any Parisian grocery store, $1.50.
- A bag of coffee. I buy Carte Noire at any grocery store, but there are other brands; Grand Mère has a cute package, $3.
- Jar of mustard. I buy Maille brand at any grocery store. Check out the two new flavors just launched—Cassis and Red Fruits, $2. Most fun when bought at Maille's own store. *Place de la Madeleine, 1er (Métro: Madeleine).*
- Box of tea or bag of tea, either from grocery store (try Elephant brand) or from Mariage Freres where 22 F will buy you a small bag of deliciously fragrant tea leaves. Mariage Freres has several stores of their own and a boutique in Galeries Lafayette.
- Anything from l'Occitane, the Provençal soap maker, including 13 F soaps. Available in all major department stores or in Occitane shops, like the one right off rue de Rivoli. If you're willing to carry it, try the lavender scented water to fill up your steam iron, 35 F! Occitane, *1 rue 29 Juillet, 1er (Métro: Tuileries).*

- A bar of French milled soap, from a made-in-France brand *(bien sur)* teamed with *gant de toilette,* a French-style washcloth, found in any linen department of a department store. The two pieces together don't have to cost more than 50 F. I like the Roger & Gallet soaps, especially the more unusual scents, such as the cherry and tomato combination.

The Best Status Gifts for Under $25

- Hermès soap, sold in the Saddle Shop. Hermès, *24 rue du Faubourg St-Honoré, 8e (Métro: Concorde).*
- Lanvin chocolates, sold in any grocery store!
- Champagne. There are plenty of good champagnes. In addition to the ones you've heard of, there are several good ones that aren't as well known in the U.S. Check out any branch of the wine chain Nicolas or a grocery store. I usually buy in grocery stores. Also note that France sells more sizes of champagne by more makers than you can imagine, so you can bring home several mini-bottles and still meet your liquor allowance.
- Anything from Diptyque, candle, soap and scent maker. This brand is not that well known in America but is a luxury brand in France and a cult item to celebs and serious shoppers. Diptyque, *34 blvd. St. Germain, 5e (Métro: St. Michel).*

The Best Shopper's Break

SALON DU THÉ BERNARDAUD
11 rue Royale, 8e (Métro: Concorde).

Pick your own dishes! That's right, if you have tea at this tea salon, they bring you a tray of gorgeous Bernardaud china, and you pick which style of china you would like everything served on. How's that for a great gimmick?

The Best Gifts for Kids

- Manitoba Jeunesse publishes these adorable French books for children—*Ma Maison, Ma*

Ferme, and *Mon École*—that lie flat like any book, but can be built into a house!, 43 F each.

- Monoprix, a chain of "popular stores," is packed with items, ranging from a selection of books (Disney translations are nice) to Legos. I also buy kids clothes here.

- Inno, a cross between a "dime store" and a grocery store, is another good bet for children's gifts. My favorite item is the miniature French shopping cart. Inno, *31–35 rue du Départ, 14e (Métro: Montparnasse)*.

- Sephora has these little animal-shaped bath gel thing-a-ma-bobs; each animal shape is a different scent and there must be 20 different ones, at about 50 cents a pop.

- CanCan Barbie. *Barbie La Dentiste* speaks French, *c'est vrai*, but I like CanCan Barbie better. Similarly, Elmo giggles in French—he's pricey (about $40) but adorable. I found him at Galeries Lafayette.

The Best Stores for Teenage Girls

H&M
118 rue Rivoli, 1er (Métro: Hotel de Ville).

LE SHOP
3 rue d'Argout, 2e (Métro: Etienne Marcel).

ZARA
44 avenue Champs Elysees, 8e (Métro: FD Roosevelt); 128 rue de Rivoli, 1er (Métro: Hotel de Ville) or place d'Opera (Métro: Opera).

There are several Zara (pronounced in the French manner, "Zah-rahhhh") shops around town, as well as representation in major department stores.

The Best New Unknown Designer Find

MARYSE CEPIÈRE AT UN DIMANCHE DANS NOS CAMPAGNES
59 rue Bonaparte, 6e (Métro: St-Germain-des-Prés).

I have no idea who Maryse Cepière is, or even how to pronounce her name. I don't think she's new to France, but she's new to me. I discovered her knits at the perfect Left Bank store, Un Dimanche dans nos Campagnes. The clothes are chic, while still being oversized, comfortable, and yet proportioned to height, so they don't overwhelm. They ain't cheap; expect to pay $250 (and more) for a knit dress.

The Best Fantasy Designer Find

LEE YOUNG HEE
109 rue du Bac, 7e (Métro: Bac or Sèvres-Babylone).

The Korean name should be a giveaway. These French clothes are inspired by Korean traditional garments, and have an edge of whimsy to them that doesn't make them practical for my lifestyle. If, however, I were going to a ball or getting married, this is where I'd go. She also has a shop in Seoul.

Runner Up

MR. GAS
44 avenue Etienne Marcel, 1er (Métro: Eitenne Marcel).

Gas has been around for years: It's a teeny, tiny jewelry shop where colorful and creative whimsies are sold. Now, "Mr. Gas" has added a clothing store next door. Funky, colorful, exotic and hip. Large sizes need not apply.

Best Kate Spade Inspirational Find

HERVÉ CHAPELIER
1 rue du Vieux-Colombier, 6e (Métro: St Germain des Pres).

I think Kate's great, but take a look at Herve Chapelier and his tote bags made of brightly colored nylon. There's a lousy selection in the major department stores, but head to his freestanding stores, such as the one on the Left Bank (above) or the other two in more BCBG neighborhoods: *3 rue Gustave Courbet, 16 e (Métro: Victor Hugo) and 53 blvd. de Courcelles, 8e (Métro: Courcelles).*

Best One Trick Pony

ANNE FONTAINE
64 rue des Saints-Peres, 6e (Métro: Sevres-Babylone); 50 rue Etienne Marcel, 2e (Métro: Etienne Marcel); 12 rue Francs-Bourgeois, 3e (Métro: St. Paul) and many more.

Ms. Anne has shops all over town and boutiques in the major department stores—she sells only one thing: white blouses. She's just opened in New York and hopes to take America by the shirttails.

♥ Best Department Store Rehab

9/13

Beautiful - like Carmikles

BON MARCHÉ
22 rue de Sèvres, (Métro: Sèvres-Babylone).

Bon Marché reinvented itself a year or so ago—this is not your *grandmere's* Bon Marché. Don't miss it for the monde, especially during sale season when all the luxuries get marked down. Even if you hate luxury, take a look at the whimsy, the fantasy, and the grocery store next door.

Most Hyped Store in Paris

COLETTE
213 rue St. Honoré, 1er (Métro: Tuileries)

This store seems to be extraordinary to the French, who can't stop talking about it even though it's been open now for four or five years. If you're an American, excuse me, but there is no there there. The merchandise is almost all American and therefore nothing to write home about. You read it here first.

The Next Colette for Those Who Care

PURPLE
9 rue Pierre-Dupont, 10e (Métro: Louis-Blanc)

Part art gallery, part Colette wannabe, part trendorama—the store everyone is looking at in order to have a new store to look at.

Chapter Two

· · · · · · ·

PARIS DETAILS

WELCOME TO PARIS

· ·

If this is your first visit to Paris, you won't notice that much of anything is different—it's just the way you saw it in pictures, in dreams. If you are returning to Paris, you'll notice that a lot of little things have changed, and very recently.

First of all, Bernard Arnault has bought up much of Paris, or tried to. What he didn't get, François Pinault has scribbled his name on. Write on, write on!

And while the tycoons have been duking it out, Karl Lagerfeld has been mooning about over the change in century, creating new philosophies for himself (too bad we missed the tag sale!) for Chanel, and for humankind. Monoprix and Prisunic have merged and created an ever upwardly mobile feel. Bon Marché has reinvented itself, so it is no longer your grandmother's department store. The beat goes on.

Paris has gotten more American and in doing so, more global and more sophisticated. As if this was even possible. Paris always sang. But the pitch is higher and deeper.

Even though Karl Lagerfeld isn't actually French (he's German by birth and Monagasque by residency) and creativity is a universal language, I look at the flowering of his originality and his change in philosophy as another example of what we go to Paris to see and to buy. Paris means style, it means genius, and it means light.

So welcome to Paris, the City of Light, where Karl Lagerfeld and I both hope to give you the sun, the moon, and the stars for at least the next century. *Bienvenue* and welcome to Paris, the *new* Paris where tons of new stores have opened and entirely new neighborhoods are being created and recreated as we speak.

After your first evening in town, you'll know why Paris has been dubbed the City of Light. In addition to all the glorious lights emanating from the buildings (even the I.M. Pei pyramid at the Louvre is lit from within), you're going to *feel* light—light-headed from the shopping opportunities you spied throughout the day, light-headed from just thinking about all the style yet to come. But you'll also feel light on your feet, especially if you've just waltzed through a fixed-price lunch at a Michelin two-star restaurant. Ah, the incredible lightness of being in Paris.

Paris is, of course, one of the world's premier shopping cities. Even people who hate to go shopping enjoy it in Paris. What's not to like? The couture-influenced ready-to-wear? The street markets? The most extravagant kids' shops in the world? Jewelers nestled together in shimmering elegance? Fruits and vegetables piled in bins as if they too were jewels? Perfumes and cosmetics at a fraction of their U.S. cost? Antiques and collectibles that are literally the envy of kings? It's not hard to go wild with glee at your good luck and good sense for having chosen such a place to visit.

PARIS NEWS

I've seen Paris move from a slow, melancholy daze during the recession to a snappy fox trot, now that some portions of the international economy are improving. While France still has plenty of its own economic problems (don't we all?), the retail scene has picked up dramatically. Few grand cities of Europe have changed as much as Paris has in the last 2 years.

If you don't get to Paris once a year, here's a quick checklist of what's new and what's hot; there's more information on these venues in the pages that follow.

- **The Left Bank** is better than ever. I thought "there goes the neighborhood," when I discovered that **Louis Vuitton** had moved in along with **Etro, Giorgio Armani,** and **Hermès.** *Au contraire.* While a teensy bit of the funky flavor is easing away, the new stores offer a funky deluxe feel that's just divine. I've never been a personal fan of Vuitton merchandise, but now I beg you, don't miss this store. You don't have to buy anything (although there's now much to tempt you)—simply stare. More designers have since come on board, including **Christian Dior** and **La Perla.**
- **Viaduc des Arts,** a massive strip mall–cum–rehab job, built under defunct train tracks right into the arches of a viaduct, could have been one of the late François Mitterrand's *grands travaux,* or big building projects. It's an ambitious rehab meant to house artisans and workshops. Not 100% successful (not all of its tenants are super), but worth following, nonetheless . . . and there has been some recent energy here to make it better than it was when the project first started. Don't go out of your way, but if you're looking to see what's happening in town, give it a try.
- The new cult hero for the wickedly rich, **Lucien Pellat-Finet** makes cashmere sweaters for women with wit, style, and grand luxury. The sweaters sell for about $1,000 in the United States (at Barney's, of course), but if you're in the in crowd, you buy in Paris. If you prefer to spend less on

your clothes, perhaps you want to visit **Le Shop,** near place des Victoires, which is considered the window where the next hot names in French fashion will pop up. It's so alive and vibrant and hot-cha-cha that you may want to dance. Over 40s might want to think twice.

- **Monoprix** and **Prisunic,** once archrivals, have merged—many old Monoprix stores have been renovated. I wonder if they are going to be called *Monoprisunic?* A fabulous Dutch fashion designer has been hired, and the clothes are hot and cheap. Oops!, excuse me, they don't like that word in Paris. Affordable, the clothes are *affordable.*

- **Duty free** has been outlawed for travelers going between EU destinations; this may not even affect you and, of course, you can still shop at the airport. But note that many airports have used the Terminal Four Heathrow model and taken on fabulous stores to seduce you into spending— without ever telling you that they're not duty-free stores!

- The **banana war** seems to be for real, so prices on many European goods will double in the U.S.—this in retaliation for EU practices in buying bananas. I won't bore you with the details (besides, you'd die laughing) so just note that French handbags with plastic in them are on the hit list. These items become a steal in France. I assume Louis Vuitton is going to reclassify all their impregnated canvas and patent leather as, uh, leather.

- *H&M arrivé!* Actually, the Swedish chain arrived a few years ago, but now this purveyor of cutting-edge and inexpensive fashion for men, women, and children has begun to build a flagship store smack dab between Galeries Lafayette and Printemps on the blvd. Haussmann, and if that doesn't make Paris sizzle, nuthin' will. Some say it will open in 2000, others say it will be 2001. Stay tuned.

KNOW BEFORE YOU GO

· ·

The French Government Tourist Office in the U.S. is an excellent source for visitor information and trip-planning advice. They have a 900 number, which costs 50¢ per minute to call: France On Call: ☎ 900/990-0040. Everyone who answers the phone speaks English, and the average call takes 5 minutes. They will mail any booklets or brochures you request (some of them have coupons for discounts), and provide you with firsthand information. They do not make actual bookings but will guide you to a local travel agent, if you need one.

If you prefer, you can call one of their several offices in the U.S. In New York, ☎ 212/315-0888; in Chicago, ☎ 312/337-6301; in Dallas, ☎ 214/720-4010; or in Los Angeles, ☎ 310/271-6665.

The French Government Tourist Office has also initiated a special program called Club France in order to provide information and discounts to American Francophiles. Membership is $75 a year (each additional family member is $35) and entitles you to a quarterly newsletter that describes current promotions, upgrade and/or discount coupons for hotels and car rentals, a Paris Museum Pass, and a few other perks. Write: Club France, c/o French Government Tourist Office, 444 Madison Ave., New York, NY 10022; or call ☎ 212/757-0229.

MORE INFORMATION, PLEASE

· ·

It's not hard to get information on Paris and on France. But all you need to get around Paris is a copy of *Paris par Arrondissement*. This is your source for street maps, bus lines, and the métro. Mine fits in the palm of my hand and is so complete, I can look up an address in the front of the book, then check a chart to find the nearest métro stop for that destination. For some reason they don't sell these babies in the U.S., so buy yours at any bookstore in

Paris . . . and at some street kiosks that also sell newspapers.

If you want to learn more, try digesting local magazines. French magazines are my secret passion—I spend a lot of my time in Paris in my tub, on a park bench, or in bed simply strolling through the pages. I can't even read French very well. Never mind. The ads alone are fabulous; the pictures make universal sense. I also "read" *Le Figaro* every day because it has good fashion coverage and covers new stores that are opening.

Figaro publishes a weekly insert to everything that's going on in the city, called *Figaroscope;* this includes special flea markets and shopping events. It appears in the paper every Wednesday.

Also consider *Pariscope,* a small-format weekly publication. It has movie listings and information about upcoming cultural events. It also lists such special events as big flea markets. A portion of it is written in English by the *Time Out* people from London. Buy it at any news kiosk.

Time Out, the weekly British cultural magazine, publishes a Paris edition in English, available at most kiosks. They also publish English-language guidebooks and annual "what's hot" guides that are sold in the U.S., as well as in English-language bookstores in Paris.

I subscribe to several French publications. They are expensive, but essential to these pages. Prices vary enormously depending on a variety of factors, so get prices on several types of magazines before you decide you can't afford this luxury. I use a French Canadian service, which seems to have slightly better prices than direct subscriptions. Call **Express Magazines,** ☎ 800/363-1310 and ask for their brochure. They speak English.

The monthly magazines seem to be affordable; a year's subscription to *French Vogue* is a little over $100, as are *Coté Sud* and *Coté Ouest,* respectively. But you can get a price break on the latter if you subscribe to both (and you want both!). I pay an outrageous $400 a year for the weekly *Madame Figaro!*

Electronically Yours

The Internet is a fabulous source for researching your upcoming trip to France. Hotels, airlines, and travel agents all have their own Web sites, which can give you a glimpse at properties . . . or more. Also note that most major brands have Web sites as to the French *grands magasins*—the big department stores. As we go to press, none of them offers e-commerce, but it's on its way to be sure. Sometimes hard-to-find information that your travel agent may not have quick access to is easily available online, such as train schedules (**www.sncf.fr**).

So many businesses have Web sites that it's impossible to give you a list. **Bonjour Paris** (www.bparis.com) is the best-known English language site, and all of the major department stores have sites. Also try:

Chanel: chanel.com

Fashion Live Magazine: www.fashionlive.com

Paris Dutyfree: www.parisdutyfree.com

Electronically Yours, Part 2

Now that I travel with my trusty laptop, I try to connect to American Online every day in order to reach out and touch. From Paris, it's not always easy. Some tips that may apply to your Internet service provider even if you aren't using AOL:

- Get the France access number, the Paris number, and the Nice number before you go—sometimes when I can't get into one, the other works. I can be desperate enough to pay long distance charges to Nice!
- If you are continually cut off and disconnected, don't curse AOL. It could be the phone lines and

the difference between digital and analog connections (don't ask). Instead, take your laptop to the hotel's business center and tap into their T-line. It saves the day for me every time.

- There are plenty of **Internet cafes** and centers around town—the easiest one I have found for my lifestyle is in Galeries Lafayette.
- New hotels have data parts in the rooms; these may or may not facilitate connecting. For $5.25 at Radio Shack, I bought a French modem connector, which is a good investment. In older hotels, an engineer will come to your room with one of these and install it for you. Regardless of the type of connection, you may or may not be able to get online. I made the Hôtel de Crillon take all my connection fees (totaling about $6) off my bill since I could not connect and I thought it was their fault. Turns out, it was a digital line and AOL needs an analog line, but I didn't know about these things.
- Investigate Hotmail (**www.hotmail.com**), a Web-based e-mail system. As long as you're near a computer with Web access (for instance, at an Internet cafe), you can get your e-mail.

GETTING THERE

. . . .

From the U.S.

While getting to Paris may seem easy enough—after all, most of the major carriers fly there—I've got a few secrets that might make getting there more fun . . . and less expensive.

The cheapest airfares are always in winter. Furthermore, winter airfares are often accompanied by promotional ticketing gimmicks, such as: buy one ticket, get one half price; buy one ticket, bring along a companion for a discounted price; or kids fly free. There are deals out there during the chilly months. Also during winter, frequent-flyer miles may go on sale.

We all know that every winter there are airfare price wars; when **Air France** announced a $269 weekend fare to Paris last winter, I think half of New York tilted into the Atlantic in a mad rush for tickets. And, of course, all the other airlines flying to France matched the fare.

Meanwhile, a new niche has been carved out—winter weekend European travel. Just about every country now has deals that allow for Thursday or Friday departures and Monday or Tuesday returns. The problem with these tickets is that you can't add the week in between; you are limited to *le weekend longue.* Conceptually speaking, people who live on the Eastern seaboard of the U.S. are flocking to European weekends like birds to Florida.

A few tricks I have learned during airfare wars: If you happen to buy a ticket at price A, and then a price war ensues making the same ticket you purchased available at price B, a better price than you paid, don't just sit there and stew. The airlines will allow you to pay a service charge and get your ticket rewritten. This charge is usually $75 to $150, but you may save money over all.

Or you buy a cheapie ticket for some dates you pick, then you pay a $150 change fee to change to different dates (must be done before the date of travel obviously) which may not have been included during the war.

Check out consolidators who will unload unsold tickets on scheduled flights for discount prices (which vary with the season, just as do regular prices). Again, no frequent-flyer miles. These tickets are great for last-minute travelers who do not qualify for 21-day advance purchase prices. You need only about 4 business days notice.

I called **Unitravel** (☎ 800/325-2222) and was offered a round-trip flight from New York to Paris for $628 plus departure taxes on Northwest Airlines during the summer peak season. You pay by credit card on the phone; they Fed Ex the tickets to you at no extra charge. They did say that their online service was even cheaper, and this made me really uncomfortable, implying that I was a chump for not surfing the Net.

Packages that include your airfare and hotel accommodations always give you good prices, especially if you can get those prices guaranteed in dollars, which is possible through many big wholesalers, airlines, and hotels. If the dollar is depressingly low, or merely unstable enough to make you nervous, look carefully at deals in which prices are frozen in U.S. dollars. Car-rental agencies also have some of these offerings.

Finally, don't forget to check out **Disneyland Paris** packages that include airfare, hotel, and transfers. Disneyland Paris has various good deals from the U.S. and Europe and then you just take the train into town.

Nouvelles Frontiers is an enormous French travel agency with offices in France and in the U.S., where they are called New Frontiers (☎ 800/366-6387). They are so big that they have their own airline, **Croseair.**

Call **Now Voyager** (☎ 212/431-1616) to volunteer to be a freelance courier; you'll get a round-trip ticket for approximately $200, although your luggage allowance will be severely restricted or nil. You get to take only one carry-on bag, measuring about 9×14×22, so the freight company can have your baggage allowance. Most flights are international and leave from New York or Newark; some departures are from Miami and Houston. Trips usually last 1 week, but there are some 2-week and a few open-ended tickets available. Bookings are for singles. If you are with another person, be prepared for your partner to go the day before or the day after you. Reservations can be made up to 2 months in advance and are nonrefundable. You pay a $50 registration fee; they take cash or credit cards (cash offers you a discount).

Air France is part owner of a domestic airline called **Air InterEurope.** For those of you who are not French residents, and want to travel beyond

Paris, Air France and Air InterEurope offer a variety of passes for travel within France. One, called "Le France pass," allows 7 days of unlimited travel within France within a 1-month period (your days of travel do not have to be consecutive). The ticket costs a flat fee ($339 at the time of writing), and you must purchase it in the U.S. before you depart for France. Call Air France for details.

Note that several new French airlines have popped up in the last year or two, mostly for intra-French travel, so Air InterEurope (previously called Air Inter) is not the only regional carrier in France. Price wars are now normal, whereas they were unheard of 2 years ago.

I've never flown **Tower Air,** but they offer deals that cannot be ignored: This charter airline was advertising business-class seats to Paris at $349 each way. This translates to a round-trip of $698 plus taxes (about $25) on their regularly scheduled 747 flights, nonstop every weekend. They also have coach seats. My friend Ken once flew coach and said it wasn't deluxe, but everything was fine. The food service wasn't wonderful, according to him; but the plane was newish, and the seats were relatively comfortable. They have their own terminal at JFK. His round-trip, coach ticket was about $520, but that was in peak season. My friend Nan flew business class and said the airline was really trying to give the big names a run for their money; ☎ 800/34-TOWER.

Don't forget the big-time tour operators. Rates are lower if you book through French tour operators/wholesalers like **Nouvelles Frontiers,** a major chain of French travel agents, which calls itself **New Frontiers** in the U.S.

From the U.K.

If you think you'll just make a quick little hop from London to Paris on a whim, you may be shocked to realize that the regular airfare between the two cities is outrageously high, depending on the day and time you fly. For a regular, round-trip ticket, figure on paying $300 to $350 per person. If you buy your ticket 14 days in advance and stay over a Saturday night, the fare will drop slightly.

However, since the opening of the Chunnel, airfares have come down dramatically, and just about every form of transportation between the U.K. and France (train, plane, ferry) has promotional deals—most require advance purchase and cannot be changed. Call both **British Airways** (☎ 800/247-9297) and **Air France** (☎ 800/237-2747) to check for fare wars, promotions, and so on.

You may also want to check out, separately, the rates offered by the two major competing British carriers (BA and Virgin) for transatlantic fares plus Paris add-ons, and then for locally priced add-ons, which could be on sale or promotion.

If you need one-way transportation between London and Paris but are keen on flying, a round-trip ticket bought in advance to include a Saturday night stay will be less expensive than a one-way ticket. Just throw away the unused portion. *C'est la vie.*

From Brussels

Don't look at me like that! Brussels happens to be just an hour and 20 minutes from Paris, thanks to brand-new, speedy train lines; you can easily fly into Brussels and out of Paris (or vice versa), or even go to Paris for the weekend from Belgium. Sometimes, when there are airfare deals and promotions, all seats in and out of Paris are sold. Try Brussels for one leg and see if you can beat the system by being a little bit clever.

Brussels has a new terminal to make the airport even more efficient. Also, **Sabena** (☎ 800/955-2000) has so many fabulous promotions these days, you have to take both the airline and Brussels quite seriously. Please note that Delta and Sabena have gone into partnership on a code-sharing basis to offer a strong Brussels hub. There are two flights a day from New York alone.

Brussels is my Paris travel tip of the decade.

From Nice

Many people like to combine the south of France with Paris, especially because the Delta nonstop flight from New York makes it so easy. Getting to Paris can be more complicated than you thought if you don't work it all out before you decide what to do and how to book the trip. If you are flying Delta in the triangular route, so to speak, you will need a train, a car, or a plane ticket to get you to Paris. Or, you can book with Air France. Since Air France has no direct flights from the U.S. to Nice, they offer an alternative that should be priced competetively when it includes Nice—you just want to lay over between legs. Note that because Delta and Air France have merged many of their flights and services, you can possibly take advantage of a mixed ticket and get it your way at a good price. The point of the game is to avoid overpaying for the Paris–Nice link.

If you are flying à la carte, you can buy an Air France ticket. On my last trip, Air France was on strike (again) and it was rough going. Most locals prefer to fly **AOM**, a local carrier that can also be booked in the U.S. through travel agents. I usually buy a round-trip ticket with a Saturday night stay over and throw away the second portion of the ticket—it's cheaper than one-way.

The train ride is 7 hours.

By Train

The Chunnel (channel tunnel) now connects Britain, France, and Belgium. You can arrive in Paris or Brussels by Chunnel in approximately 3 hours. There is no shopping on the train itself. There's a cutie pie fancy shop in Folkestone, where you board **Le Shuttle,** the car service for passenger cars, but for assorted complicated and political reasons, there are no duty-free shops in any of the international Eurostar train stations or on the trains themselves. The stores you see there are fake duty-free shops.

Do not get confused and think that all trains now use the Chunnel. Old-fashioned train service between the two cities, where you and/or your car board a ferry for the crossing, still exists. To ride a train through the Chunnel, you must book through **Eurostar** (☎ 800/677-8585); you can also book through **RailEurope** (☎ 800/4-EURAIL). Then book for either London–Paris, or London–Brussels.

BritRail USA has several packages that allow you to choose which method you'd like to use for getting from the U.K. to the continent; their Continental Capitals Circuit connects London with Paris, Brussels, and Amsterdam. The pass costs a flat fee (about $275 for second class and $350 for first class) and is good for a period of 6 months after the date of issue. It gives you unlimited stopovers in those four cities; call ☎ 212/575-2667 for more information.

There are other BritRail passes, geared to travel to specific countries (such as the BritFrance pass) that enable you to save money on train travel. If you buy some of these products, you get an automatic discount (about 30%!) off your Chunnel train ticket. Note that the Eurostar ticket is not part of any pass currently available; it must be bought as an add-on.

RailEurope (☎ 800/4-EURAIL) not only has tons of train passes but also books transatlantic flights, hotels, car rentals—the works. One of the greatest things about their system is that there are different prices based on age (youth passes, seniors, etc.) as well as on the number of people traveling together. Not only do they believe the more the merrier, they also think the more the cheaper.

Note that French trains and Eurostar now have frequent-flyer plans just like airlines. Also note that there are 1-day round-trip low-cost train tix for those who just want a taste of another destination. If you are in Paris and want to hop to London, this works in your favor, as you get an extra hour in the day with the time change.

ARRIVING IN PARIS
. . . .

I don't know how to break this news to you gently, so here goes: It is now impossible to arrive at Orly Airport from the U.S. This means you should be prepared to face the music at Charles De Gaulle International Airport.

Orly is to the south of Paris, not as far away from town as CDG. Expect a taxi to the 1er to cost you approximately $40, including tip. Orly is now being used for intra-European flights, so if you are coming into Paris from London, Nice, or elsewhere in the EU, do book through Orly and save yourself some time and money.

If you are arriving from the U.S., you are stuck with Charles de Gaulle International Airport (CDG). CDG is composed of two parts, Terminal 1 and 2. Terminal 1 has various satellites, Terminal 2 has pods designated A to D. I have been lost in those pods, and I want to tell you it was not pretty.

A taxi to the 1er from CDG will cost about $50 to $60. This price includes tip and the traditional surcharge for luggage. Do note that most French taxis are small; if you have a lot of luggage, hold out for a Mercedes taxi. If you have a lot of family, plus a lot of luggage, expect to need two taxis. Or you can send one person and all the luggage in a taxi and let the other members of the family take public transportation. Air France offers bus service from Étoile (take a taxi to your hotel from there); or you can take Roissy Rail, which lets you off at either the Gare du Nord or Châtelet, both in-town locations.

There are two lines of bus service, aside from Air France: One drops you at Nation; the other, at Gare de l'Est. For English-language information about transport at CDG, call ☎ 01/48-62-22-80.

You may buy individual tickets for public transportation. Use a package of six tickets (good for families) or show your *carte orange* (see below).

GETTING AROUND PARIS

Paris is laid out in a system of zones called *arrondissements,* which circle around from inside to outside. When France adopted the Zip code method for its mail, Parisians incorporated the arrondissement number into their Zip codes as the last two digits. Thus a Zip code of 75016 means the address is in the 16th arrondissement (16e).

If you see a number with a small *e* written after it, this number signifies the arrondissement. The first arrondissement, however, is written 1er. Knowing the proper arrondissement is essential to getting around rapidly in Paris. It is also a shorthand system for many people to sum up everything a place can or may become—simply by where it is located, or by how far it is from something that is acceptably chic.

Think about arrondissements when planning your shopping expeditions. Check the map frequently, however, since you may think that 1er and 16e are far apart, when in actuality. you can walk the distance, and have a great time doing so. (Take the Rue du Faubourg St-Honoré toward the Champs-Elysées and you even get a tour of the 8e thrown in.)

With its wonderful transportation system, Paris is a pretty easy city to navigate. Tourists are usually urged to ride the métro, but buses are available and often a treat—you can see where you're going and get a free tour along the way. Your edition of *Paris par Arrondissement* usually has bus routes as well as a métro map. Métro maps are handed out free at your hotel and are printed in almost every guidebook. Keep one in your wallet at all times.

By Métro

There are many métro ticket plans for easiest access to the city. If you can speak a little bit of French and

Paris by Arrondissement

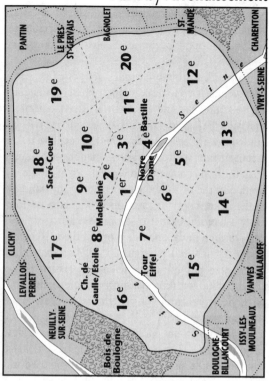

visit Paris often enough to take the time to do this, buy a *carte orange*. It is exactly what it sounds like: a small orange card, which bears a passport-type photo of yourself. (Bring a photo with you, or use the photo booth in the Concorde station.)

The *carte orange* is good for unlimited travel on bus or métro *for a 1-week period, Monday to Monday*. Once you have your permanent orange card, with your photo in place, you will then only have to buy a coupon for each week you want to travel—I've had the same orange card for about 15 years and was shocked on this past trip to learn that a new, stream-lined version has been introduced. I was so excited that I got a *carte orange* for the Mona Lisa. I may spring for one for Dr. Gachet next trip.

The *carte orange* is about half the price of the weekly ticket pushed for tourists, called **"Sesame."** Bargain shopping begins at the métro station, *mes amis.*

Note: You probably cannot get your first *carte orange* unless you speak enough French to negotiate the purchase and can answer a few questions that will be asked; touristy-type tourists will be guided toward other kinds of more expensive ticket arrangements, such as the above-mentioned Sesame. I ask the hotel concierge to write down everything I need, and then I slide the paper under the window at the ticket booth at the Concorde métro station. Only a handful of métro stations do a first-timers' *carte orange,* and Concorde is one of them. Remember, you will need a passport photo. Also remember where you put the card when you return home (I keep mine with my passport) because once you have the actual card, you bring it back with you on each subsequent trip.

If you just want individual tickets, please buy them by *carnet.* The *carnet* is made up of 10 tickets, can be bought at any station, and can be used for the bus or the métro. An individual ticket to the métro costs about $1 a ride; with the *carnet,* the price drops significantly.

Paris Visite is a transportation pass providing travel for 3 to 5 days (depending on what you buy); it costs up to $30 but includes rides to the airport, outlying suburbs, and even Versailles, and is an awfully good deal if you plan to use it. The pass comes in a black case in which you insert something that looks remarkably like the same coupon used in a *carte orange.* This pass is sold at RATP stations (big métro stations or RER stations—I look at the acronym and think "rapid transit"), SNCF stations (French national trains), and ADP (airports de Paris) booths—at either airport, Orly or CDG.

There are Travelcard passes, good for unlimited 1-day travel that cost about $5, but remember, the *carte orange* costs about $10, and it's good for a whole week. You can't go to Versailles on the *carte orange,* but it only costs about $5 (round-trip) for a regular RER ticket to Versailles anyway.

By Bus

Paris buses take the same *coupons* as the métro, or real money. They are much slower than the underground, but you get to see the sights as you go by. For bus information for the airport, see page 000.

Since I now stay at the Concorde-St. Lazare so often, and this hotel is across the street from one of the major bus terminals, I take the bus more often than I used to. Most drivers do not speak much English, although they are friendly to tourists and will tell you when you get to your stop. Write down the name of your stop and show it to the driver when you board the bus. You can say, "*ditez moi*" (from the song from *South Pacific*) and point to the address of the bus stop. Allow a half hour to get to nearby places and 1 hour to get all the way across town.

By Car

If you plan to visit the countryside or Disneyland Paris, you may want to rent a car. As long as you avoid driving around the place de la Concorde, you'll be fine. As an added convenience, most major car-rental agencies will allow you to drop the car at a hotel, saving you the time and trouble of returning it yourself.

I once returned a car at the Inter-Continental on a Sunday, but then worried it wouldn't be picked up until Monday, and I would be charged for an extra day. Many phone calls later, I discovered the clock stopped ticking the minute the concierge notified the agency (Hertz) that we were ready. I needn't have worried.

Should you be renting a car in Paris from **Kemwel,** ask them to fax you a map with the location of the pickup point (Citer at Gare du Nord) marked, since you'll have to navigate a number of tricky one-way streets to get there. Confirm their hours of operation as well, as they may not be what you expect. Isn't travel fun?

If you intend to drive around Paris (silly you), be sure you know about parking regulations and how to work the meters, which provide a ticket that proves you've paid for curbside parking. (Display it prominently in your windshield.) Just because you don't see a meter like we have in the U.S. doesn't mean that parking is free.

If you prefer a car and driver, call **Carey France** at ☎ 1/42-65-54-20, or their American headquarters at ☎ 800/336-4646. Their fax number in France is 1/42-65-25-93. Or try **Euro Limo** (☎ 1/40-11-30-30, fax 1/40-11-25-84). You can request a limo, a sedan, or even a van.

PHONING HOME

Using a French pay phone is not particularly difficult, especially if you use a French Telecom *telecarte*. You can buy one at any newsstand. Another way to save is to use a direct-dialing service through your long-distance carrier at home. For **AT&T,** call 0-800-99-00-11; for **MCI,** call 0-800-99-00-19; for **Sprint,** use 0-800-99-00-87.

Of course, the most expensive way to phone home is from your hotel room. Very few of Paris's fanciest hotels have pay phones that take phone cards in their lobbies, making it inconvenient to save a franc. One that does, however, is the **Paris Inter-Continental,** right in the heart of the best Right Bank shopping. In fact, it has two pay phones: one that accepts *telecartes,* and another than accepts credit cards. Both charge France Telecom rates. I spoke to Cannes from the latter for 2 minutes for $2, billed directly to my Visa card. Not a big bargain, but a lot less than you might otherwise be charged.

Now then, here is the most exciting thing of all—many stores have just introduced telephone cards along the American model. I bought mine at

Printemps, but FNAC has them, as do many other stores. You can use this phone card from a hotel and it's amazing. I spoke to a friend in the U.S. for over a half hour for 50 F, less than $10! These phone cards require some reading in French to catch onto how they work; if your French isn't too good, get the concierge of the hotel to read the card to you or have someone at the store when you buy it explain it all. It's not hard, but because my French isn't very good, I struggled at first.

On my last trip to Paris, I sprang for a French mobile telephone. It changed my life. Though you may not be in France as often as I am, there are three new pay-as-you-go phone systems, each costs 980 F and is available at FNAC and many other places. Prices around town seem to be fixed.

Of the three systems, I think NOMAD is the easiest because you can refill your units via credit card from the phone itself. On other systems you have to buy another card. The three systems are **NOMAD, Mobicarte,** and **SFR Entree Libre.** The magic words that you are looking for in any phone (if you aren't living in France) are *sans abonnement*—this means "without subscription."

SFR is actually an operating system, so this is just one of their many products. In France, all phones receive calls for free.

POSTCARDS FROM THE EDGE
. . . .

Postcards in Paris are as original and arty as the city itself—there are truly thousands of designs and styles to choose from, but watch out, many of them cost between $1–$2 each! The enormously cute, large-sized Disney cards (sold in Paris, not Disneyland Paris) cost even more! The better the postcard design, the higher the price. Look before you leap.

You can buy postcards for a mere 1 F each if you shop the tourist traps carefully; you may even luck out and find 15 cards for 10 F; 12 cards for 10 F is more easily done. Walk along the Rue de Rivoli, where the tourist traps are thick, checking prices as you go. The price per card drops the higher uptown you go (away from Concorde, toward the Louvre), and the better the bulk deals get. Tourist traps near Notre Dame also sell postcards for 1 F each and often offer bulk deals.

You can buy stamps at a PTT (post office), tobacco shop, or from your hotel concierge. Postage to the U.S. (even for a postcard) is rather pricey, but if you have friends in other EU countries, it's a bargain.

SHOPPING HOURS

Shopping hours in Paris are extremely irregular and independent. Welcome to France. Thankfully, they are big-city hours, so you needn't worry about a lot of downtime, as in Italy or even the French provinces. There are plenty of shopping opportunities even on Sunday and Monday, and finally there's some serious late-night shopping.

Monday can be a tad moody, but generally speaking, *stores are open Monday, or part of Monday*. Those stores that tend toward Monday morning closings will open anytime from noon on, sometimes 1, 2, or even 3pm. For the most part, they are small stores. The department stores and branches of the major chains are open on Monday morning; about 50% of the stores on the Left Bank in the prime shopping areas are open.

During the rest of the week, most stores consider 10am to 7pm to be standard hours of operation, but there are so many variations of this rule, such as it is, that you can lose your mind. Some stores open every morning at 10am except one day of the week when they open at 9:30am. Some stores are open until 10pm on Thursday nights only. A few stores are open until 9pm or 8pm every weekday, especially in high-traffic areas.

My favorite is Au Printemps, which opens not at 9:30am but at 9:35am! It's impossible to know or keep track of every store's hours. Other stores have a few weird twists to their hours as well, like Hermès—which closes for lunch only on Mondays.

In summer, many stores close for lunch on Saturday, but stay open later in the evening. Some stores are open for lunch during the week, but close for lunch on Saturday, and then reopen. (Hermès does this also.)

France has about 15 bank holidays a year; stores may close on these holidays. Beware the month of May! Not only does May have about 10 holidays in it, but it's hard to know when stores will be open. May 1 is a huge holiday and everything is closed. May 8, however, is a so-so holiday and stores may or may not be open—check ads in *Le Figaro*. Your hotel concierge may not know. Also note that openings may be related to the part of town. On May 8 I was shut out in the 16th arrondissement, but found most other neighborhoods in Paris were open. Go figure.

The entire month of August may be unusual. Most of France closes down on August 15 for Pentecost, but some stores close for the entire month of August, or just from August 14 to August 31. Bastille Day, July 14, is a holiday (stores are closed), but some small Parisian retailers open up, if only for a few hours, to take advantage of the crowds in the streets.

Bonne chance, as we say.

Sunday in the Park with Georges

Although traditional Parisian retail is closed on Sunday, there is still an enormous amount of shopping going on. Aside from the flea market business, which has always been hot on Sunday, nowadays entire neighborhoods are jumping on Sunday. Check out **the Louvre,** with the adjoining mall **Carrousel du Louvre, the Marais,** and **Virgin Megastore** on the Champs-Elysées. In fact, lots of the stores on the Champs-Elysées are open on Sundays starting at noon. The main shopping street of the **Île St-Louis** is also open on Sundays.

Many stores that open on Sunday are closed on Monday.

Antiquing on Sunday is a national hobby; don't forget to check the newspapers, or ask your concierge about any special shows or events which might be planned for the weekend. From February through May, the weekends are dense with special events—many of which highlight shows for antiques and/or *brocante* (used items, not necessarily antique).

When the weather is good, shops in the main flow of tourist traffic may open on a Sunday just to catch the extra business. Every now and then a duty-free shop will open up; tourist traps near popular attractions are almost always open on Sunday afternoons. By 5pm on a Sunday, though, it's hard to find any place that's open.

Exceptional Openings

The French government allows retailers to have five exceptional openings on Sundays during the year. These are most often taken around Christmas, but there's usually one in September or October for back-to-school (which is called *Rentrè* in French). Often openings on holidays in May are also known as exceptional. Exceptional openings are usually advertised in French newspapers like *Le Figaro*.

SALE PERIODS

Officially, the French government sets the dates of the sales, and there are only two sales periods: one in winter (January) and one in summer (June–July). However, many retailers, strapped for cash, offer assorted promotions and discounts these days. A few of them, like Hermès, have special events held outside the store. These events are advertised and listed in papers; check the page called *Le Carnet du Jour* in *Le Figaro* for sale ads.

The big department stores turn their sale promotions into big mega-deals with banners all over the front of the stores and enticing titles like "The 7 Days" or whatever. You don't need to speak French to get the picture—the ads and banners at the store sites make it quite clear.

The thing that I find most frightening about French sales is that they last a set amount of time and are then over. The sale merchandise does not stay marked down! I fell in love with a tablecloth at a department store. On sale it cost $150, which I thought was a little high for my budget, so I decided to think about it. Lo and behold, when I went back, it cost $200!

PERSONAL NEEDS

Pharmacies are marked with a green neon cross; at least one in each neighborhood must be open on Sunday. When a pharmacy is closed, the nearest open pharmacy is indicated on a sign in the window.

Condoms are sold from machines in all métro stations and at pharmacies.

If you need a book in English, **Brentano's** is at 37 avenue de la Opéra; **W.H. Smith,** 248 rue de Rivoli. Both sell American and British books and periodicals. Most luxury hotels sell the London newspapers or at least the Sunday editions. There's also a small cadre of Left Bank bookstores that sell books in English and serve as hangouts for expats.

AIRPORT SHOPPING

Both Orly and CDG have more than their share of shopping opportunities for visitors—in fact, the shopping is so brisk in these airports that they have their own shopping bag. Stores at CDG are fancier than those at Orly, but you will have no trouble dropping a few, or a few hundred, francs. Prices at the airport duty-free shops may be slightly cheaper than at comparable retail stores in Paris, but not much, and may be confused because of the recent change in duty-free laws.

You should have already purchased your cosmetic and fragrance bargains in Paris at the duty-free shops that offer 20% to 40% savings; you will save only 13% at the duty-free stores at the airport. The selection at the airport may be better than the selection on your airplane, but the airline's prices can be better. It pays to take the duty-free price list from your plane when you arrive and save it for comparison when you're shopping at the airport at the end of your trip. I also keep a Saks Fifth Avenue price list in my wallet for each of the fragrances that I like. Saks prints them constantly in mailers, bill stuffers, ads, and so on. You'd be surprised how often a duty-free price can be the same as the Saks Fifth Avenue price!

Duty-free shopping is now stranger than ever, so if you are buying something just because you *think* it's cheaper—ask!

Legally speaking, you may not buy duty-free goods if you are leaving for another EU destination. If you are departing the EU, you may buy at the duty-free price (13% less than regular retail).

Chapter Three

· · · · · · · · ·

MONEY MATTERS

UNIFICATION & YOU

· ·

The EU (European Union) has officially transferred and united its currency into the long anticipated euro, which is at present solely an electronic currency. It exists in computers and on price tags and bills, but there are no actual euros in existence yet (discounting the chocolate ones you can buy at any candy store).

If euros on price tags confuse you, calm down. Since the euro-to-franc ratio is very close to the dollar-to-franc ratio when the dollar is trading at six francs per dollar, you can actually consider them at parity in order to get a quick fix on a price.

Now then, here's the only tricky part. The relationship of the dollar to the euro will always fluctuate, but the relationship of the franc to the euro is fixed and cannot change. One euro equals 6.55 francs. See, that didn't hurt a bit, now, did it? The dollar is very strong against the euro as I write this (about $1.09), but that doesn't mean anything to you and won't until you are actually buying euros, some time in 2002 probably.

Will the so-called unification of Europe affect your shopping habits? Not really. Even though in the end you can easily comparison shop in euros without conversions, without a Web site that lists all the prices in the world, it is impossible to compare prices in all the different countries, euros or not. For those who are visiting just Paris, very few major changes have come about because of the introduction of euros. Not to worry.

THE BANANA WARS

Yes, we have no bananas, or more precisely, yes we have no Chiquita bananas in Paris. That is because the EU imports its bananas from colonial countries—the United States is really peeved about this. And the European Union doesn't like U.S. and Canadian beef because our cattle are fed hormones.

So ticked are the various parties that they have instituted a series of embargoes and tariffs on specific European goods so that they will cost double in the U.S. what they cost in Europe. The list is pretty silly, but it includes German coffeemakers and French handbags made with plastic. Should you be craving one of these, buy it in France where the price will be significantly lower than in the U.S.

FRENCH DELUXE

The concept of name brands was invented in France hundreds of years ago, based on the very simple, and correct, assumption that people would pay anything for the very best quality. This notion remains at the core of French marketing today.

Brands are fiercely marketed in order to keep their image, sales are strictly regulated by the government (the French government only allows two legal sale periods during the year), and makers of fakes are hunted down and prosecuted. All of this is done not only to protect the images of deluxe brands but also to protect the shopper who paid full price. Discounts are limited to duty-free stores. And for the ditty on duty free, see below.

Because the deluxe philosophy is so innately French, French consumers believe in it with all their hearts. They have been happily brainwashed. French men and women save their money and make their wish lists before Christmas and birthdays to include deluxe goods from French luxury houses. I have French girlfriends who have a list of the items they "must" have; when an item on their wish list materializes, I think they are more relieved than grateful. It would be hard to face their friends without these items.

Americans may have trouble understanding the difference between the concepts of status and deluxe goods. Status items are bought because the labels impress either the owner or the owners' circle of friends. Deluxe goods are meaningful because of their beauty and quality of workmanship; they've been created to last forever.

Because these two kinds of goods are produced and sold with two different objectives in mind, don't be surprised by the protective French attitude you may encounter. Certain luxury or deluxe goods are actually considered national treasures. You may even consider French salespeople in such luxury stores to be rude. They're not rude; you just don't know the system.

ALAS, POOR DUTY FREE
. . . .

Duty free between EU destinations was eliminated July 1, 1999. To adapt, airports have brought in the big guns from BAA, the worlds leading authority on jazzy airport shopping (Heathrow to Pittsburgh), and they have begun to redo the shopping malls in the European airports to make sure the shopping ops are so attractive that you never realize that duty free is gone.

But wait, duty free is not totally gone. It is just outlawed between EU destinations. If you are departing the EU for a non-EU country you may purchase items at the duty-free price. Some items will have two prices on them. When you go to pay, you are charged the higher price after you produce your boarding pass if you are going to an EU city. Some airports are keeping old duty-free prices and paying the difference.

CURRENCY EXCHANGE

Exchanging currency in a foreign country can be downright depressing. I do most of my money changing through the use of French ATM machines (called *distributeurs*), but then my bank at home charges me $5 per hit. My old bank charged $3, which I liked better.

I also buy traveler's checks in French francs before I leave home—because the time and aggravation involved in exchanging money in Paris can drive you nuts. When the U.S. dollar is strong against the franc, I even stock up.

The rate announced in the paper (it's in the *Herald Tribune* every day) is the official bank exchange rate and is not usually available to tourists. Even by trading your money at a bank, you will not get the same rate of exchange that's announced in the papers. And you will pay a fee for the bank's services. I've stood in lines at banks for 20 or 30 minutes to try to save $3 and realized it was a total waste of my time. If you exchange a traveler's check each day, expect to get a lousy rate and pay $5 per exchange.

I've also been to those Exchange booths that dot the rue Rivoli and the Champs-Elysées and found that even if they advertise a great rate of exchange, there is usually a hidden hook—a $10 fee!

You may get a better rate of exchange for a traveler's check than for cash because there is less paperwork involved. But the rate of exchange you get anywhere is usually not negotiable with that establishment. While you can shop for the best rate available, you cannot haggle for a better rate from a certain source.

Hotels generally give the least favorable rate of exchange, but they do not charge a fee to guests. The bank may not give you a better rate anyhow. As far as I'm concerned, if there's no line and the people are pleasant, this is the best bet!

Shops may negotiate on the rate of exchange they'll give you. Say the item you buy costs the equivalent of $40, and you sign over a $50 U.S. traveler's check. The shopkeeper may ask you the rate of exchange, or say something like, "Let's see. Today the dollar is trading at . . ." Then, he (or you) will pull out a calculator and figure out how much change you will get. If you have bought a lot, you may ask for a more favorable rate of exchange on your change or bargain a bit. But exclusive shops will be insulted at this maneuver. Use credit cards there, anyway.

The best rate is generally offered by American Express. Their main office is on rue Scribe, across the street from the Opéra and the Le Grand Hôtel Inter-Continental. This is a convenient place to visit (*grands magasins* are a block away!) and can save you money if you're a cardholder (they won't charge you a commission). Other financial services are provided as well.

If you are going to Brussels and want correct change, do not exchange money in France first (even at American Express), because you will be charged to change your U.S. dollars to French francs, and then your French francs to Belgian francs! The American Express office once gave me Belgian money that had been out of circulation for over 3 years and was totally worthless.

If you want to change money back to dollars when you leave a country, remember that you will pay a higher rate for them. You are now "buying" dollars rather than "selling" them. Therefore, never change more money than you think you will need, unless you plan to stockpile for another trip.

Have some foreign currency on hand for arrival. After a lengthy transatlantic flight, you will not want to stand in line at some airport booth just to get your cab fare. You'll pay a very high rate of exchange and be wasting your precious bathtub time. Your home bank or local currency exchange office can sell you small amounts of foreign currency. No matter how much of a premium you pay for this money, the convenience will be worth it. I get $100 worth of currency for each country I visit to have on me on arrival; I buy it at the airport before I depart. This pays for the taxi to the hotel, tips, and the immediate necessities until I decide where to change the rest of my money.

Keep track of what you pay for your currency. If you are going to several countries, or you must make several money-changing trips to the cashier, write down the sums. When you get home and wonder what you did with all the money you used to have, it'll be easier to trace your cash. When you are budgeting, adjust to the rate you paid for the money, not the rate you read in the newspaper.

Keep a rough estimate of the conversion rate in your mind. Know the conversion rate for $50 and $100 so that in an instant you can make a judgment about a purchase. If you're still interested in an item, slow down and figure out the accurate price.

HOW TO GET CASH OVERSEAS

Go to **American Express** for quick cash. Card members may draw on their cards for cash advances or may cash personal checks. *Never travel without your checkbook.*

It's all a relatively simple transaction—you write a personal check at a special desk and show your card, it is approved, then you go to another desk and get the money in the currency you request. Allow about a half hour for the whole process, unless there are long lines. Usually you get the credit advance on your card at the same desk.

ATM Machines

Sacré cash card! This is without doubt the easiest and possibly best way for exchanging money—*le bank machine.*

Bank cash machines are being used by everyone in Europe and are everywhere. Just look for the Cirrus and NYSE logo, as some bank machines are only for local bank cards.

Strange Change

See page 64 for tips on spotting fake 10 F pieces, which are legion these days.

TIPS ON TIPPING

Tipping in Paris can be confusing because a service charge is added to all restaurant and hotel bills. While you do not have to add a tip to a restaurant check, it's often done—simply round up the bill or plunk down a few extra francs. It's all the waiter will see of your real tip; think 5% of the total.

Also note that tipping has gone up dramatically lately. Figure 10 F per suitcase when tipping bellboys at luxury hotels—5 F at three stars. Give 5 F to doormen who hail you a taxi.

Round up for taxi drivers or give 10% for longer rides (such as to the airport).

SEND MONEY

You can have money sent to you from home, a process that usually takes about 2 days. Money can be wired through **Western Union** (someone brings them cash or a certified check, and WU does the rest—this may take up to a week). Call Western Union at ☎ 800/325-6000 in the U.S. You can also get cash with an international money order, which is cleared by telex through the bank where you cash it. Money can be wired from bank to bank, but this only works when your American bank has branches in Europe or a relationship with a French bank. Banks usually charge a large fee for doing you this favor.

In addition, American Express can arrange for a Money Gram, a check for up to $500 that can be sent to you by family or friends at home. You then cash it at the American Express office in Paris. Call ☎ 800/543-4080 in the U.S. for details.

PAYING UP
. . . .
Whether you use cash, traveler's checks, or a credit card, you are probably paying for your purchase in a currency that is not American dollars. Airports and airplanes often take dollars anywhere in the world, and you can tip a bellboy with a dollar bill, if need be, but in France you're going to need French francs.

I think you'll do best using a credit card. Plastic is the safest to use, provides you with a record of your purchases (for U.S. Customs as well as your books), and makes returns a lot easier. Credit-card companies, because they often are associated with banks, also give the best exchange rates. You may even "make money" by charging a purchase to a credit card because the price your credit-card company gives you on an exchange ratio is almost always better than what you can get for cash in a foreign country.

One thing to note about credit-card charges: Your purchase is posted in dollars the day your credit slip clears the credit-card company (or bank) office, not the day of your purchase. If the dollar goes up in the 2- or 3-day lag between these transactions, you make money; if the dollar loses strength, you pay. However, the differential is usually no more or no less than what you would suffer on the streets with a volatile exchange rate.

If you go to a shop that does not honor any of the cards you hold, but does have a display of cards in the window, ask them to pull out their credit forms to find the names (and pictures) of their reciprocal bank cards. Chances are you can make a match. Access, a common European credit card, happens to be the same as MasterCard—yet this is rarely advertised.

If you happen to be given a book of discount coupons by your hotel or tour guide, you will also notice that you get a 10% discount for cash, but only a 5% discount when you use credit cards. Storekeepers much prefer you to pay in cash. Remember this also when you are bargaining at flea markets. A credit-card transaction costs the retailer 2% to 5%. If you pay cash, you should be able to get that amount as a discount.

Traveler's checks are a must—for safety's sake. Shop around a bit, compare the various companies that issue checks, and make sure your checks are insured against theft or loss. I happen to use American Express traveler's checks, but they are not the only safe game in town; choose your type of check by what you can get without paying a fee. If you are a member of **AAA** (American Automobile Association), you can get American Express traveler's checks without paying a fee—this alone is worth AAA's membership dues.

I also use AAA to obtain traveler's checks in foreign currency. They don't come in every currency, but they are available in French francs. You may have to order ahead. If you don't travel to France frequently, you don't want more than you can use, but a few hundred dollars' worth of francs will make changing money that much easier, since you are not converting currency. Do watch the rates for a few weeks while you contemplate this purchase; once you buy, you are locked into a rate.

American Express now offers a "Global Moneypac," which provides foreign cash and/or traveler's checks in the currencies you'll need for your trip. Call ☎ 800/414-6914 in the U.S., and pay with your American Express or Optima credit card. They'll charge a commission, and there's an extra fee if you need courier delivery. Currencies available are: French francs, English sterling, Japanese yen, Swiss francs, Deutsche marks, and Canadian dollars. You're on your own for that trip to Italy.

Finally, when you are trying to figure out how much things cost, remember to divide by the rate you paid for your money, not the bank rate.

DÉTAXE

. . . .

Détaxe is the refund you get on TVA, the value-added tax of 20.6% that is levied on all goods sold in France. It's similar to sales tax in the U.S. The French pay it automatically. Tourists can get a refund on it.

The basic détaxe system works pretty much like this:

You are shopping in a store with prices marked on the merchandise. This is the true price of the item that any tourist or any national must pay. If you are a French national, you pay the price without thinking twice. If you are a tourist who plans to leave the country within 6 months, you may qualify for a détaxe refund. But wait: There's a hitch. Each store, on an individual basis, establishes the amount of money you must spend to qualify for the refund. You must immediately ask a salesperson, "What is the minimum expenditure in this store for the export refund?" While the rate varies from shop to shop, the minimum is set by law. Currently the minimum for a détaxe refund is 1,200 F for a person spending this amount or more in one store on a single day.

Once you know the minimum, you must decide if you will make a small purchase now, and come back another time for a bigger haul, or if you will hoard receipts. Only you know how much time your schedule permits for shopping or what your bottom-line budget is. Spending to save doesn't always make sense. Keep the discount in perspective.

If you are going to another European country, consider the export tax credit policy there. The tax-free program in Italy is now working, and requires a *lower* expenditure to qualify for the refund. If you are going on to Italy from France, you may want to make your big purchases there. If you're planning to visit England next, you can get a VAT refund on most purchases made there. Usually, you need only to spend £50 to qualify, but that, too, is flexible. (Harrods makes you spend £75 before you get a refund.)

Balance local good buys against foreign détaxe credits as well. In other words, perfume is not a good buy in England, so who cares if you get a 15% refund, when the markup is much higher than in France? France or the French West Indies are absolutely the best places in the world to buy French perfume—no discount plan or VAT refund plan should dissuade you.

If you go for the détaxe refund, budget your time to allow for the paperwork. It takes about 15 minutes to fill out each store's forms, and may take 20 to 60 minutes for you to receive the forms back, especially if you are shopping in a big department store during the tourist season. But you never know—I've zipped through the line in less than 5 minutes. Allow more time than you need, just in case.

You will need your passport number (but not necessarily the passport itself) to fill out the paperwork. The space that asks for your address is asking for the name of your hotel. You do not need to provide its address. After the papers are filled out, they will be given back to you along with an envelope. Sometimes the envelope has a stamp on it; sometimes it is blank (if the latter, you must affix a stamp to it before you leave the country). At other times, it has a special government frank that serves as a stamp. If you don't understand what's on your envelope, ask.

When you're at the airport, go to the Customs official who services the détaxe papers. Do this before you clear regular Customs or send off your luggage. The Customs officer has the right to ask you to show him or her the merchandise you bought and are taking out of the country. Whether the officer sees your purchases or not, he or she will stamp the papers, keeping a set (which will be processed) and giving you another set. Place this set in the envelope, and mail the envelope to the shop where you made your purchases. Usually the envelope is preprinted with the shop's name and address or has been hand-addressed by the shop for you. Sometimes, however, the Customs officer keeps the specially franked envelopes. Don't worry, they'll be mailed.

Please note: Since unification in 1993, you now claim your détaxe when you leave your final EU destination to return to the U.S. If you are going on to Belgium from France, you claim everything as you exit Belgium and process your paperwork there. You'll get the French laws and the French discounts, but the paperwork itself is done at Belgian customs. Ditto for Britain, Italy, and elsewhere in the EU.

When the papers get back to the shop and the government has notified the shop that their set of papers has been registered, the store will then grant you the discount through a refund. This can be done on your credit card (they will have made a dual pressing), or through a personal check, which will come to you later in the mail (see below).

So that's how the system works. Now, here are the fine points: *The way in which you get your discount is somewhat negotiable!* At the time of purchase, discuss your options for the refund with the retailer. Depending on how much you have bought, how big a store it is, or how cute you are, you may get a more favorable situation. At Galeries Lafayette, you have five different choices of how to take the refund. Here are two different and popular ways in which you can get the refund, in order of preference to the tourist:

- The retailer sells you the merchandise at the cheapest price possible, including the discount, and takes a loss on income until the government reimburses him or her. For example: The bottle of fragrance you want costs $50. The discount is $7.50. The best possible deal you could ever get is for the retailer to charge you $42.50 flat, give you the détaxe papers, and explain to you that he will not get the rest of his money unless you process the papers properly. Being as honorable as you are, of course you process the papers.
- You pay for the purchase, at the regular retail price, with a major credit card. Your card is passed through a second time for a refund slip, marked for the amount of the détaxe. You sign both slips at the time of the purchase. When the papers come back to the retailer, the shop puts through the credit slip. The credit may appear on the same monthly statement as the original bill, or on a subsequent bill. Just remember to check that the credit goes through.

With the most common method, you pay the regular retail price with cash, traveler's check, or credit card. You're given the forms and go through the refund process as described above, get on your plane, and go home. Several months later (usually about 3) you get a check in the mail, made out for the refund. This check is in the currency of the country in which you made the purchase and will have to be converted to dollars and cents, a process for which your bank may charge you a percentage or a fee. Or you can go to a currency broker and get the money in the currency of origin to save for your next trip to that country. Either way, it's a pain in the neck.

Note: The tax refund at department stores is 13%—the store takes the rest for fees. The refund at designer shops and boutiques is 14%; same thinking. Only a few rare stores actually give you a 20% discount.

Détaxe on Trains & Ferries

If you leave Paris by train—as I do frequently—you may be in a panic about your détaxe refund. Not to worry. As mentioned above, you now apply for the refund as you leave the EU. If your train is taking you to another EU country, you do not even have to think about filing for your détaxe refund in France.

If your train (or ferry) is taking you to a non-EU country, you will need to do the paperwork on board the train. No problem. Shortly after you board the international train, the conductor for your car will poke his head into your cabin, introduce himself (he speaks many languages), ask for your passport, and give you the Customs papers for the crossing of international borders. If you are on the sleeper, he handles the paperwork in the middle of the night while you sleep. If you have détaxe papers, provide them at this time. You can act nervous and fuss a bit, but this guy knows exactly what to do. It is customary to provide a small tip for him when you depart anyway; if he has secured your papers you may want to add to the tip.

ONE LAST CALCULATING THOUGHT
· ·

Unless you have a Ph.D. in mathematics from MIT, I suggest you keep a calculator in your purse. Furthermore, it should be the kind that uses batteries. Solar calculators are very cute, but your purse is dark inside, and many shops are, too. There's nothing worse than trying to do a hard bit of negotiating when your calculator won't calculate. If you use your calculator frequently, or if your children like to play with it as a toy, buy new batteries before you leave on the trip.

U.S. Customs and Duties Tips

To make your reentry into the U.S. as smooth as possible, follow these tips:

- Know the rules and stick to them!
- Don't try to smuggle anything.
- Be polite and cooperative (up until the point when they ask you to strip, anyway. . .).

Remember:

- You are allowed to bring in $400 worth of merchandise per person, duty free. (Books are not included, as they are duty free.) Before you leave the U.S., verify this amount with one of the U.S. Customs offices. Each member of the family is entitled to the deduction; this includes infants.
- Currently, you pay a flat 10% duty on the next $1,000 worth of merchandise.
- Duties thereafter are based on the type of product. They vary tremendously per item.
- The "head of the family" can make a joint declaration for all family members. Whoever is the head of the family, however, should take the responsibility for answering any questions the Customs officers may ask. Answer questions honestly, firmly, and politely. Have receipts ready, and make sure they match the information on the landing card. Don't be forced into a story that won't wash under questioning. If you tell a little lie, you'll be labeled as a fibber, and they'll tear your luggage apart.
- Have the Customs registration slips for your personally owned goods in your wallet or easily available. If you wear a Cartier watch, be able to produce the registration slip. If you cannot prove that you took a foreign-made item out of the U.S. with you, you may be forced to pay duty on it. If you own such items but have no registration or sales slips, take photos or

Polaroids of the goods and have them notarized in the U.S. before you depart. The notary seal and date will prove you had the goods in the U.S. before you left the country.

- The unsolicited gifts you mailed from abroad do not count in the $400-per-person rate. If the value of the gift is more than $50, you pay duty when the package comes into the country. Remember, it's only one unsolicited gift per person. Don't mail to yourself.

- Do not attempt to bring in any illegal food items—dairy products, meats, fruits, or vegetables (coffee is okay). Generally speaking, if it's alive, it's verboten. Any creamy French cheese is illegal, but a hard or cured cheese is legal.

- Antiques must be 100 years old to be duty free. Provenance papers will help (so will permission to export the antiquity, since it could be an item of national cultural significance). Any bona fide work of art is duty free, whether it was painted 50 years ago or just yesterday; the artist need not be famous.

- Dress for success. People who look like "hippies" get stopped at Customs more than average folks. Women who look like a million dollars, who are dragging their fur coats, have first-class baggage tags on their luggage, and carry Gucci handbags, but declare they have bought nothing, are equally suspicious.

- Elephant ivory is illegal to import. Antique ivory pieces may be brought into the country if you have papers stating their provenance.

- The amount of Customs allowance is expected to change. If you are a big shopper, check before you leave to see if there's any news.

If you do not have a calculator with you but are contemplating a large purchase, ask the store to provide a calculator or to "run the numbers" for you. The difference between dividing by 5 and 5.3 can matter; likewise 5.8 is nice, but 6.2 is nicer.

Chapter Four

· · · · · · ·

SHOPPING STRATEGIES

PARIS PLANS

· ·

Unless you have scads of time on your hands, you'll find that shopping in Paris involves making choices: You'll always be sorry you didn't get to one neighborhood or another, but then you'll have an excuse for returning to the City of Light. No matter how little time you have, you'll have no trouble spending your budget or finding something worth buying.

A map is called a *plan* in French, so start planning for your savings before you leave home—or as soon as you arrive at your hotel. By studying a map, you'll get a feel for the relationship between the sights you want to see, the places you want to eat, and the areas you want to shop. Make plans with your *plan* in hand or arrive with a schedule.

If you have a map at home, spend a little time doing what I do: Make charts that outline each day and your goals for that day. I rarely get everything done (I go much slower than I think I will), but at least my time, directions, transportation, and shopping priorities have been thought out and organized to maximize my Paris power.

Be sure to consider what kind of métro pass to buy, as well. Some of these are pegged to the day of the week, so pay attention before you arrive. That way, no matter how much jet lag clouds your brain on arrival, you're ready to start saving.

BARGAIN SMARTS

. . . .

Prices in Paris are not low, so to sniff out the bargains you're going to need some background information. The bargains go to the shopper who is ready to recognize them, and that means doing some homework.

If you have favorite designers or acquisition targets for your trip, shop the major department stores and U.S.-based boutiques for comparison prices. Don't assume you will get a bargain on a Parisian purchase. Many international designers and retailers set prices that are virtually the same all around the world. Even so, within that structure, you can find a deal.

If you do not live in a city that has a lot of European merchandise, do some shopping through *Vogue* and *Harper's Bazaar*. In the ads for the designer boutiques, you'll find phone numbers. Call and ask about prices and sales. Don't be afraid to explain that you are contemplating a shopping trip to Europe and are doing some comparison pricing. If you live in a city that dresses conservatively, you'll find clothing in Paris to be much more vibrant and exciting. If you think creatively, you'll find a way to adapt it to your lifestyle.

Read French magazines to get familiar with the French look and the hottest shops. They can cost a fortune (sometimes $14 a magazine in the United States), but many libraries have them. Many French magazines now have U.S. and U.K. editions that do not have the foreign advertising you want, but will keep you in touch with the look.

Understand the licensing process. Designers sell the rights to their names and often their designs to various makers around the world. Two men's suits may bear an identical label—that of a well-known French designer—but will fit differently because they are manufactured differently.

French cosmetics and fragrances can be extraordinarily less expensive in France, or just marginally so. Know prices before you leave home. Also note that the marketing concept of giving a gift with a purchase is pretty much an American thing. While you can find it in Europe on occasion, you won't get as good a gift. The value of the gift in the U.S. may indeed exceed the value of the discount when you buy it retail in France.

Don't be fooled into thinking that merchandise with foreign-sounding names is made in Europe, or is French, or offers a bargain.

Because Americans are so taken with European names, many American-made products have foreign, especially French, names. Since the biggest rage in France these days is American-made products, don't be lured into buying something in France that could be bought at home for less.

BEST BUYS IN PARIS

. . . .

Perfumes, Cosmetics & Hair Care   Perfume savings get to the heart-stopping level once you make the commitment to spend enough to qualify for the détaxe (1,200 F). Beyond that, actual savings on discounted perfumes are getting hard to find because of changing business practices in France and a united crackdown by the big-name fragrance and makeup makers to try to stop non-détaxe-related discounting. This is aimed mostly at French locals, but may also impact you. Know your U.S. prices and understand that new laws have been passed within the last year, so that what you paid last trip or how discounts were handled at that time could be very different now.

I tend to buy fragrances that have just been introduced in Paris and are not yet available in the U.S. as gift items for my American friends because of their novelty value; therefore, price isn't an issue.

If you find your beauty creams are no longer the bargain they once were, it may be time to visit a *parapharmacie*. These stores carry drugstore brands of beauty products—no Chanel or Yves Saint Laurent—at a 20% discount. This is the place to load up on fancy hair care products, skin creams, bath products, and possibly even face powder. Barney's New York has made Leclerc all the rage; now they have it everywhere in Paris.

Limoges   Buy Limoges boxes in pretty shapes— fruits, vegetables, animals, and so on. Each box costs between $75 to $100 in Paris, but twice as much in the U.S.

Hermès   Hermès Paris prices (with a détaxe refund) are definitely lower than in New York. In addition, you can frequently find Hermès bargains at various airport duty-free shops and in airline duty-free catalogs that are even better than Paris retail prices. London may also be less expensive than Paris! And here's a shocker: I flew different legs of my last trip on two different airlines and the price for Hermès products on the airlines was different.

Baccarat   All French glassware can be dramatically less expensive in France, but the cost of shipping it abroad voids the savings. However, have you seen the Baccarat crystal medallions and butterflies that hang from a silk cord? They are drop-dead chic and cost approximately $135 in the U.S. and in France. Get onto an airplane that has Baccarat in its duty-free catalog, and lo and behold, the same trinket sells for about $60. Or buy at regular French retail for about $70. This is a serious bargain.

Candies, Foodstuffs & Chocolates   These make great gifts, especially when wrapped in the distinctive packaging of one of Paris's premier food palaces. I buy Maille's tomato soup–colored "Provençale" mustard in grocery stores (no fancy wrap for me, thanks) and give it to foodies around the world—it's unique and special. I haven't found it in any U.S. specialty stores yet. Some Maille flavors are available in the U.S. (and U.K.), but not this particular one. Maille has its own shop at place de la Madeleine.

I also stock up on caramelized almonds in beautiful tin boxes (under $10 £6.50), or create baskets containing a variety of fancy foodstuffs. Foods make fabulous gifts and souvenirs in the $2 to $10 price range.

Collectibles It's pretty hard to give advice about the ever-changing collectibles market, but the things that caught my eye have all turned out to be bargains when I compared prices at American flea markets (why didn't I buy more?). I bought an empty postcard album—probably from the turn of the century—at the flea market in Vanves, in perfect condition, for $10. I saw a similar one in a dealers' show in Greenwich, Connecticut, for $150. I bought a funky straw hat from the 1950s for $40 and a country-style tablecloth for $5. I thought these were fair prices; I hope you'll agree.

Stockings I have a hard time finding stockings (and tights) that are long enough for my frame in the U.S. and the U.K. Not so in France. I also like to wear a garter belt and stockings sometimes; fancy stockings (with lace-border tops) are easy to find in Paris—far easier than in other countries. I can also count on the French for gorgeous garter belts.

Kitsch I'll admit up front that I adore kitsch. I can't help but buy kitschy souvenirs for myself and my friends. My usual hangout for fun junk is the rue de Rivoli. Every visit I find another reason to buy a pencil with the Eiffel Tower attached by a slim gold chain, a bath sponge that looks like the French flag, a scarf with tacky illustrations of Paris's best sights, boxer shorts emblazoned with baguettes, or a T-shirt from the Sorbonne. These items are carefully priced with tourists in mind and never cost more than $10. While the more tasteful part of me wants to advise *you not to load up on tacky gifts and instead save your money for something worthwhile, the truth is, I can't stop buying (and using) this junk.

LESS-THAN-STELLAR BUYS

· ·

Some things are simply not a bargain in any sense. Unless you are desperate, avoid buying: **American-made goods.** Whether they be designer items, such as a Ralph Lauren jacket or a pair of Joan & David shoes, or mass-market items like a GAP T-shirt or a pair of Levis, American-made goods are rarely good buys. Ditto for British goods (Aquascutum, Hilditch & Key, or Marks & Spencer), men's business attire, electrical goods (wrong voltage), and Coca-Cola purchased at bars, cafes, or hotels. Postcards priced at $1 or more are no bargain (see p. 31 for how you can do better), and neither are massive amounts of Disneyland Paris souvenirs. Unless they are on sale or you qualify for a détaxe refund (or you've just sold the movie rights to your life's story), big-name designer clothes are another less-than-good buy.

THE MOSCOW RULE OF SHOPPING

· ·

The Moscow Rule of Shopping is one of my most basic shopping rules and has nothing to do with shopping in Moscow, so please pay attention. Now: The average shopper, in her or his pursuit of the ideal bargain, does not buy an item she wants when she first sees it because she's not convinced she won't find it elsewhere for less money. She wants to see everything available, then return for the purchase of choice. This is a rather normal thought process. If you've ever lived in a former Iron Curtain country, however, you know that you must buy something the minute you see it because if you hesitate—it will be gone. Hence the title of my international law: the Moscow Rule of Shopping.

Naturally you can't compare the selection in Paris to what's on hand in Moscow (even today Russians would swoon at the airport shopping alone), but the fundamental principle is still applicable.

When you are on a trip, you probably will not have the time to compare prices and then return to a certain shop; you will never be able to backtrack through cities, and even if you could, the item might be gone by the time you got back, anyway. What to do? The same thing they do in Moscow: Buy it when you see it, understanding that you may never see it again. But remember, since you are not shopping in Moscow and you may see the same item again, weigh these questions carefully before you go buy:

- Is this a touristy type of item that I am bound to find all over town?
- Is this an item I can't live without, even if I am overpaying?
- Is this a reputable shop, and can I trust what they tell me about the availability of such items?
- Is the quality of this particular item so spectacular that it is unlikely it could be matched at this price?

If you have good reason to buy it when you see it, do so. The Moscow Rule of Shopping breaks down if you are an antiques or bric-a-brac shopper, since you never know whether you can find another of an old or a used item, whether you can find it in the same condition, or whether the price will be higher or lower. It's very hard to price collectibles, so consider doing a lot of shopping for an item before you buy anything. This is easy in Paris, where there are a zillion markets that sell much the same type of merchandise in the collectibles area. At a certain point you just have to buy what you love and be satisfied that you love it.

THE INTERNATIONAL ICON RULE OF SHOPPING
. . . .
And so it came to pass that I had to give a business gift to a French businessman whom I do not know very well. It had to be expensive (approximately

$100) and it had to be prestigious. Since I had never had a personal conversation with him, I decided that God had created ties for this very purpose.

I carefully shopped all the designer stores and settled on a drop-dead chic Prada tie. It came elegantly wrapped up, complete with a card testifying to its authenticity. However, I also bought a fake designer tie from a street market for $10 and wrapped that in an Hermès box.

When it came time for the presentation of the gifts, the businessman seized the Hermès box like a particularly gleeful child at a birthday party and said, "You bought me an Hermès tie. You shouldn't have."

I quickly added that it wasn't an Hermès tie and handed him the Prada box with great ceremony. He smiled weakly at the Prada box, exclaimed that the tie was very nice, and promptly forgot about it.

When I replayed the scene in my mind, I realized that a Frenchman is interested only in French status symbols, unlike Americans, who respond to status items from many countries. Despite the EU and the so-called unification of Europe, Europeans are still regional people who want status and luxury goods from the houses they know best. Despite the fact that an Hermès tie and a Prada tie cost virtually the same amount, the Prada tie was lost on a Frenchman.

Then, it happened to me in reverse. I bought a French tie for an American businessman who represents French hotels, figuring it was the perfect gift. It was not, however, a Hermès tie. It was a famous French brand, and any Frenchman would have known its status, but my American friend did not. He smiled weakly. Even as I explained to him what the tie meant and where it was from, I knew that for the same amount of money I would have looked like a genius if I'd simply bought him a Hermès tie.

So in the hope that you'll learn from my missteps, here are a few thoughts to bear in mind. First, if you have to give an international business/status gift, make sure the person to whom you are presenting the gift recognizes the name you have chosen. If you must give an American gift to a European, make sure the European knows the American name.

Second, the next time you complain about high prices in designer shops, think twice. Remember that these high retail prices cover the cost of international advertising and image making, which in turn bestows importance on the gift you choose.

Finally, never buy faux anything and try to pass it off as the real thing.

FRANC-LY MY DEAR

· ·

You can moan and groan about the good old days when $1 was equal to 10 F, but I call that negative thinking. Instead, remember back to when the dollar was equal to 4 F, which is where the equation stood for years and years. (If you are not old enough to remember, you'll just have to trust me here.)

Now that you've readjusted your thinking, things aren't looking so bad, are they? It's all a matter of perspective! The recession proved to even the French that the 1980s are over. The fanciest hotels in town (well, some of them) have lowered prices or begun to add value. Led by Claude Terrail of the famous Tour d'Argent, restaurants—and I'm talking about famous tables with multistarred Michelin chefs—have added on fixed-price meals, so that just about anyone can afford to eat at the best tables in Paris.

There are tricks out there so that Paris can give you more bang for your franc than in past years. You can save on transportation, meals, and more. Combine your luxury hotel room with some down-and-dirty consumer facts and enjoy the best of both worlds. Here are just a few tips:

- Buy Cokes and mineral water at the grocery store and keep them in your minibar. Every chic Frenchwoman in Europe carries a large tote bag with a plastic bottle of mineral water. If you really want to save money, avoid drinking Coke completely—it's expensive everywhere in Europe. If you must splurge, enjoy one Coke in your room—after you've bought a six-pack at the market. A whole six-pack costs almost as much as one minibar Coke!

- Buy food from fresh markets (one of Paris's most beautiful natural resources), supermarkets, and traiteurs who sell ready-cooked gourmet meals— hot or cold. You can eat a fabulous French meal for $5 to $10 per person this way. An entire rotisserie chicken, which feeds four, costs no more than $10 and can cost even less (depending on the size and quality of the chicken). Pizza is another good buy.

- Eat your fancy meals at starred Michelin restaurants that offer fixed-price meals.

- Get into the hotel dining room game. Lately, it's become trendy for hotels to acquire a one-star Michelin chef in order to attract guests and locals alike. Some of the one-star chefs have even earned two stars! These hotel restaurants are competing so fiercely with each other that they watch their prices carefully. You can eat a three-course gourmet meal at several one-star restaurants in Paris for the fixed price of 220 F to 250 F ($40 to $50), including tax and gratuity! Some of the most famous restaurants in Paris cost only slightly more. See page 00 for more on good deals on good eats.

- Do your gift shopping either in duty-free stores (not at the airport; the Paris streets are crammed with them), *parapharmacies,* flea markets, or the *hypermarché;* don't scorn those tacky tourist traps for great $3 to $5 gift items. You can also find small gifts at Inno or Monoprix—even at métro stops.

ACCUMULATING RECEIPTS

Most stores, even mom-and-pop shops and little perfume shops, will allow you to accumulate your receipts over a 6-month period until they total 1,200 F and you're able to apply for a détaxe refund. Department stores claim that a law passed in 1997 insists that all the purchases must be made in 1 day and cannot be accumulated, although they will let everyone in one family combine receipts. Also, department stores are open late on Thursday nights so you can go back for another crack at it then.

DEPARTMENT STORE DISCOUNTS & DEALS

The three major department stores in Paris, **Galeries Lafayette, Au Printemps,** and **Bon Marché,** all offer a flat 10% discount to tourists.

This discount card has nothing to do with détaxe and applies to all goods in the store, except in leased departments, which are usually luggage and fine jewelry. In order to get this discount, you need a coupon. These coupons are given away in most hotels and even through U.S. travel agents. Go to the welcome desk or ask someone the minute you enter the store then walk around with the coupon in your hand; I always forget to use mine.

Do not be surprised if you are asked to pay at a central cashier rather than the nearest cashier; this has to do with the discount card and the store's accounting process. It's a pain, but nothing in life is free.

FIDELITY CARDS

Fidelity cards are used all over the world, but seem to be particularly popular in France, especially in midrange designer shops and *parapharmacies.* This is a small card, like a credit card, that is stamped or punched every time you make a purchase. Make a certain number of purchases or reach a total franc value and receive a discount or a gift.

SHOPPING SCAMS

. . . .

Imagine my surprise one day when Pascale-Agnès grabbed the change out of my hand and began inspecting it very carefully. "We have to make sure it's not fake!" she announced.

Sure enough, there's been a flood of faux 10 F pieces; there are over eight million in circulation today. *Travel & Leisure* says the fakes are redder in color with a bad fit between the silver core and the brass edge. Pascale-Agnès says badly etched lines give away a fake, particularly the arm holding the torch, which has fuzzy edges on a counterfeit piece.

Meanwhile, many of my friends who live in Paris are complaining about being shortchanged—mostly by taxi drivers but also by vendors. Stand there and count your change. I don't think I've ever been cheated outright in a store in Paris, but I have fallen into a few shopping canyons where a smarter person might have worn a parachute.

At a perfume shop in Paris (not my regular one), I asked the price of the perfume of one of my favorite scents. The price I was given sounded fair; not a bargain, but fair. I decided to make the purchase. The entire time that I was doing this, I was assuming that we were talking about 1 ounce of perfume. I never asked specifically, "What is the price for 1 ounce of Tocade?" When I got home, I discovered that I had bought a 1/4-ounce bottle of Tocade in a very, very fancy, but very, very tiny atomizer.

Here's another size-count story. I priced a roll of French tricolor ribbon at the flea market at Vanves. It was a full roll; the asking price was 10 F. I had trouble arguing with that. I found a second full roll of ribbon and asked the price for two rolls. I was told 20 F. I said, "That's no bargain. I want a deal."

So the vendor offered me all of the tricolor he had in a box on the ground for 50 F. I was overwhelmed by my good fortune. I handed over the 50 F. Hours later, I took out all the rolls of ribbon and rewound them, so that each spool was filled with ribbon, just like the first two. I had four spools of ribbon, or 40 F worth!

Had I rewound the spools at the flea market, or even lined up all the spools and said to the guy, "Hey buddy, this isn't the equivalent of five spools, how about 40 F?," then I'm sure he would have gladly taken 40 F. But I was stupid.

GETTING TO KNOW YOU

Personal relationships are very important in France. People continue to do business with the same people, indeed the same salesperson, in the same stores and markets for years, even generations. This is cultural, but it also helps the customer make sure he or she is not cheated.

When you find stores you like, spend the time to develop a personal relationship. Reinforce the connection with faxes or little notes during the year, announcing when you will return to Paris. Go so far as to make an appointment, if you feel this is warranted. The more you are known—and this truly takes years of repeat business—the more chance you'll have of getting a discount or a family price and extra perks.

DUTY-FREE SHOPPING STRATEGIES

Discount is a dirty word in France. In recent years, a few upstarts began to discount major names so that locals could get a fraction of the price breaks that non-EU passport holders get through duty-free shops. These discount sources so threatened the big-name makers and department stores that makers now limit the amount of goods released to discounters and the amount of discount allowed.

Few shops use the word *discount* at all. The proper name to hide behind is "duty free." Paris is famous for its duty-free shops. It is one of the few cities in the world where there is a lot of duty-free-style shopping, not just at the airport but on city streets. These shops take on a whole new importance now that duty free between EU destinations has been outlawed and airport shopping has begun to change focus.

Most non-airport duty-free shops sell makeup, fragrances, and deluxe gift items—designer earrings, scarves, ties, and even pens. Some of accessories have been created specifically for the enormous duty-free business and are not sold through the designer boutiques. Duty-free stores like to tell you that they give a 40% discount. The truth is, the notion of a 40% discount is based on the days when the luxury tax on real perfume (not *eau de toilette*) was 18%. Then you were getting a 20% discount off the top and an additional 18% discount on the détaxe. Because France has lowered the luxury tax on perfume, the amount of the détaxe refund has also been lowered.

In reality, expect to get a 20% discount without too much trouble; a 25% discount, if you are lucky; and no further discount unless you qualify for a détaxe refund. If you do get a 25% discount and also qualify for a détaxe refund, your total savings will be 45%!

Duty-free shops are good places to buy fragrances and cosmetics, even though the prices on these items are controlled and may offer you little or no savings over U.S. prices, especially if you shop at discounters.

On American brands, savings are iffy.

On French brands, savings tend to vary enormously.

This is where homework pays off. Saving $1 on a Lancôme mascara is not my idea of anything to brag about. Sometimes the savings are related to the cost of the dollar. When the dollar was high, I saved $4 on a Lancôme mascara. Now the dollar is lower, and Lancôme prices are higher. Life goes on. But there are enormous savings to be made if you qualify for a détaxe refund and shop wisely.

Note that in the department stores, the export rebate is 13%. In luxury shops it is 14%.

SPECIAL-EVENT RETAILING

. . . .

Paris is filled with special shopping events. Watch for the **Braderie de Paris,** held in December and June at the Porte de Versailles. It's rather like a church bazaar. An ability to speak French will help, but is not required. All the big designers donate items for sale; there are bargains by the ton. Ask your concierge for details and the exact dates, although the event is advertised in magazines and papers. (I know you read *Madame Figaro* when you are in town, so you probably know it all anyway.) There is easy access by métro.

Hermès has twice yearly sales that can only be described as world-class sporting events. Held in March and October, the exact dates of the sale are revealed only moments before in newspaper ads. The sales have become such an event that they are no longer held at the store. The average wait in line is 4 hours before admission; items are marked down to just about half price. Unfortunately, a code is worked into your purchase that tells the world your item was bought on sale. It is not obvious, but look for a teeny-tiny S in a scarf.

The event you really want to catch, however, is the **Biennale Internationale des Antiquaires,** the single biggest, most important antiques event in the world. It's held only every other year, usually in September, at the Grand Palais, which is roughly halfway between the place de la Concorde and the Rond Point. It's most easily reached by *mètro.*

Check the design trades for the actual dates or ask your concierge. You need not be a designer to attend.

Annual antiques shows are held at the Grand Palais each year from late November through early December, and they, too, are wonderful. But if you ever make it to the big event, you will never forget it.

There are also a number of antiques shows that happen at the same time every year and become special events to plan trips around. April or May in Paris means only one thing: time for the **Brocante de Bastille.** Celebrated outside, in stalls planted around the canal at Bastille, it is truly a magical shopping affair to remember.

For information about any of the big shopping events, look in *Allo Paris* or *Figaroscope*. **The French Government Tourist Office** in New York (☎ 212/ 315-0888) can supply you with the dates of these special events as well.

RENTING COUTURE

In Paris for a special occasion, such as New Year's Eve or your 25th wedding anniversary? Why not rent a couture gown for that big night out? The French do. The proper place to rent is **Sommier,** 3 Passage Brady, 10e. Since French women want only the finest quality, but are too practical to buy a couture gown for a once-in-a-lifetime formal event, they rent. If it's been your dream to wear a couture gown, you can have a very good choice for about $100 to $150.

MAKEUP & PERFUME SHOPPING TIPS

Perfume and makeup are possibly the absolute best buys in Paris. I'm talking French brands here. If you understand the ins and outs of the system and are willing to do some work, you can score gigantic savings. There will be a quiz next Friday.

Makeup in France is different from French makeup in the U.S. This is because makeup (even French brands) sold in the United States must be made according to FDA regulations, regardless of whether it's manufactured here or in France. When you get to France, the names of your favorite products may be the same or different, and even makeup with the same name may not be identical in shade. In addition, some products available in France are not sold in the U.S. at all. This can be because they haven't been launched yet or because the FDA has not approved them.

French perfume is also different in France than in the U.S., mainly because it is made with potato alcohol (yes, you can drink it—just like Scarlett O'Hara), while Anglo-Saxon countries use cereal alcohol. Potato alcohol increases the staying power of the fragrance, as well as the actual fragrance—to some small degree. If you've ever shopped for perfume in the Caribbean, you know that certain stores make a big brouhaha over the fact that they import directly from France. Now you know why that's important. The French version is considered the best or most authentic version.

Many American brands you see in France are made in France (or Europe) for the European market, such as Estée Lauder and Elizabeth Arden. You may save on these items when détaxe is credited to your purchase, but generally you do not save on American brands in Europe.

If you ship your beauty buys, you automatically get a 40% discount; you need not buy 1,200 F worth of merchandise. But the cost of postage can be high on beauty products that are in heavy jars. The cost of shipping fragrance is surprisingly modest. Discuss shipping costs before you get into any mail-order deals.

French perfumes are always introduced in France before they come out internationally. This lead time may be as much as a year ahead. If you want to keep up with the newest fragrances, go to your favorite duty-free store and ask specifically for the newest. If you are stumped for a gift for the person who has everything, consider one of these new fragrances. The biggest spring launch comes in time for Mother's Day in France, which is usually a different day than in the U.S., but it is always in spring—May or early June.

The converse of this rule also applies. Some older scents are taken off the market in the U.S. and U.K. because the sales figures aren't strong enough to support them. These fragrances are still sold in France. I saw an American woman at Catherine doing a gang-busters business in Fidji, which she says is no longer sold in the U.S.

Finally, some scents are never brought to the U.S. at all. Guerlain is big on this.

The amount of the basic discount on perfume and cosmetics varies from one shop to the next, as does the system by which you gain your détaxe refund. Ask at several shops until you find a program that makes you comfortable, or simply go for a flat discount and avoid the fuss.

Chapter Five

· · · · · · ·

SLEEPING IN PARIS

ARE YOU SLEEPING?
· ·

Some of the world's best hotels are in Paris; thankfully they are cheaper than in London. But the really fancy ones have gotten a lot fancier in the last year and more expensive. Even mid-priced hotels can be expensive; furthermore, you can stay in a fabulous hotel or you can stay in a terrible hotel for the exact same amount of money. That's why I do so much hotel research and keep looking for the best buys.

The kind of trip you have is very much related to the hotel you book. Please take the time to research value and make sure you don't get burned. Also remember the importance of "the $50 difference" (see p. 78) because sometimes you have to spend a little more to save a lot more. Even if you love the hotel you are staying in, spend a little bit of time during your trip to do some research for future trips. It's good to have backup plans.

When pricing hotels, especially during promotions, make sure to read the fine print and understand what you're getting. Some hotels require a minimum stay of 2 consecutive nights for you to qualify for a bargain price. Some "deals" are only on weekends. Bear in mind as well that the price listed may be per person or per room. Also, several promotions may be offered simultaneously, leaving you confused as to which one is really the best.

Please remember that July and August are high season in terms of airfare prices, but they are low season in terms of hotel rooms in Paris. Some of the best deals of the year can be made during this time period, so ask around.

Here are a few more of my hotel booking secrets:

- **Think winter.** The rack rate (the official room rate) at a luxury hotel in Paris is generally between $300 and $500 a night or more for a double room. Don't flinch. It's rare that anyone has to pay rack rate. Paris is most attractive and most fully booked in May and June and in September and October. Those are not good months to get a break on a fancy hotel room. Think December. Think January. Even February.
- **Work with hotel associations and chains.** Most hotels are members of associations or chains that have blanket promotions. Leading Hotels of the World offers a fabulous corporate rate at all their hotels. Most hotels have rates frozen in U.S. dollars for at least a portion of the year, especially when they are in a promotional period. These invariably have to be booked in the United States, but usually offer incredible value. Some hotels do the special rates for certain months; others offer these rates year-round!
- **Never assume that all hotels in a particular chain are equal.** Even if you are talking about big American hotel chains, such as Hilton or Sheraton, you will find hotels in every category of style and price within the same chain. Concorde Hotels, one of the most famous hotel chains in France, which has plenty of hotels in the moderate price range, also has the Crillon, one of the fanciest and most expensive hotels in Paris. By the same token, it's not unusual for a booking agent from any chain of hotels to try to trade you from one hotel in the chain to another hotel, especially in a

similar price bracket. Don't do it without knowing the properties.

- **Think package tours.** Airlines and tour operators often offer you the same trip you could plan
for yourself with the kind of hotels you really
want to stay at, but for less money. Check it all
out. Beware, however: On a packaged tour, you
may not get as good a room as you would get on
your own, and your chances of being upgraded
are lower.

- **Think opening day . . . or reopening day.** Several
of Paris's most famous hotels have been closed
for renovations and are just now reopening in
December of 1999. To woo back their regular
clients and to introduce the public to their new
splendors, they have some pretty amazing introductory deals and perks. Check out the Four
Seasons Georges V, the Hôtel Meurice, and the
Plaza Athenée—all recently redone and drop-
dead fabulous (with prices to match).

- **Think competition.** While the Georges V was
closed in order to transform itself into the Four
Seasons, two neighboring hotels increased their
business—the deluxe Prince de Galles, next door
to the Georges V, and the Queen Elizabeth, a four-
star around the corner. With the Four Seasons
now open, try these hotels—they may try to lure
you with price cuts.

Believe me, there are tons of fabulous hotels in
Paris. Given the proper amount of advance notice,
you should have no problem getting something great
at the price you want. Once you know your favorite neighborhoods in Paris, spend some time devel-
oping your own network of nearby hotels that fit
your needs and means. It is always acceptable to
walk into a hotel, ask for a brochure or a tariff card,
and request to see a room or two. You do not even
need to tip the person who shows you around.

HOTEL CHAINS & ASSOCIATIONS

. . . .

If you prefer to book all your reservations in one easy phone call or don't want any surprises, almost every major hotel chain in the world has a property in Paris. I've found that the big American chains offer the same type of room you expect, while the smaller European chains can be very uneven in what they offer. I have listed only major chains or associations with properties in the most convenient neighborhoods for shopping.

U.S.-Based Hotel Chains

Inter-Continental: Two hotels that don't feel like members of a hotel chain, both in fabulous locations, and offering the best promotional rates in the business. You can even get frequent-flyer mileage points. The flagship property has just been renovated.

Both Inter-Continental hotels are great, but bear in mind that Le Grand Hôtel Inter-Continental caters to tour groups, has approximately 1,000 rooms, and can resemble Grand Central Terminal at 9am. A very stylish Grand Central Terminal, but you get the idea. The rooms are tiny. The location, especially for shoppers, is beyond sensational. The restaurants on the property are fabulous. The nearby transportation choices are the best in Paris. If you prefer a more elegant atmosphere, the Paris Inter-Continental is the right choice. And yes, it's one of the big hotels that was recently refurbished. ☎ 800/327-0200 in the U.S. for reservations.

Westin-Demeure: Demure little French Demeure ain't so shy anymore. This French hotel chain recently merged with Westin Hotels to offer French glamour with American reservation systems. There are five luxury properties in Paris, including my adored Hôtel Castille. Le Parc, nestled in the 16th arrondissement, is where Alain Ducasse has his new restaurant. There isn't a more chic address in town, especially for a foodie. But then, foodies may like Le Marignan, next door to M. Ducasse's newest creation—Spoon. This hotel is walking distance to the Champs-Elysées and the avenue Montaigne. Hotel guests do get preference for dinner reservations and can even order room service from the restaurant. The hotels are dotted across the 8th and 16th arrondissements; the whole chain is a really good find. ☎ 800/228-3000 in the U.S. for reservations.

Sheraton: In Paris, Sheraton ITT offers us the Prince of Wales (Hôtel Prince de Galles), part of Sheraton's St. Regis Collection of grand dame hotels. The property is next door to the famed Georges V and is currently having a price war with Four Seasons now that Georges V has reopened. Rather conveniently situated near the Champs-Elysées, this hotel is aptly named. Furthermore, they have frequent promotions and airline mileage packages; it is drop-dead gorgeous in the intimate but gold ormolu tradition. ☎ 800/325-3535 in the U.S. for reservations.

Marriott: They have opened a nice little shopping hotel right above Sephora on the Champs-Elysées— you can't beat the location. The hotel is extraordinarily deep, so don't let the front door deceive you. The hotel strives to be discreet up front, but go up to the lobby, explore the hotel, and you will be smitten. Sunday brunch outside on the terrace is a must-do. Note: Since this hotel opened, it invariably sells out and may not be very flexible on rates. ☎ 800/228-9290 in the U.S. for reservations.

Hyatt: A little off the beaten path (but not by much), this hotel looks new and spiffy despite the fact that it's now been here for several years. Located in the St. Augustin part of the 8th arrondissement, it's just a block from the Madeleine and the heart of Paris shopping, so it's officially the Hyatt Regency Madeleine. Along with the hotel is a moderne cafe, Café M, which is a good place for you to have a shopping break and check out the hotel for another stay. ☎ 800/233-1234 in the U.S.

Hilton: There's a Hilton at each Paris airport as well as a large Hilton right near the Eiffel Tower. This isn't the best shopping location in the world, but it does have many promotional prices and price breaks, including 3 nights for the price of 2 on a Spring Weekend Breaks deal. Don't miss the restaurant, Pacific Eiffel. ☎ 800/HILTONS in the U.S. for reservations.

European Hotel Chains & Associations

Relais & Châteaux: Nothing stands for luxury more than this organization, representing small luxury properties all over the world. In Paris, their holdings include the Hôtel de Crillon. The phone situation is tricky, since the toll-free number works in only some states. If it doesn't in yours, call the New York number. ☎ 800/860-4930 or 212/856-0115 in the U.S. for reservations.

Forte & Meridien Hotels: Hôtel Meridien was offering such a fabulous winter weekend promotional rate last year that they filled up and turned away guests. Definitely worth looking into. ☎ 800/225-5843 in the U.S. for reservations.

Warwick: Warwick is a very small international chain with a great deal of variety among its hotels. Hôtel Westminster in Paris is a winner; see page 83. ☎ 800/223-3652 in the U.S. for reservations.

Sofitel: I've always been nervous about hotels represented by Sofitel because there are thousands of them, and they are very mixed. You must judge each one on an individual basis. I did, accidentally, bump into a few small, intimate three- and four-star Sofitels in prime shopping areas and thought they looked fine. Ask about Sofitel Pullman, not far from Étoile. ☎ 800/SOFITEL in the U.S. for reservations.

Concorde: Concorde is an unusual chain because it's really two different hotel chains in one: a set of drop-dead luxury hotels, which are among the fanciest in the world (Hôtel de Crillon, The Martinez, La Mamounia), and a set of perfectly fine but not as luxurious four-star hotels. Some of these are in old buildings, in various states of repair and disrepair, and others are in brand-new, modern high-rises.

I almost always stay in Concorde hotels, but that's because I've gotten to know so many on an individual basis and can control the surprise factor. The group publishes its own guide with color pictures of each property that helps in choosing but isn't failsafe. You can't go wrong with the Hôtel du Louvre, one of my faves (see p. 82). The Hôtel Concorde St. Lazare is the best secret in Paris. The Hôtel Ambassador, with its split personality—half businessperson's hotel and half shopper's delight—is another one to consider. For business travelers, it's close to the Bourse, yet for shoppers, you're just 1 block from Galeries Lafayette. And best yet, the Ambassador has a super restaurant expected to earn its one-star Michelin rating that it gave up when they revamped. ☎ 800/888-4747 in the U.S. for reservations.

BOOKING DEALS

• •

Sometimes the big hotel associations have their own promotions or deals. I call **Leading Hotels of the World** (☎ 800/223-6800) at the drop of my cell phone for their corporate rates and specialty promotions. Less fancy is the **Utell** organization (☎ 800/448-8355), which books thousands of hotels internationally and often has specials, especially weekend deals. They recently had an offering with Hôtel Normandy that made my heart stop—$215 per night (with breakfast) on weekends including May and June. I thought I was the only person who knew about the Normandy—a great find 1 block from the Hôtel du Louvre.

THE $50 DIFFERENCE

· ·

Many people book the hotel with the lowest rate, figuring it represents the best value. But frequently, a more expensive hotel—or a slightly higher package rate—turns out to be cheaper, if you add in the extras. Does the more expensive hotel have a better location that saves money on your transportation costs? Does their rate include breakfast, while the less expensive hotel's doesn't? The more people traveling with you (or sharing one room), the more vital this information is. Breakfast for a family of four can easily be $50. Hell, in a really good hotel, continental breakfast for two can be $50. Think also about what kind of breakfast is included. Is it a continental breakfast or a buffet? You'll notice a big difference between the two by the time lunch rolls around.

Make sure that tax and service are included in the price quoted to you as well, and then figure this into your comparison. Sometimes U.S. dollar promotions do not include tax and service. Finally, remember that Paris has a 7 F per night room tax; this is rarely included in any rate sheet and therefore should not be taken into consideration when you're calculating your $50 difference.

THE GENERAL MANAGER'S SECRET

· ·

The general manager (GM in English, DG in French) of every hotel in the world has only one bottom line: to sell hotel rooms. He must book a 40% occupancy rate just to break even. In order to fill rooms, a GM will do whatever it takes. (Usually, there are a few palace hotels that prefer to be empty rather than cut deals, but this is rare.)

I am not saying that every GM will cut a deal with you or that you should always call or fax the

GM directly. I am saying that it pays to go out of your way to meet the GM, especially if you have decided to have a regular relationship with a hotel. The GM has the ability to give you a better rate; to upgrade you to a better room, to send you a bottle of champagne or wine or a bowl of fruit, or to do something else that adds an extra touch of value to your choice. The GM has the ability to make you feel like a valuable customer, which will always enhance your stay.

Here's the best part: While the GM does not have time to have breakfast with you and the kids, he very much wants some type of relationship with you so that you will feel a connection to the hotel and will return. If he moves to another hotel (they all move to another hotel), he'll want your name and address so he can notify you, much like your hairdresser.

If you have no time to meet the GM, write a follow-up letter after your visit and wait for his reply and business card. Networking pays, especially in a competitive market like Paris. Once you have his name and business card, the next time you want a reservation, contact the GM directly by fax. If you book with him and not a reservation service, the hotel saves a commission. You may turn that into a discount or an upgrade for yourself and your family.

Should you choose a hotel without knowing the name of the GM you want to approach, simply call the toll-free number of their U.S. reservations office and ask for the name (and correct spelling) of the GM of your chosen hotel and the fax number. Hotels change GMs quite often, so verify the name if you already have one to make sure your GM is still there. If your own contact has moved on, but you want to return to the hotel anyway, write to the new GM and explain that you knew the former GM and tell what he did for you.

TECHNOLOGICAL REPORT

· ·

If plugging in your laptop and getting online is important to you, you may well want to consider the age of the hotel, or its most recent renovation, when you begin to book. Older hotels do not have data ports, although they will send an engineer to your room with an adapter to modify your phone jack. All new hotels have data ports.

Note that even your phone cord may need an adapter. After I had great difficulty connecting online, one hotel told me calmly, "Ah yes, madame, that is because you are using a 45-35 line and in France you must use a 45-11. I will send it right to your room."

HOTELS IN THE 'HOOD

· ·

For years I stayed in the same part of Paris, where I became an expert in the hotels and the promotions offered. "My" Paris consisted of the portion of the city where the first and eighth arrondissements join, and I love it because it is the heart of the Right Bank shopping experience.

This last year I have shifted neighborhoods slightly, and while I am still partial to this Concorde coeur, I have also put together a new network of hotels closer to the grands magasins (big department stores)—these hotels also cost less money than the Crillon and the Meurice.

Concorde Coeur

HÔTEL DE CRILLON
10 place de la Concorde, 8e (Mètro: Concorde).

Instead of raving on about how gorgeous this converted palace is, or how much fun it is to sit at the base of the Champs-Elysées and be a block from the rue du Faubourg St-Honoré, let me tell you a story that sums up the essence of why the Crillon is considered one of the best hotels in the world.

I once arrived in Paris for a stay at the hotel and received a package from my girlfriend Jill, who then lived in St-Paul-de-Vence in the south of France. I wanted to thank her, but realized I had brought the wrong telephone book with me and did not have her number. Furthermore, I knew that she uses a professional name, which is not her legal name, so she was unlikely to be listed.

Christian, the head concierge, first checked Minitel by the address (which I did know by heart), but found St-Paul too small to be cross-referenced by address. He checked under her professional name, but as I suspected, Jill had no phone listing in Minitel under that name.

Next, Christian called the concierge of the Relais & Châteaux hotel in St-Paul and sent him to Jill's home. He asked Jill for her phone number, then called back the Crillon and gave it to Christian. *Voilà!*

You tell me where you can find another concierge like that!

If you are pinching pennies, the Crillon is not for you. If you are on business or are a get-it-done person who demands the best, look no further. If you must have a data port in your room, this hotel is not for you. But your room will have a crystal chandelier. It's all a matter of choice.

There are a number of packages and promotions with dollar rates, which can make the hotel almost affordable. In addition, there are weekend and honeymoon specials, including one that includes dinner and breaks down to be good value. The restaurant in the Crillon is one of the most famous in Paris; the chef, who replaced the famous Christian Constant, has earned his stars, so it's safe to say that a stay that includes dinner is a memory in the making. The hotel has a shopping package complete with limo—as if you needed a car and driver to get the half block from the hotel to Hermès.

Member, Leading Hotels of the World (☎ 800/223-6800); Relais & Châteaux (☎ 212/856-0115). For reservations, call ☎ 800/888-4747 in the U.S. In France call ☎ 1/44-71-15-00; fax 1/44-71-15-02.

HÔTEL MEURICE
228 rue de Rivoli, 1 er (Métro: Concorde or Tuileries)

For over 20 years the Hôtel Meurice has been my main squeeze in Paris; many of the big events of my life happened in this hotel. I also used to love to send people here because it was drop-dead fancy without being as expensive as the Crillon or the Ritz. Not anymore, folks.

The sultan of Brunei has bought this hotel and merged it into The Audley Group along with the Dorchester in London. After extensive renovation, the hotel has emerged fancier than before—and more expensive, although there are some introductory promotional prices.

Regulars please note that the front door of the hotel has been moved directly to the rue de Rivoli (next door to Angelina); there are more bells and whistles in a room than you can stand, including direct data port, *bien sur.* The gun stations have been removed from the roof, the roof has been broken apart, and a whole new set of apartments—with views that are to die for—have sprung into life.

The hotel has chosen to compete with the hotel *grand dames* on all levels of grand including new technology with old world service and decorations. I just miss the $335 price tags from old-time winter promotional rates. For reservations from the U.S. call Leading Hotels of the World ☎ 800/223-6800. Local phone: ☎ 1/44-58-10-10.

HÔTEL DU LOUVRE
Place André Malraux, 1er (Métro: Palais-Royal).

This is a smallish, old-fashioned hotel that's a member of the Concorde group; it has just been spruced up to heightened charm. In this one little plot of land you have the owners of the Crillon as your landlord and the benefit of a fabulous discount program—you can get a room at the Louvre for around $200 per night.

The hotel overlooks the Garnier Opéra and is situated directly across the street from the Musée du Louvre. Its modern rooms are decorated in Laura Ashley–inspired French style. My favorite room has a gabled roof, blue-and-white *toile de Jouy* everywhere, and a gigantic bathroom with glass doors that overlook the Opéra.

Another room, sort of a suite dream, had a tiny room for my son, Aaron, on the left, and a master bedroom for my husband, Mike, and me. It was laid out more like a mini-apartment than a hotel suite and was beautifully decorated. Both of these fifth-floor rooms are great places if you're traveling with kids.

The only drawback to the Hôtel du Louvre is that tour groups have discovered it. But the location, the price, and the charm more than make up for the bother of sharing it with others. ☎ 800/888-4747 in the U.S. for reservations. In France call ☎ 1/44-58-38-38; fax 1/44-58-38-01.

LE CASTILLE
37 rue Cambon, 1er (Métro: Tuileries or Concorde).

This is a relatively new hotel. The rooms are relatively small, but they are fresh and gorgeous, with chintz and trim and fancy bathrooms. The difference between a standard room and a deluxe room is negligible. The breakfast room is adorable. Rates vary enormously with the season, but you can sometimes make a week-long deal; expect to pay about $300 per night. ☎ 800/949-7562 in the U.S. for reservations. In France call ☎ 1/44-58-44-58; fax 1/44-58-44-00.

Haussmann Haunts

HÔTEL WESTMINSTER
13 rue de la Paix, 2e (Métro: Opéra).

I am a little reluctant to tell you about this hotel because it's already hard to get a room here in May, and I don't want to ruin it. Honesty insists that I shout: "Have I got a deal for you!" This hotel could be the cheapest luxury hotel in Paris. When you add in its great location (a block from the place Vendôme, a block from the Garnier Opéra), and its Michelin one-star chef, Emmanuel Hodencq, who offers an affordable, fixed-price three-course gourmet meal, the deal just gets better.

Here are just a few details, so you can laugh all the way to your fax machine: The hotel is in the same building as Cartier (this beats breakfast at Tiffany's by a long shot); the rooms have just been redecorated; and the building was built in the early 1800s, with high ceilings, crystal chandeliers, wonderful moldings, wide corridors, and window boxes filled with geraniums. The lobby may not be much to look at, and some of the rooms up in the roof are tiny, but this is a find.

As at all Paris hotels, the rate varies with the season, but you can usually get a promotional rate, frozen in dollars, for under $300 per night. Because this hotel is a member of the Warwick chain, it always offers *Born to Shop* readers the best rate possible, which is currently around $280 depending on availability. You may fax the hotel's general manager, Mr. Volker Zach, directly and request a *Born to Shop* rate. No modems, but they will provide an adapter; business center on premises.

Call ☎ 800/223-3652 in the U.S. for reservations. In France call ☎ 1/42-61-57-46; fax 1/42-60-30-66.

CONCORDE ST-LAZARE
108 rue St-Lazare, 8e (Métro: St-Lazare)

If I'm not at the Crillon or the Meurice in Paris, you are very likely to find me here, my secret find—a landmark hotel with a lobby as grand as the Crillon, but rates that are much, much lower. That's because the hotel is used mostly by tour groups or savvy Europeans on vacation with the kids. Don't let that stop you as the hotel has been renovated; there are phone lines galore and a data port right in the wall at the desk in deluxe rooms. There's a tea set and electric pot in the pantry and the world's best bath amenities from Annick Goutal.

Location-wise, I am nuts for this hotel. It's near one of the major bus stops, near a train station, near three métro lines, and walking distance from everything you need anyway. If you are in Paris for only a few days and want to get to shopping right out your door, you have everything a sneeze away.

Meanwhile, there's a nice cafe, a great breakfast buffet served upstairs, and a hidden billiards rooms (restored to *belle epoque* grandeur) that makes this hotel the best buy in Paris at $200 to $250 per night. The general manager is very smart and goes out of his way for shopping guests. He makes his own shopping reports (with maps) of all the Paris areas and offers tours to certain groups that book packages. There's also a weekly general manager's cocktail party so you can talk to him in person.

Note: I stay in this hotel a lot and have had an assortment of rooms. Recently I got a small and unattractive room possibly meant for Cinderella. Out of curiosity, I asked the front desk how much the room would cost for someone who didn't book it through a package (I was on a rate) and I was told that this room sold for almost $400 a night. I burst out laughing, although I would have been crying if I were paying that price (you can get the Crillon for not much more). When you pick a hotel based on price, make sure you are getting good value.

Book through Concorde Hotels in the U.S. (☎ 800/888-4747). Local phone: ☎ 01/40-08-44-44.

AMBASSADOR
16 blvd. Haussmann, 9e (Métro: Chausée d'Antin)

The *grande dame* hotel where Lindbergh landed and celebrated in Paris, is a convenient 1 block from Galeries Lafayette. It has excellent prices and packages. Ask about the deal whereby you get a free chauffeur-driven pickup at the airport—it may be worth upgrading to this room level. The hotel is fancier than the St-Lazare and only slightly more expensive. It's also 1 block from many fast-food restaurants and movie theaters where English-language movies play. The new restaurant, "16," has an award-winning chef who is going for his Michelin star. Rooms have several phone lines and a data port, and bathroom amenities are by Annick Goutal. Who could ask for anything more?

MILLENNIUM COMMODORE
12 blvd. Haussmann, 9e
(Métro: Chaussée-d'Antin)

This is one of those 1927 luxury hotels that was closed and fell apart and was never heard from again until a year or two ago when a small chain (Millennium) bought it and sank zillions of francs into it, and *voilà!* what a find. Now then, first a warning about the location—this hotel is a little bit over there. My theory is that what you lack in location, you gain in luxury. Luxury-wise, it is to die for, and technologically you could sing for days—three phone lines, including direct data ports.

From a price point of view, it's very tricky. Promotional rates make the hotel $299 a night if you book 3 nights, and then you get the fourth night free. This is a fabulous deal. However, rack rates are way too high to swallow, so ask for a deal. To book in the U.S., call ☎ 800/465-6486.

LEFT BANK HOTELS

Many will tell you that you haven't been to the true Paris if you haven't stayed on the Left Bank. I have stayed on the Left Bank and generally find the hotels smaller, and the rooms smaller still. I'm personally happier on the Right Bank, but if you want small and charming and truly French—the Left Bank it is.

Note: Meridien has a hotel in the high-rise tower at Montparnasse, which is available in many package tours. This hotel does not fit into the small and charming category; however, it is modern and convenient. And for those nitpickers in the bunch, yes, the Hilton is also a Left Bank hotel.

HÔTEL MONTALEMBERT
3 rue de Montalembert, 7e (Métro: rue du Bac).

If you want a charming but very chic hotel in a great shopping location search no further. There are only 50 rooms here, and each is decorated to the nines. While the rates are between $300 and $400 a night, there are packages for several nights that make it more affordable. This is without a doubt the fanciest hotel on the Left Bank. Call ☎ 800/447-7462 in the U.S. for reservations. In France call ☎ 1/45-48-68-11.

HÔTEL DE SEINE
52 rue de Seine, 6e (Métro: St-Germain-des-Prés).

Since the rue du Buci is one of my favorite streets in Paris, it's no surprise I love this small hotel nestled in the heart of the Left Bank, just half a block from the rue du Buci. They don't take credit cards, but a double room was $133 when I last poked in; just have a few extra traveler's checks on hand. The feel is country French, but there are color TVs and all the amenities you need—even hair dryers. Left Bank hotels are always tiny, so don't expect Texas proportions. ☎ 1/46-34-22-80.

RELAIS CHRISTINE
3 rue Christine, 6e (Métro: Odéon)

Just down the street from the market at rue du Buci and rue de Seine, this hotel is charming beyond words in full medieval style and great for families because it has lofts and apartments. It's not inexpensive, but it's perfect. Local phone: ☎ 1/43-26-71-80.

Chapter Six

· · · · · ·

DINING IN PARIS

PARIS ON A ROLL

· ·

It's hard to get a really bad meal in Paris. The trick is to find a good meal that's not too expensive. You can count on me to have a nosh at every crêpe stand I pass; I've even been to McDonald's and am not ashamed to tell. I stand by that old tourist standby, **Café de Flore**. While it may cost $13 for coffee and croissants for two, it beats the $50 I'd have to pay for the exact same breakfast at my fancy hotel. And there's nothing better than the early morning air, a French newspaper, and a seat in one of the world's greatest theaters to start your day.

I have graduated from pizza to *pannini*, the newest fast-food craze in Paris. I seem to eat one meal a day at a branch of **Toastissimo**. I still eat a lot of pizza; pizza places are easy to find in every neighborhood. I eat a lot of picnics bought from grocery stores I pass by as I wander; you can shop the grocery stores of the rue du Buci or the rue Cler any day of the week or do special market days.

I've also tested the offerings in the food court at Le Carrousel du Louvre, which is an American-style shopping mall attached to the Louvre. It's on a mezzanine level above the stores, and the food is great. My favorite is **Hector, le Poulet**. On a recent visit, Ian and I had a superb lunch there. We purchased a bottle of wine (from the wine-and-cheese vendor—wine is not sold at Hector's), two bottles of mineral water, and two chicken meals for $20.

I cover additional simple, fast, and affordable lunch and dinner choices below. Of course, I also love to eat at Michelin-starred restaurants, particularly when my schedule's more leisurely and I can order from a fixed-price menu and save. So you'll find my favorite formal dining choices listed below as well. In these listings, if both a fax and phone number are provided, you may want to fax ahead for a reservation. These restaurants are in greater demand than others.

SNACK & SHOP

. . . .

If you are out alone or merely want a quick, easy lunch so that you can continue your explorations of Paris (and your shopping), perhaps you want to stop by any of these addresses.

Please note that I pick a "Snack & Shop" location based on a combination of factors: location in relation to good shopping, degree of visual stimulation, price, and quality of food. If you want to eat every meal in a Michelin one-star restaurant, or if you plan your day around where you'll have lunch, these suggestions may not be for you.

Right Bank

SALON DE THÉ BERNARDAUD
11 rue Royale, 8e (Métro: Concorde).

If you follow no other tip from me in your life, you owe it to both of us to please visit this restaurant, preferably for tea. But you can also have breakfast, lunch, or dinner.

What's so special about tea here is how it's served. You are brought a silver tray laden with teacups. Pick the pattern you like best and your tea—and snack or meal—will be served in this pattern. Isn't that just the best gimmick ever? Especially since Bernardaud is one of the finest makers of French porcelain in history.

You can get here one of two ways. Step directly behind the Crillon (for the back approach), or walk through the small Galerie Royale mall. If you arrive via the mall, you'll see just a few seats. You can take your tea here or move to the dining area inside with celadon-colored ragged walls. Don't forget to buy an ashtray for 50 F when you leave. Open Monday through Saturday, 8:30am to 7pm.

ANGELINA
228 rue de Rivoli, 1er (Métro: Concorde or Tuileries).

If you've ever heard of Rumpelmayer's, the famed New York ice-cream parlor, then you'll understand the idea behind Angelina—a Parisian tearoom opened by René Rumpelmayer in 1903. Famous for its hot chocolate, the restaurant also happens to be a great place for breakfast, lunch, or dinner. Salads and easy snacks are a breeze; pastries and desserts are simply the house specialty.

Prices are low to moderate; there is a fixed-price full meal, but I usually order a salad or light fare, so I can go for a dessert. They open for breakfast at 9:30am and are located in the first arron-dissement, a great place to shop that's convenient to the rue de Rivoli and the Louvre. There is also a branch of Angelina in Galeries Lafayette on the 3rd floor.

LADURÉE
16 rue Royale, 1er (Métro: Concorde).

I'm a regular for the quiche and salad at lunch. Eat upstairs or downstairs, or take food to go. There's also a branch inside Printemps and a large branch on the Champs-Elysées where you can eat outside on the sidewalk.

CAFÉ MARLY
Palais du Louvre, 1er (Métro: Musée-du-Louvre or Tuileries).

Once before you die, you have to eat or have coffee at the Café Marly overlooking the I.M. Pei pyramid in the courtyard of the Louvre. You may sit outside, weather permitting, or in any of the small salons filled with smoke and well-heeled locals. Despite its nature, this cafe serves locals as well as visiting firemen. Off-hours are less crowded; yes, you can sit with a coffee for hours, and pay only for the coffee. Light lunch is easy to do, be it a hamburger or a salmon platter. Open daily, 8am to 2am.

LA CHOPE DES VOSGES
22 place des Vosges, 3e (Métro: St-Paul).

If you're shopping the Marais, this is the place for you. Located right on the place des Vosges—in the heart of the Marais—this visually charming restaurant offers lunch and dinner, or simply tea, which is served from 3 to 7pm. With its old-fashioned front, stone interior, and wood beams, this is a cozy multilevel space. Lunch is about $22.

DESIGNER & RETAIL DINING
. . . .

For the last few years, the fanciest designer boutiques in Paris have been adding cafes or small restaurants for shoppers, right on the premises—often in the midst of the shopping experience. The trend was started by Lanvin, but has been picked up by several other designers and is spreading to regular retail—even Emporio Armani has a large cafe.

Check out: **Lanvin's Café Bleu,** 15 rue du Faubourg St-Honoré, in the men's shop, lower level. On a recent visit, I went for the brunch, while Pascale-Agnès had terrific ravioli. I eat here often (it's a few steps from the Hôtel de Crillon), and just have a salad. On the tiny avenue Montaigne, there's **Joseph,** at no. 14.

Teens and 'tweens may prefer **Virgin Café,** 156 ave. des Champs-Elysées, although a serious lunch for two can run $40 per person.

DEPARTMENT STORE DINING
. . . .

The major department stores, which make a true effort to bring in tourists of all nationalities, have restaurants geared to a quick meal or a well-earned coffee break. There's a big competition between them, so when one store gets one name, the other strives to outdo it.

AU PRINTEMPS
64 blvd. Haussmann, 9e (Métro: Chausée-d'Antin).

Café Flo, on the 6th floor, is actually a chain of restaurants and food shops with an excellent reputation; it has taken over the space directly beneath the cupola at Printemps to offer easy meals. You can indicate your choice by pointing to a photo. Lunch starts at 59 F; there is also an 89 F menu that includes wine. Ladurée is on another floor, and there's a coffee bar called Express Flo on the teenage floor (3rd floor).

GALERIES LAFAYETTE
40 blvd. Haussmann, 9e (Métro: Chausée-d'Antin).

There are six restaurants in the store and more in Gourmet Lafayette, the store's gourmet grocery store next door. In summer, you can also eat on the seventh-floor terrace. On the sixth floor is Café Lafayette, a sit-down restaurant, as well as a self-service cafeteria. There's a branch of the famous Angelina on the third floor, as well as the very chic Lina's Sandwiches on the first floor. If you'd rather go lightly, there's sushi on the fifth floor.

SAMARITANE
2 quai du Louvre, 1er (Métro: Musée-du-Louvre or Hôtel-de-Ville).

At Toupary, this very French department store's restaurant, only dinner is served. You'll understand why as soon as you enter: The lights and view are spectacular. Designed by the American designer Hilton McConnico, who is the rage of Paris design, this is a special place. Reservations are essential. ☎ 1/40-41-29-29. Closed Sunday.

FAMOUS FOOD HALLS

. . . .

While it's easy to take home a picnic from any of the famous food halls, most of them permit you to dine in as well.

HÉDIARD
21 place de la Madeleine, 8e (Métro: Madeleine).

This gastronomical house of wonders was redone a few years ago in a series of small dens and salons. Now the displays of everything from fresh and dried fruit and wine to spices are as tantalizing as ever. Upstairs is a very chic restaurant. The spicy entries (and there are plenty) are marked, as this is, after all, a spice house. Reservations are advised: ☎ 01/43-12-88-99. Closed Sunday.

FAUCHON
26 place de la Madeleine, 8e (Métro: Madeleine).

In the renovations at Fauchon, part of the greengrocer has been relocated and a fancy Belle-Epoque tea salon has opened up. You can sip tea, read, and write postcards in glory. Open 8am–7pm Monday through Saturday, closed on Sundays. Check out upstairs as well.

LENÔTRE
48 ave. Victor Hugo, 16e (Métro: Victor-Hugo).

Although famous for its chocolate, Lenôtre has a salon for everything—chocolates, gourmet foods for dinner parties, cocktail nibbles, coffee, and more. You can have a meal or a snack.

MUSEUM DINING

Check out: **Le Grand Louvre,** in the Louvre. Closed Tuesday, but otherwise open from noon to 3pm and 7 to 10pm. **Café Marly,** on the Louvre property, see above. **Café Beaubourg,** 100 rue St-Martin, right across from the Centre Pompidou—an alternative to the top-floor cafe within the museum itself. **Musée d'Orsay Restaurant,** 1 rue de Bellechasse, closed on Tuesday, but otherwise open from 9am to 6:45pm.

And don't miss **Les Monuments,** in the Palais de Chaillot, which houses three museums (but no madwoman). My buddy Christian Constant, from Les Ambassadeurs in the Hôtel de Crillon, has taken over the food situation there.

GROCERY STORES

There are grocery stores situated in neighborhoods frequented by tourists, so unless you're staying in one of the outlying arrondissements, you won't have to go out of your way to get to one. All the best shopping neighborhoods also have their share of grocery stores, so you can easily buy a picnic or do some of your souvenir shopping in one. The markets listed below are big, modern supermarkets chosen for their location; you will be near one or all of them as you explore Paris. And don't neglect any Monoprix you come across.

Left Bank

INNO
31 rue du Départ, 14e (Métro: Montparnasse/Bienvenue).

They have a running joke with me at the Crillon: I am the only guest at this super-posh hotel who also shops at Inno, a combination dime store/grocery on the Left Bank. I love it for its full basement grocery department with prepared foods, its excellent wine and champagne area, and the bakery upstairs. Check out the automated track for the shopping carts. It's something you'll see elsewhere in Europe, but not in the United States.

MONOPRIX GOURMET
*50 rue de Rennes, 6e
(Métro: St-Germain-des-Prés).*

This recently became a more upscale branch of Monoprix to befit the rising stature of the street address and the fact that Giorgio Armani has moved in next door. Don't be fooled by the small street-level space; downstairs is an entire world of food shopping. Open Monday through Saturday, 9am to 9pm.

LE GRAND ÉPICERIE
*Le Bon Marché, 38 rue de Sèvres, 7e
(Métro: Sèvres-Babylone).*

This grocery store is actually part of Le Bon Marché, although it is housed in a separate building from the mother store. (There's a flea market upstairs!) In the street-level grocery, you'll find everything imaginable, including Fauchon and regional food-stuffs from all over France and the EU. There's a good wine and champagne department, a bakery, and prepared foods. Don't mind the other American tourists.

Right Bank

LAFAYETTE GOURMET
52 blvd. Haussmann, 9e (Métro: Chausée-d'Antin).

This store is inside Galeries Lafayette Men's Store, up one flight. You can do your gourmet grocery shopping here, as well as have lunch; there are various serving areas in a circle surrounding a kiosk. Despite its location near the fancy food temples along the place du Madeleine, this store is just as fancy but not nearly as expensive as Fauchon or Hédiard. Don't miss it for the world. Open Monday, Tuesday, Wednesday, Friday, Saturday, and Sunday, 9am to 8pm; Thursday, 9am to 9pm.

MONOPRIX CHAMPS-ELYSÉES
109 rue de la Boetie, 8e (Métro: F-D-Roosevelt).

Not as fancy as Lafayette Gourmet, but handy, Monoprix grocery stores can supply basic needs. This branch is open late, usually until midnight in summer and 10pm in winter. You'll also find Monoprix grocery stores in Monoprix St-Augustin, place St-Augustin (Métro: St-Augustin).

THE DISCIPLES
· ·

If you keep up with the latest chefs, then you are probably into the group of young chefs I call The Disciples. They trained with the most famous chefs in France and are now out on their own. A meal with them costs less than at one of the restaurants at a palace hotel and will put you on the cutting edge of table talk.

LES BOOKINISTES
53 quai des Grands-Augustins, 6e
(Métro: St-Germain-des-Prés or Odéon).

The chef trained with Guy Savoy, and this restaurant is one of several in the Savoy Group. A fixed-price two-course lunch costs just over $25 per person (without wine), whereas a three-course lunch is about $35. Reservations are imperative: ☎ 01/43-25-45-94. It's closed for lunch on Saturday and Sunday, but open for dinner both nights; believe me, finding a great place to eat on Sunday nights is hard.

LES ELYSÉES DU VERNET
Hôtel Vernet, 25 rue Vernet, 8e
(Métro: F-D-Roosevelt).

This restaurant is small, intimate, and formal, with a ceiling designed by Gustav Eiffel (yes, that Eiffel); it currently holds two Michelin stars. The chef was trained by none other than Alain Ducasse. A complete lunch is about $65 per person; a dinner, about $70. It's located right behind the Champs-Elysées, so don't let the address throw you. In fact, you can get there easily if you cut through Chez Clément (123 ave. des Champs-Elysées), another restaurant favorite of mine. Fax ahead (1/44-31-85-69) for reservations with as much notice as possible.

LE JARDIN
Hôtel Royal Monceau, 37 ave. Hoche, 8e
(Métro: Étoile-Charles-de-Gaulle).

Located on the far side of l'Étoile, the restaurant is in a garden, as the name implies. In winter, it's sort of like a gazebo inside a rocket ship; in summer, the doors open to reveal the garden setting. This chef also trained with Alain Ducasse; he has one Michelin star. Lunch is about $56 per person; dinner, $67. Book by fax, 1/42-99-89-92.

L'HÔTEL ASTOR
11 rue d'Astorg, 8e (Métro: Madeleine).

The small but intimate dining room has two Michelin stars and is the baby of none other than chef Joel Robuchon, who retired from Jamin and yet opened this hotel almost immediately after.

Though Robuchon does not do the regular cooking, his influence is felt and the famed mashed potatoes are all they are said to be. Robuchon is called the director; the actual chef is Eric Lecerf. There are several dégustation menus to chose from, or you can order off the menu, leaving room of course for the famous desserts—many of which were created by Robuchon himself. Reservations ☎ 01/53-05-05-20.

The Baby Ducasses

If you want to do Ducasse but on a more informal and slightly more affordable scale, try either **Il Cortile**—a one-star Michelin Italian restaurant in the Hôtel Castile (try the garden in summer) or **Spoon Food & Wine**, where you dine on "world cuisine" from a mix-and-match menu. The macaroni and cheese is to simply die for. While Spoon has gotten a tremendous amount of press and is known to be created by M. Ducasse, few people know about Il Cortile, which is worth investigating because of the delicate palate and the wonderful crowd, which is not at all touristy.

SPOON FOOD & WINE
14 rue de Marignan, 8e (Métro: F-D-Roosevelt).
☎ 01/40-76-34-44

IL CORTILE
37 rue Cambon, 1er (Métro: Concorde).
☎ 01/44-58-45-67

Chapter Seven

. . . .

RIGHT BANK SHOPPING NEIGHBORHOODS

THE BASTILLE IS UP

. . . .

Paris is a city of neighborhoods. Thanks to the Seine, there are Right Bank neighborhoods and Left Bank neighborhoods, and then all those arrondissements. But don't make the mistake of assuming the word *arrondissement* is synonymous with "neighborhood." Single arrondissements can hold several distinctly different neighborhoods, and there are neighborhoods that straddle portions of two or more arrondissements. The French call their neighborhoods *quartiers;* often I give them my own names to simplify it all from an American perspective.

This chapter covers the best shopping neighborhoods on the Right Bank; the following chapter features the best shopping neighborhoods on the Left Bank. Since I tend to be a Right Bank person, this chapter comes first. But as the Left Bank may be the most exciting news on the Paris shopping scene, you won't want to miss it, even if, like me, you've always considered yourself a Right Bank type.

Now that we've got that straight, a few words about orientation. I tend to categorize sections of arrondissements into separate neighborhoods by their landmarks and stores. The Bronx may not be up and the Battery may not be down in this town, but the way I look at it, the Bastille is uptown and the Arc de Triomphe is downtown.

As a tourist, you'll probably stick to a dozen or so neighborhoods that are must-see, must-return-to areas. Some you visit just for their shopping, but mostly you wander for everything they offer—sights, shopping, dining, and more. There are streets that fulfill all your fantasies of what Paris should be. While the city limits of Paris may sprawl all the way to the highway loop Périphérique (and beyond), my parts of town are compact and easy to manage. See chapter 11 for shopping tours; in this chapter and the next, I give you an overview of the best *quartiers* of Paris.

RIGHT BANK ARRONDISSEMENTS

The First (1er)

The 1er is a prime shopping area, with several high-rent neighborhoods and four main districts: Louvre, Halles, Palais-Royal, and Vendôme (Tuileries). It's a rather large district with many shopping moods and modes.

You'll find the city's fanciest designer boutiques on the **rue du Faubourg St-Honoré** (which actually crosses into the 8e), and some wonderful boutiques on the **rue St-Honoré**. But it's also where you'll find tourist trap heaven (the **rue de Rivoli**) and some of the city's best museum shops, as well as the mall of the **Louvre**. Not to mention a big antiques center (right across the street from the mall) and the **Palais-Royal**. The most amazing thing about the 1er is its diversity of shopping opportunities.

The Second (2e)

The 2e is called Bourse and consists of four areas: Gaillon, Vivienne, Mail, and Bonne-Nouvelle. It is mostly a business district—basically the Wall Street of Paris—with some border areas for shoppers.

The Right Bank

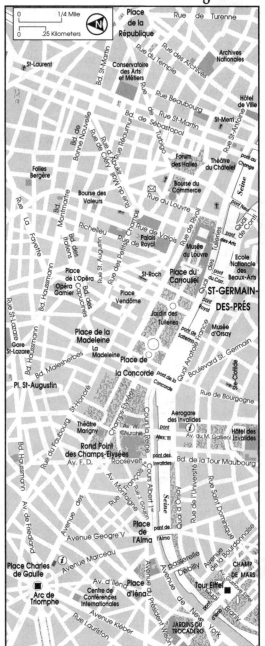

You may not find yourself in the 2e unless you are doing business or have the heart of a *garmento* and want to visit the **Sentier,** or garment center. There are tons of little wholesale-only shops in the Sentier, where if you have nerve you can ask if they'll sell to you. (Many will.) Glamorous, however, it is not.

The **Galerie Vivienne** is in the 2e; this is one of the most famous *passages* in Paris and is at the edge of place des Victoires. There are also a few hidden upscale treasures in and around here. Victoires is on the border of the 1er and 2e, and it is one of the highlights of Paris because of its designer and avant-garde shops. Kitchen supply houses (see p. 264) arehere as well. You'll find them near the mall **Forum des Halles,** but also near rue Étienne Marcel, which is chockablock with designer stores. Many of the big-name jewelers on the far side of place Vendôme (**Cartier** and so on) are in the 2e, even though the 1er is across the street. All in all, the 2e has a good bit to offer after all.

The Third (3e)

Nicknamed either Temple or Marais, the 3e has become popular with the renaissance of the Marais and the **place des Vosges** (on the border of the 3e and 4e). This is a must-do experience. To most visitors, the 3e *is* the place des Vosges, not just the square itself, but the tiny, curvy little streets, arcades, shops, and offbeat finds all around it. It's everything you've dreamed Paris would be. To be totally accurate, the **Picasso Museum** is in the 3e and the place des Vosges is in the 4e, but the spirit which connects them allows most visitors to lump them together.

The 3e has several yummy museums in it and much historical perspective; it also has some edges of funkiness to it. There's a big covered market called the **Carreau du Temple,** where you can find old clothes (*fripes*) and some nice handcrafted items. It's open every day except Monday. When you're here, don't get confused between rue du Temple and boulevard du Temple. Boulevard du Temple, and the part of the neighborhood that backs up to place de la République, is a middle-class neighborhood with a good number of discounters and rather shabby outlets that probably aren't worth investigating, especially if you are a rue du Faubourg St-Honoré kind of customer.

The Fourth (4e)

This neighborhood backs up on the Marais and the place des Vosges and is a very grand and wonderful place to live: I have fallen in love with the place du Marche St-Catherine and want to live there. Not far away there is a famous and very colorful old Jewish neighborhood.

The **Village St-Paul** is in this *quartier* as well (antiques galore), and you are a stone's throw from Bastille and the new opera house. Once you cross the boulevard Bourdon at the canal, you are in the 12e, but never mind, you are now in an area of town considered very *branché* (with it). I prefer to hang around in the Marais portions of the street and then head down the rue Rivoli, which has many chain stores, a good branch of **Monoprix,** and a few discounters.

The 4e also includes the **Île St-Louis,** whose local church is the **Cathédrale de Notre-Dame.** There is some very pleasant tourist shopping near the church as well as the very touristy but fun shopping on the Île St-Louis's main thoroughfare, rue St-Louis En Isle, which begins almost immediately after you cross the tiny bridge from the rear end of the Notre-Dame and set foot onto the Île St-Louis.

The Eighth (8e)

The 8e, which is nestled between the 1er and the 16e, connects the rue du Faubourg St-Honoré with the **Champs-Elysées,** thus stretching right across some of the best shopping in the world. To me, the real soul of the 8e lies directly behind the Hôtel de

Crillon, where you have not only the rue du Faubourg St-Honoré but also the boulevard de la Madeleine, and the tiny rue Boissy d'Anglas, which is now packed with great stores stretching from the Crillon all the way to the place de la Madeleine. The 8e is probably the single most shopping-dense district in Paris.

The Ninth (9e)

The 9e sits on the far side of the 2e and the back end of the 8e; it is famous to most of the world as the location of some big department stores, including the two French icons **Au Printemps** and **Galeries Lafayette.** There's also a giant **Marks & Spencer,** and the Dutch-owned **C&A. H&M,** from Sweden, is coming soon.

Originally, the 9e owed its fame to the St-Lazare train station, which brought shoppers to the big department stores on boulevard Haussmann. Meanwhile, two new train connections have just opened— the Meteor line and the Eoes line, a connection directly to the Gare du Nord so that you can get from the Eurostar to the stores in a hop, skip, and jump.

A small mall, **Passage du Havre,** opened about a year or two ago—it's between the train station (St. Lazare) and Printemps. Do you wonder why I am so fond of the Hôtel Concorde-St-Lazare?

The Tenth (10e)

Wholesale, did you say you like wholesale? Well, the 10e is one of the many wholesale neighborhoods in Paris. It's known for its fur, glass, china, and coiffure suppliers, but also for its hookers, hoods, and dealers, particularly around St-Denis. It has a strong ethnic mix as well.

Not one of your must-see, must-write-home-about areas. Both the **Gare du Nord** and the **Gare de l'Est** are in the 10e, as is the **rue de Paradis**—a street filled with shops selling glass and china and crystal and, yes, those little Limoges boxes.

The Eleventh (11e)

République is a middle-class neighborhood. There are some discounters, but mostly this is not a neighborhood you would go out of your way to shop in, simply because there is little that is special here. The furniture business stretches along the **rue St-Antoine,** but it's not the kind of furniture you're looking for.

The Twelfth (12e)

This is the arrondissement of the moment—gathering no moss as it rolls across Paris from the far side of Bastille toward Gare de Lyon. The biggest news here is **Le Viaduc des Arts,** a very long stretch of street under an elevated train track that has been turned into boutiques and artisans' workshops. Not far away is the **place d'Aligre,** with a great food market and a small flea market. You can walk from Le Viaduc des Arts to place d'Aligre.

Tons of American artists live around here; the area is quite hip. But this is a very large arrondissement with a lot of different neighborhoods. What you get around the place de la Bastille is very different from what you get down the street at Ledru-Rollin and dramatically different from other parts.

Primarily, it is design, art gallery, and furniture territory. For bargain hunters, a not-so-touristy but terrific place to shop is the place d'Aligre. An open market, **Beauvau St-Antoine,** fills the streets every day except Monday until 1pm. It backs up to a covered market of the same name. At the open market, vendors sell fruit and vegetables, flowers, and *fripes*. Meat, fish, and fowl are sold in the covered market.

The Sixteenth (16e)

To many Parisians, there's only one arrondissement in Paris, and its number is 16. The districts are Auteuil, Passy, Chaillot, Muette, and Porte Dauphine. What more could a yuppie want?

Rue de Passy is a terrific find for someone who wants to shop and see the real Paris, as experienced by the BCBG (*bon chic, bon genre*) crowd who hangs out in this district. The well-heeled residents of the 16e have their own park, the Bois, and it's very chic to live close to the park. More important, the 16e has lots of resale shops. The 8e and the 16e bump heads over couture shopping—*ooh la la!*

The Seventeenth (17e)

Another fashionable district, or at least parts of it are. The acceptable neighborhoods for the BCBG set are Péreire, Ternes, and Monceau. Otherwise, this arrondissement is mostly residential.

The Eighteenth (18e)

You've heard of the 18e because it includes **Montmartre**. Other districts are Clignancourt, Pigalle, Chapelle, and Goutte-d'Or. This is a very scenic part of Paris, a part that tourists like to visit in order to confirm their fantasies of Paris, and also the site of some of the fabric markets that design students haunt. (All students of shopping also know that Clignancourt means flea market in French.)

While the 18e was once charming and famous (*Irma la Douce* was shot here), now it is a less-than-charming place. The **place du Tertre**, near Sacré-Coeur, is crammed with tourists and con men. The fabric markets of St-Pierre near Sacré-Coeur are wonderful, but very funky. In fact, the 18e is funkiness personified.

The Nineteenth (19e)

This is really getting out of the swing of things, especially when you get to Villette, the part of this arrondissement that's at the edge of the highway that encompasses Paris. There's no shopping reason to visit.

The Twentieth (20e)

Maurice Chevalier made this area famous when he sang about Ménilmontant, but other than that historical fact, there isn't too much going on in this residential neighborhood, inhabited by people who can't afford high rents in other parts of town.

The famous Pére-Lachaise cemetery is here; the only piece of retailing advice I have regarding the cemetery is to make sure you buy a map of the gravestones; otherwise, you will never find Jim Morrison's.

THE SHOPPING QUARTIERS

Luckily for visitors, the prime shopping areas in the sprawling city of Paris are concentrated in a few neighborhoods. Despite the fact that many new stores come on board each year, the really good ones are smart enough to open in existing high-traffic areas.

The neighborhoods below are listed in rough geographic order, starting with the 8e arrondissement and fanning outward along the Right Bank. I've deferred a bit to tourist timetables. Let's face it: Everyone wants to go to Notre-Dame. You may as well know how to shop your way there.

Because there is so much to see and do in Paris, the best way to tackle the city is by neighborhood. Decide which museums and monuments you care about and what kind of shopping experiences are important to you personally. Then use a map to see how the pieces all fit together to maximize your day.

I consider lunch, and tea, an essential part of the shopping experience, and you'll find recommendations in each neighborhood description. For more information on these picks and others, see chapter 6.

When it comes to shopping in Paris, you must decide if you are just looking or if you actually want to buy something. Do you want a fantasy experience or a real-people French experience? Do you mind crowds of tourists, or would you prefer to be surrounded by the people whose home you have invaded? Is your time so limited that you just want the one address that will give you the most value? Please answer these questions for yourself as you read up on my favorite shopping districts and browsing treats.

Allons-y.

Champs-Elysées, 8e

Métro: F-D-Roosevelt.

Shopping Scene: Outdoor mall.

Where to Have Lunch: Lo Sushi, 8 rue de Berri. The "in" restaurant of the moment for locals who are nuts for the conveyor belt that dishes out the sushi; interior designs are by Andrée Putnam, the *grande dame* of French architectural design.

Where to Have Tea or Coffee: Ladurée, 75 ave. des Champs-Elysées (this also good for lunch).

Where to Have Drinks: Le Bar de l'Étoile, 12 rue de Presbourg—so hot you can barely stand yourself. Don't gawk too much.

What's new? Talk about a makeover. In the last 2 years the Champs-Elysées has changed a lot—some of it has been changing for a long time: the **Disney Store, Virgin Megastore,** and flagship **Sephora** brought new life to the most famous street in Paris. Now we have a new branch of the tearoom **Ladurée,** a new **GAP,** a branch of **FNAC** to compete with Virgin, and, at the far end near l'Étoile, the new **Louis Vuitton**—one of the few stores where you can buy the Marc Jacobs clothing line for Vuitton. More important, the feel of the street is very new.

The sidewalk has been widened to allow for more strolling, and everything is kept clean and neat. Sundays and holidays are a day to promenade; stores open at noon on Sundays. The **Monoprix** is open until midnight in season and 10pm in winter.

Along the way you'll see numerous car show-rooms, perfume showrooms, drugstores, airline offices, cafes, and change booths. A few big-name designers have stores here; **Galerie du Claridge**—another mini-mall—has two levels (go downstairs, too) and has the best selection among the kind of shops you want to see; most of them are big-name designers. There's a newish *parapharmacie,* **Paraland,** on the Vuitton side of the street.

Indeed, years ago I thought only one side of the street (Monoprix side) was worth shopping, but Ladurée and Vuitton have changed all that, and smart strollers will take it all in.

If you travel with your children, don't miss **Monoprix** for cheap clothes, cheap toys, and the grocery store on the downstairs level. Even if you don't travel with children, don't miss this store for cheap, fun makeup, plastic shopping totes, grocery giftables, and fun novelties.

If time is precious, you might want to make sure you've paid homage at **Monprix** (109 rue La Boétie), pressed your nose (and toes) to the glass at **Charles Jourdan** (68 ave. des Champs-Elysées), and made a hearty tour of **Light** (93 ave. des Champs-Elysées). Light is one of those stores that, on first glance, you're ready to pass over, but on second glance, you realize you've misjudged. Its young, kicky (often cheaply made) clothes are trendsetters. This is af-fordable street fashion from the best street. The store is a known resource for buyers and designers from around the world. You can dash into **FNAC's** street-level telephone store to buy your French mobile phone or Nomad system, or down the escalators for the music store, although CDs tend to be very pricey in France.

If you want to walk from the ridiculous to the sublime, just cross to the other side of the Champs-Elysées and cut over 2 blocks to avenue Montaigne, the single most prestigious address a store can have in Paris. This is an easy walk, unless you have already done your grocery shopping at Monoprix or have two dozen jars of Maille mustard in your handbag.

Avenue Montaigne, 8e

Métro: F-D-Roosevelt or Alma-Marceau.

Shopping Scene: The rich, the chic, and the insatiably curious.

Where to Have Lunch: Plaza Athenée, newly renovated deluxe hotel with newly renovated luncheon choices including (in spring) outdoors in the courtyard or indoors in the Relais. This is power hitting, make sure you are dressed appropriately.

Where to Have Tea or Coffee: Joseph Café, in Joseph store (#14) or if you head to the Champs-Elysées, then **Ladurée.**

What's new? Well, the Plaza Athenée has totally renewed itself while stores keep opening, moving around, and sprucing up. Calvin Klein opened a men's store—certainly this is the place to be if you're looking for big-name designer fashions.

You want the Paris that dreams are made of? You want stores that are drop-dead fancy, where the women who patronize them wear couture and carry little doggies under their arms? Little doggies with couture hair ribbons, right? You want architecture and trees with little lights in them, and even a view of the Eiffel Tower? *Ici.*

The avenue Montaigne has become a monument to itself. **Dior** and **Ricci** have always been here. For years, the **Chanel** boutique was a secret jealously guarded by those in the know. Then **Louis Vuitton** built its glitzy flagship store here, and Montaigne became the mega-address it is now. **Escada** has moved in, as has **Inès de la Fressange,** with her oak leaf logo motif and preppy clothes in pastel colors. Of course, the Italians also came: **Krizia, Ferragamo, Max Mara,** and **Dolce & Gabana.** The shopping pace continues to quicken; the international mix is a crazy salad: from **Jil Sander** (German) to **Calvin Klein** (American).

One stroll down the 2 blocks of retail in this short street will give you a look at these famous names, as well as **Loewe, Thierry Mugler, Ungaro, Porthault, Céline, Christian Lacroix,** and **Valentino.** Some of the other stores are old-fashioned French shops that deserve a visit just to soak up atmosphere; try **Au Duc de Praslin** (a candy and nuts store) and **Parfums Caron** with its giant glass bottles filled with perfumes and its offerings of scents not carried in department stores in Paris, let alone in America.

Rue du Faubourg St-Honoré, 8e

Métro: Concorde.

Shopping Scene: Tourists with their noses pressed to the glass; rich regulars from out of town.

Where to Have Lunch: Café Bleu, Lanvin Homme, 15 rue du Faubourg St-Honoré, for a quick and affordable bite, or **L'Obelsik** at Hôtel de Crillon for something divine but not too over the top.

Where to Have Tea or Coffee: Bernardaud, 11 rue Royale or the Hôtel de Crillon, which has a gorgeous courtyard open in spring and summer for tea and/or champagne.

What's new? Well, **Thierry Mugler** has moved into the space vacated by Au Bain Marie next door to where the Buddha Bar has taken root and behind the Hôtel de Crillon. So the names are still moving into this area, despite the rumors of its death.

During the recession, when rents were low and morale was lower, new faces moved into this otherwise posh real estate, so the feel to the street has changed. GAP hasn't opened here, but it's more commercial than it used to be. Still, the rep goes on and Hermès doesn't quit.

Façonnable has moved in, but so have **La Perla** (jazzy lingerie and bathing suits), **JP Tod's** and even **Lolita Lempicka.** Old standbys stretch from **Hermès** to **Sonia Rykiel** with international big names thrown in (**Versace, Ferragamo,** etc.)

Are you actually going to buy anything on the Faubourg? That's up to you and your budget; surely during a sale period, you've got a good shot at it. And yes, I've found affordable items at Hermès. If you've never been before, you simply have to go, if only once.

Now then, one tiny grammatical point from someone who doesn't speak French. The word *faubourg*, a noun, means small street. There are thousands of addresses in Paris that carry the word *faubourg*. Because of the fame of this particular faubourg, it is often referred to merely as "the Faubourg."

Rue St-Honoré, 1er

Métro: Concorde or Tuileries.

Shopping Scene: Locals and smart shoppers who love to poke around and enjoy.

Where to Have Lunch: Ladurée (an old-fashioned French tearoom), 16 rue Royale, or **Pizzeria Venus** (a neighborhood pizza joint), 326 rue St-Honoré.

Where to Have Tea: Ladurée, see above; or **Angelina** (an icon tea salon), 226 rue de Rivoli.

What's new? Actually, not that much. The news is around the corner at the Hôtel Meurice, newly re-opened and splendid. As for the rue St. Honoré, well, this is not your typical neighborhood. In fact, you may not have realized it exists, or you might think it's part of the Faubourg, even though it's not.

This is my secret Paris. From the Hôtel du Louvre, where it is funky and neighborhoody; to the rue de Castiglione, where it begins to get hoity-toity; to the rue Royale, where it becomes super-fancy and eventually turns into the rue du Faubourg St-Honoré, this is the real Paris. It's authentic and untouristed, especially the totally hidden place du Marché St-Honoré. Don't miss this chance.

Plenty of designer shops are located on the rue St-Honoré (**Laura Ashley, Longchamp, Lacoste**), but the area also offers quite a few mom-and-pop retailers. The farther you get from the rue Royale, the more casual the neighborhood gets. Be sure to wander onto the tiny place du Marché St-Honoré with some designer and would-be designer shops, as well as several food shops and groceries.

Get a look at places like **Biberon & Fils** (334 rue St-Honoré), which is actually an office supply store. Stand far enough back in the street to get a look at the entire storefront. It is preserved just as it was in 1836 and is often featured on postcards and in movies.

If you're out on a stroll take the rue St-Honoré to the Comédie Française. Here you can hang a right and go to the Louvre, or take a left and shop in the arcades at the Palais-Royal, moving right along to Victoires and the 2e. Or you can hit the rue de Rivoli and circle back toward Concorde while you visit all the tourist traps and stop by Angelina's for tea. The arcade of the Palais-Royal is the essence of all Paris retail to me. You can have your Faubourg. I'll play the Palais.

Victoires, 2e

Métro: Palais-Royal.

Shopping Scene: Chic trendsetters.

Where to Have Lunch: Le Grand Véfour (weekdays only; expensively divine and famous), 17 rue Beaujolais, ☎ 1/42-96-56-27.

Where to Have Tea or Coffee: At **Priori Thé** (cute and perfect), Galerie Vivienne.

What's new? Actually **Kaat Tilley,** a wild *créateur* from Brussels has moved into the area, but otherwise things are pretty stable.

If you want to have a wonderful shopping experience that's very French, very uptown, and quite special, this is it. But it's not easy to reach, and you'll need to walk quite a bit. For example, the métro station I've given above, Palais-Royal, is a ways from where this neighborhood starts at the place des Victoires. That said, this neighborhood between neighborhoods is a sensational stroll.

You'll find the place des Victoires nestled behind the Palais-Royal, where the 1er and the 2e connect. Facing the place is a circle of hotels; the ground floor of each has been converted to retail space. The spokes of streets shooting out of the place represent various retail streets as well, and they are filled with more wonderful shops.

Rue Étienne Marcel is the major drag, and it has long housed some of the big *créateurs* (designers). You can save this area for last, and depart the neighborhood by browsing this street before heading toward the Forum des Halles or the Beaubourg. Or you can start your stroll from the Étienne-Marcel métro stop and work backward.

Between place des Victoires and the Palais-Royal (a distance of only a few blocks), you've got the rue des Petits-Champs, which has a lot of showrooms and charming shops on it, as well as the Galerie Vivienne, one of Paris's famed *passages,* the covered alleys of stores that were the first mini-malls.

As for the place des Victoires itself, there's **Esprit, Cacharel,** and **Thierry Mugler,** but you will enjoy simply going from door to door around the circle and then branching out into the small streets. Victoire is one of the most famous names in France for ladies who want a pulled-together chic look that's just right. Don't miss **Henry Cottons,** an Italian, Ralph Lauren, weekend-chic sort of place with great architecture. Although the address is written as place des Victoires, the entrance is on the rue Étienne Marcel.

Don't forget to check your trusty map before you leave Victoires—because the location is so superb, you can continue in any number of directions. You can easily walk to the Forum des Halles or Opéra, or to the boulevard Haussmann and the big department stores, or simply to the rue de Rivoli and the Louvre. The world starts at Victoires, and it's a magnificent world.

Sentier, 2e

Métro: Bourse.

Shopping Scene: *Garmento*.

Some people have printer's ink in their veins; I've got garment center in my blood. If you do, too, you may want to go from Victoires into the Sentier—the wholesale garment district in Paris.

From place des Victoires, follow rue d'Aboukir, which leads you from the 1er into the 2e. *Be fore-warned:* The Sentier may not be your kind of place; it sure ain't fancy here. This area is very much like New York's Seventh Avenue—men with pushcarts piled high with fabric, little showrooms that may or may not let you buy from them, hookers in certain doorways, junk in bins, metal racks and forklifts, and mannequins without arms.

There are few big-name designer names here, and there are no guarantees that you will find what you want. Any time you want to buy something in the Sentier, simply play dumb American: Ask the price and see what happens. For the most part, the area is closed tight on weekends. A few shops are open on Saturday, but Saturday is not the day to tour the neighborhood and see it all. Sunday is totally dead.

If you're not sure about exploring this neighborhood in depth, you may want to walk from place des Victoires on the rue Étienne Marcel. It'll give you a chance to take in designer shops, some wholesale places, and land you right at the rue Montmartre, for more garment shopping before you move on to the mall Forum des Halles and the Beaubourg.

You'll also get the wholesale kitchen stores on this route (see p. 264).

Rue de Rivoli, Part One, 8e–1er

Métro: Concorde, Tuileries, or Musée-du-Louvre.

Shopping Scene: International tourists.

Where to Have Lunch: Angelina (salads and pastries), 226 rue de Rivoli; Food Court, **Le Carrousel du Louvre** (an American-style food court, but great), 109 rue de Rivoli, or **Café Marly**, see below.

Where to Have Tea: Café Marly (once, before you die), Louvre, 93 rue de Rivoli.

The rue de Rivoli is the main drag that runs along the back side of the Louvre. Since the Louvre was once a fortress, you will understand why it seems to go on forever. They just don't build them like that anymore. Exit the métro at Concorde and face away from the Eiffel Tower. You are ready to walk. I call this part of the street "Part One" because it is the main tourist area. The rue de Rivoli continues after the Louvre, but has an entirely different character. Part One has a few chic shops on it toward the Hôtel de Crillon end, but soon becomes a good street for bookstores, such as **W. H. Smith & Son**. As you get closer to the Louvre, the stores get more and more touristy. Yep, there's tons of tourist traps here, all in a row.

Rue de Rivoli, Part Two, 1er–4e

Métro: Musée-du-Louvre or Hôtel-de-Ville.

Shopping Scene: Real.

Where to Have Lunch: Le Carrousel du Louvre (see above).

Where to Have Tea or Coffee: See the Marais, page 124.

The touristy stuff ends at **Le Louvre des Antiquaires**, but the street itself—rue de Rivoli—continues forever and has many stores on it. By the time you get up near the Hôtel de Ville, there's the giant department store **BHV**, which has a basement filled with wonderful hardware and gadgets for the home. Then there's another giant department store, this one with four parts, **La Samaritaine.** Keep strolling along the rue de Rivoli, and you'll find one of my faves, **à l'Olivier,** at no. 23.

The rue de Rivoli will change names to become the rue St-Antoine, leading directly to the Bastille. Along the way there's some junk shops and discounters, as well as the path to the place des Vosges and/or the Village St-Paul.

Jean-Paul Gaultier has a shop on rue St-Antoine (no. 30); this is **Galerie Gaultier,** a new concept that has all sorts of designs (clothing and products for the home) in one space; there are similar stores in London and Tokyo. It's a long hike all the way from BHV to Bastille, but it can be very rewarding. See page 123 for the Bastille neighborhood, which connects directly to this one, if you're strong enough to keep on walking.

Place Vendôme, 1er

Métro: Tuileries.

Where to Have Lunch: The Ritz, *bien sur.*

Where to Have Tea: If you didn't have lunch at **The Ritz,** there's always tea.

What's new? Well, I think the news is still to come as an entire block is being torn down and rehabilitated. Otherwise, this is simply a neighborhood that says "Paris" and is the home to the new Tiffany store. Place Vendôme is conveniently located between Opéra and rue de Rivoli. It's a subneighborhood of rue de Faubourg St-Honoré and rue St-Honoré, so you'll be eating elsewhere but dreaming here—unless you want to splurge for a visit to The Ritz, where two can eat outside, or in the bar for about $100.

Formerly one of the finest residential areas in Paris, the place Vendôme is surrounded by old hotels that now house either jewelry shops, banks, insurance companies, or all three. There's also a hotel that you can still spend the night in—The Ritz. Besides the big jewelry firms, like **Van Cleef & Arpels** and **Cartier,** some ready-to-wear kings have moved in—like **Giorgio Armani, Natori,** and even **Armani's**

Emporio. Natori is a little hard to find, but it's on the rear side of the **Chanel** jewelry store. (You do know, *chèrie,* that Chanel now makes the real thing as well as costume, don't you? And that it, too, has a jewelry store in this 18-karat neighborhood.)

The far side of the place Vendôme is the rue de la Paix, which dead-ends 2 blocks later into Opéra. There are more jewelers here (including Tiffany & Co.) and a few other retailers. Don't confuse **Charvet** (a men's store) with **Chaumet,** a jeweler. It just so happens that there are several men's haberdashers on this street—everyone from **Alain** (Figaret) to **Zegna.** Figaret is not quite as famous as others in the neighborhood, but is a local hero nonetheless.

The **American Express** office is on rue Scribe, right beside Opéra. How convenient.

Department Store Heaven, 9e

Métro: Chausée-d'Antin.

Shopping Scene: In summer, a zoo. At other times of the year, middle- to upper-middle-class French from the suburbs and out of town mixed with an international crowd.

Where to Have Lunch: Galeries Lafayette, Au Printemps, or **Toastissimo** in Passage du Havre; see pages 93–94.

Where to Have Tea or Coffee: Galeries Lafayette, Lafayette Gourmet, or **Café Flo,** see above. There's a branch of **Angelina,** the famous tea shop known for its hot chocolate, at Galeries Lafayette; **Ladurée** is in Printemps.

What's new? The two major department stores are reinventing themselves in front of our very eyes. Two floors of **Printemps** have been jazzed up enough to make you think this is Saks Fifth Avenue. (After that, forget it.) **Galeries Lafayette** has just begun its long climb; stay tuned.

This 3-block-long and 2-block-deep jumble of merchandise, pushcarts, strollers, and shoppers is a central trading area. I frequently call it "the Zoo." If you insist on seeing it, go early in the morning (9:30am), when you are strong and crowds aren't in full swing. Winter is far less zoo-like than summer.

Check out **Lafayette Gourmet,** the grocery store attached to Galeries Lafayette—it's fabulous.

The other department stores, lined up in a row here, are **Marks & Spencer, C&A,** and **Au Printemps,** which sits opposite.

Boulevard Haussmann hits the rue Tronchet a block after the string of department stores. Take a left and walk 2 blocks to the place de la Madeleine, where **Fauchon** and many other food landmarks are located. Take a left and you're at the **Passage du Havre,** a great mall with one of many stores you want to visit, including **Sephora** and the French version of **The Nature Company.**

After you have finished up here, be sure you're standing at the Madeleine: Facing away from the Madeleine turn right at **Gucci** for the Faubourg, or walk straight ahead for place de la Concorde and the Crillon . . . or go left for the new **Conran Store.** Choices, choices, choices.

Place de la Madeleine and the rue Royale are lined with big-name stores, including **Polo/Ralph Lauren** and the showrooms for the glass and porcelain shops. A new mini-mall is just blossoming due, no doubt, to the success of the American-style mall **Les Trois Quartiers.** Now this area is a big mall destination; there's branches of **Kenzo, Weill, Chacok, Body Shop, Marina Rinaldi, Burma, Dorothée Bis, Agatha, Mondi, Georges Rech, Rodier Homme, Stéphane Kelian,** and a huge perfume shop called **Silver Moon. Le Cedre Rouge,** sort of the French version of Pottery Barn, anchors the newer mall space across the street from **Les Trois Quartiers.** If you continue along the rue Royale, it brings you to the place de la Concorde. You haven't done it at all if you don't stop into **Bernardaud** for tea. If you're not too tired, please make time for Hidden Madeleine (see below).

Several areas overlay each other near here and can be considered one big neighborhood.

9\14\00 Wonderful day —

Madeleine, 8e

Métro: Madeleine.

Shopping Scene: Upscale international.

Where to Have Lunch: Hédiard, 21 place de la Madeleine.

Where to Have Tea or Coffee: Fauchon Thé, 26 place de la Madeleine.

What's new? Fauchon has all but gutted itself and started over. Indeed, the heart of this area is the string of famous food shops that stand almost in a row—**Hédiard, Fauchon, Nicolas** (the wine shop), **Maison de la Truffe,** and more. Almost all of these stores have many opportunities for you to eat; you can come back for lunch every day and try a new place. Fauchon has several places to eat, including a charming restaurant, one flight upstairs, and a coffee shop on the lower level (SS). Most of these food stores sell take-out food as well. Don't miss the mustard kings from Dijon, **Maille,** on the other side. Dijon mustard is one of the items on the duty list for the banana wars, so load up now.

Hidden Madeleine, Parts One and Two, 8e

Métro: Madeleine or Concorde.

Shopping Scene: Secret chic.

Where to Have Lunch: See "Madeleine," immediately above.

Where to Have Tea: Bernardaud, 11 rue Royale.

Part One: The **rue Boissy d'Anglas** is the street that runs behind the Hôtel de Crillon, from the place de la Concorde right past **Hermès,** down to the place de la Madeleine. It's kind of narrow and doesn't see that many tourists. What it does see are a lot of chic fashion editors and in-the-know types who pop in and out of their favorite stores, secure in the thought that the tourists are on the Faubourg and haven't caught on.

If you cut through the Passage de la Madeleine, just off the place de la Madeleine, which begins with a very good duty-free perfume shop, it leads you right to the chic part of the rue Boissy d'Anglas. Walk toward Concorde, to your left. Don't stop until you get to the Passage Royale, which will lead you to tea at **Bernardaud.** Along the way there's yet another passage that you have to explore if you are going to see the **Chanel** shoe store, which sells only Chanel shoes.

Part Two: I've nicknamed **rue Vignon** "Honey Street," because it is the home of the **Maison de Miel,** one of the leading specialists in French honey. This street runs on the other side of **Fauchon,** just as the rue Boissy d'Anglas runs behind Hédiard. Vignon has a few smaller clothing shops on it as well as other places I like to explore. It's chic without being touristy. This is one of my favorite streets in Paris, and I often use it as my route for cutting over to the *grands magasins.* There's several fast-food places here although I am partial to **Tarte Julie,** where you can sit down or have take-away. For some reason, there are three plus-size shops on this street, near the far end at rue Tronchet.

Victor Hugo, 16e

Métro: Victor-Hugo.

Shopping Scene: Chic, French, and rich . . . with dogs.

Where to Have Lunch: Maison Prunier (decadently chic and expensive), 16 ave. Victor-Hugo, reservations needed ☎ 1/44-17-35-85, closed Monday.

Where to Have Tea or Coffee: Lenôtre (famed chocolate and pastry house), 48 ave. Victor-Hugo, ☎ 1/45-02-21-21.

What's new? Well, **Yves Saint Laurent** chose this neighborhood to unveil the new "look" for his boutiques—they will roll out internationally in the next few years, but you can see the flagship right here on Victor-Hugo.

Victor-Hugo is one of the fanciest shopping streets in Paris, safely nestled into an uptown residential neighborhood. Years ago, many big-name international designers had shops here. Most of them have moved, giving the neighborhood an intimate feel. Most of the shoppers here today appear to be regulars who live nearby. This isn't the kind of street you visit to actually shop; you come here to get a feel for a certain part of Paris, with a lifestyle that is totally unknown in America.

Passy, 16e

Métro: Passy or La Muette.

Shopping Scene: Rich casual, with a black velvet headband and pearls.

Where to Have Lunch: Le Toit de Passy, 94 ave. Paul-Doumer, may need a reservation, ☎ 1/45-24-55-37.

What's new? Well, **Franck et Fils** has been redone, but don't look now, it's not Bon Marché. Passy is the main commercial street of one of the nicest districts of one of the nicest arrondissements in Paris. It has a little of everything and is convenient to other neighborhoods. You can visit Passy on your way to the Eiffel Tower, Trocadéro, or the resale shops of the 16e, or you can catch the métro and be anywhere else in minutes. If possible, do Passy on a Saturday morning because then you will really be French.

The street has been booming ever since **Passy Plaza,** an American-style mall with that number one American tenant, GAP, opened. Go to Passy Plaza for a lesson in French yuppie sociology. Shop the supermarket in the lower level, shop the various branches of American and British big names, and go to the French candy store. Check out **Franck et**

Fils, a swanky department store, and **Sephora** (no. 50), which isn't a duty-free store, but has an immense selection of brands. **Prisunic** also has a branch on Passy. There are numerous big-name boutiques that range from **Descamps** to **Max Mara**. This is a fun, let's-pretend neighborhood: You can stroll the street and pretend you are part of the French upper-middle class.

Shopper's tip: When you get to the end of Passy (where the Max Mara shop is located), you'll find a back street called rue Paul-Doumer. If you love home furnishings, tabletop, and good design, you'll find a few winners along this tiny street (there's a branch of **Souleiado**). Forget about shopping this neighborhood on Monday until at least the afternoon.

Bastille, 4e–12e

Métro: St-Paul or Bastille.

Shopping Scene: Hip.

Where to Have Lunch: Bofinger (legendary bistro), 6 rue de la Bastille, reservations, ☎ 1/42-72-05-23, or **Barrio Latino** 46-48 rue du Faubourg–Saint-Antoine, 12e reservations, ☎ 1/55-78-84-75.

Don't look now, but Bastille is chic. Dare I say it? People are losing their heads over this up-and-coming neighborhood! Bastille is benefiting from the rebirth of the nearby Marais, one arrondissement over, and the ugly but renowned new opera house. The artists have moved in; so have the Americans (to live, not to set up shop). Long known for its home furnishings stores, the district is now taking on some galleries and interior design shops of note.

To see it all, take the métro to either St-Paul or Bastille. You can walk along the rue St-Antoine toward the column in the center of the place de la Bastille. This gives you the real-people view. If you want a more glamorous view, walk along the Seine, then cut in toward the Opéra along the residential boulevard Bourdon.

Once you've gotten to the opera house, you want to walk uptown along the rue Daumensil toward Gare Lyon because that's where the real story is—**Le Viaduc des Arts,** an enormous restoration project. Here, the arches under a train viaduct have been filled in with boutiques, showrooms, and artisans' shops.

Marais/Place des Vosges, 3e–4e

Métro: St-Paul.

Shopping Scene: Fabulous, funky fun.

Where to Have Lunch: Le Loir dans la Théière (cute and charming, serves a light lunch), 3 rue des Rosiers.

Where to Have Tea or Coffee: Mariage Frères (seriously cute and famous), 30 rue du Bourg-Tibourg, ☎ 1/42-72-28-11.

The rebirth of the Marais is no longer news, but new shops continue to open here, making it a pleasurable area to explore every time you visit Paris. Take the métro to St-Paul and follow the signs toward place des Vosges. Or taxi to the **Musée Picasso** and wander until you end up at the place des Vosges. (This is difficult wandering; you will need a map if you start at the Picasso Museum.)

The area between the church of St. Paul and the Seine hosts the **Village St-Paul** for antiques. The Marais lies nestled behind the other side of the rue St-Antoine and is hidden from view as you emerge from the métro. You may be disoriented when you come above ground. I've gotten lost a number of times. That's why taking a taxi here is a good idea. There's also no hint of charm until you reach the Marais.

While the heart of the neighborhood is the place des Vosges, this is a pretty big neighborhood with lots of tiny, meandering streets that you can simply wander. Take in designer shops like **Popy Moreni** and **Issey Miyake** in an arcade that surrounds the place. The side streets are dense with opportunities:

from the chic charm of **Romeo Gigli** to the American country looks of **Chevignon.** In between there's a bunch of funky little shops selling everything from high-end hats to vintage clothing. Check out antiques at **Les Deux Orphelines** (21 place des Vosges) and modern, contemporary housewares and style at **Villa Marais,** 40 des Francs Bourgeois. Many stores are open on Sunday afternoon, but the entire area is dead on Monday.

The main shopping drag is rue Francs Bourgeois; look for it on a map when you are finding your way from the Picasso Museum.

Montmartre, 18e

Métro: Anvers.

Shopping Scene: Uphill, it's touristy; down by the métro, it's discount heaven, but very *declassé.*

Where to Have Lunch: There are many touristy cafes around the place du Tertre; I'd leave the neighborhood for lunch.

Mon Dieu, what a schlep! I investigated the famous place du Tertre in Montmartre, where the artists supposedly hang out, and was royally ripped off. I'm not certain which facet of the adventure came closer to giving me a heart attack—the number of stairs I climbed to get to the church, or the fact that the portrait artists run price scams. I was told "150," which I assumed was French francs ($30), but portrait artists were quoting U.S. dollars. After handing over the caricatures, they demanded $150 for each! It was a very unpleasant (and expensive) scene.

Paris 2000   9/11 – 9/18

Hotel du Levant

Chapter Eight   #21

18, rue di la Harpe

LEFT BANK SHOPPING
NEIGHBORHOODS

75005 Paris

RIVE GAUCHE

. . . .

To many, the essence of Paris is the Left Bank. I see it as several different villages—all with different personalities—nestled together. If you're the type who just likes to wander, go to the 6e and spend the day, or even the week. If your time is precious, perhaps you'd like to use my method of coping. After all, Gaul may be divided into three parts, but I've divided the shopping portions of the Left Bank and an area of one or two arrondissements, into several.

In other words, there's more to the Left Bank that just the 6e. I don't happen to like the 5e that much—it's too full of students and funk for my taste—but I adore the 7e. My part of the 7e can easily connect to the 6e, so I have listed it below as if it were a subdivision of the 6e. Purists, forgive me.

LEFT BANK ARRONDISSEMENTS

. . . .

The Fifth (5e)

This is the famous **Latin Quarter,** or student quarter, which is also called Panthéon. It's filled with little cafes and restaurants; it's paradise for book hunters.

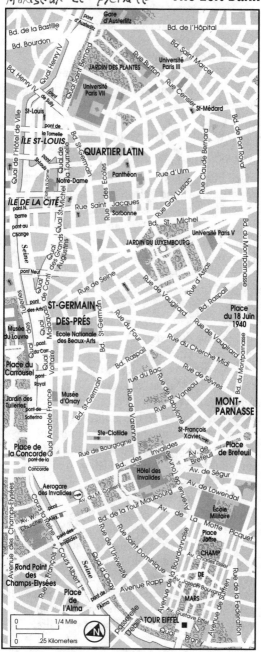

Bd. de la Bastille
Bd. Bourdon
Gare d'Austerlitz
pont d'Austerlitz
Bd. de l'Hôpital
Bd. Henry IV
pont de Sully
Quai Saint Bernard
Rue Buffon
Bd. Saint Marcel
Université Paris III
JARDIN DES PLANTES
Rue Censier
Université Paris VII
St-Médard
St-Louis
Quai de l'Hôtel de Ville
pont de la Tournelle
ÎLE ST-LOUIS
Quai de la Tournelle
Bd. St-Germain
QUARTIER LATIN
Bd. de Port Royal
Rue Claude Bernard
Notre-Dame
Panthéon
Rue d'Ulm
ÎLE DE LA CITÉ
pont N.
Dame
pont au Change
Rue Saint Jacques
Rue des Écoles
Sorbonne
Rue Gay Lussac
Bd. St. Michel
Université Paris V
Seine
pont Neuf
Quai de Conti
Quai des Grands Augustins
JARDIN DU LUXEMBOURG
Rue d'Assas
Bd. du Montparnasse
Tuileries
pont des Arts
Rue de Seine
Rue de Vaugirard
Bd. Raspail
Place du 18 Juin 1940
Musée du Louvre
Quai Malaquais
Quai Voltaire
ST-GERMAIN-DES-PRÉS
Bd. St-Germain
Rue du Four
Rue de Vaugirard
Rue du Cherche Midi
Place du Carrousel
pont du Carr.
pont Royal
École Nationale des Beaux-Arts
Bd. Raspail
rue du Bac
Rue de Sèvres
Bd. du Montparnasse
Jardin des Tuileries
pont de Solferino
Quai Anatole France
Musée d'Orsay
Rue de Varenne
Rue de Babylone
Rue Vaneau
MONT-PARNASSE
Place de la Concorde
pont de la Concorde
Ste-Clotilde
Rue de Bourgogne
Bd. des Invalides
St-François Xavier
Place de Breteuil
Aerogare des Invalides
Av. de M. Gallieni
Hôtel des Invalides
Av. de Breteuil
Av. de Ségur
Cours des Champs-Élysées
Av. W. Churchill
pont Alex III
Bd. de la Tour Maubourg
Rue Saint Dominique
Av. de La Motte Picquet
Av. de Lowendal
École Militaire
Place Joffre
Rond Point des Champs-Élysées
Rue François 1er
Cours Albert 1er
pont des Invalides
Quai d'Orsay
Av. de la Bourdonnais
Av. Charles Risler
CHAMP DE MARS
Rue de la Fédération
Place de l'Alma
pont de l'Alma
Seine
Avenue Rapp
Av. Joseph Bouvard
Av. de la Motte Picquet
Av. de Suffren
passerelle Debilly
Quai Branly
TOUR EIFFEL
Av. Gustave Eiffel

0   1/4 Mile

0   .25 Kilometers

N

There are shops selling *fripes* and jeans, as that seems to be all that people around here wear. This is the funkiest part of the Left Bank, just above the chic part of the boulevard St-Germain. There are good stores in the 5e—if you're a **Diptyque** candle and soap and scent freak, you'll find their store is here.

9/13/00

The Sixth (6e)

With the enormous changes in retail that have taken place in the 6e, you'd think I'd say, "There goes the neighborhood." Instead, one of Paris's best shopping districts has simply become better. This is one of the most Parisian arrondissements for tourists and shoppers. It's often called Luxembourg because the Jardin du Luxembourg is here, or St-Germain-des-Prés because of the church and boulevard of the same name. Let's just call it heaven and be done with it.

The district has everything. On the **rue de Buci** and the **rue du Seine,** there's a street market piled high with fruit, vegetables, and flowers—great for picking up picnic supplies. Prices tend to be higher than at other street markets in Paris because of the number of tourists who shop here, but it's so luscious, who cares? The antiques business is also clustered here, and there are a number of one-of-a-kind boutiques. But the area is no longer small and funky. Led by **Sonia Rykiel,** who came in years ago, a herd of major designers—**Louis Vuitton, Hermès, Christian Dior**—has moved into this prime real estate. Their shops are tasteful (and then some!) and respectful to the soul of the neighborhood. Even the American-style mall at the **Marché St-Germain** is an addition to the neighborhood. And, of course, many of Hemingway's favorite cafes and haunts are here. This is a prime place for sitting at a sidewalk cafe, watching all of Paris walk by, and having the time of your life.

The Seventh (7e)

Difficult to get around because of its lack of métro connections, the 7e is a mostly wealthy residential area, with just a handful of shopping addresses. The real story here is the **rue Cler,** which reigns as the street for serious food. Foodies from all over the world work this 2-block street, take notes, taste everything, and discuss their finds for years. The main shopping streets are the **rue de Grenelle** (which is also partially in the 6e) and the **rue St-Dominique.** There are many small shops for rich ladies who just can't go so far as the crass rue du Faubourg St-Honoré or the crasser still avenue des Champs-Elysées.

The portion of the 7e that lies next to the 6e forms an invisible barrier much like that between the 1er and the 8e on the Right Bank; it is impossible to know where one begins and the other ends. The closer you get to the 6e while still in the 7e, the more you are in an enclave of hidden good taste. My favorite part is the **rue du Bac,** which lies partly in the 7e and partly in the 6e. It is crammed with wonderful shops for the neighborhood's rich residents—there's everything from fancy pastry shops and linen shops to fashion boutiques and tabletop temples. More chic still is the **rue du Pré-aux-Clercs,** which took me years to discover. Along 1 block, some of the best talent in the world is lined up on both sides of the street. Shhh, don't tell the tourists.

The Thirteenth (13e)

One of the largest arrondissements in Paris, the 13e is mostly residential and of little interest to tourists. Its districts are Italie, Gobelins, and Austerlitz. Part of it is known as the French Chinatown. You can pass. And yet, on my last visit to Paris I went to a yummy *brocante* market in this area and absolutely loved it. Very real.

The Fourteenth (14e)

Looking for a Sonia Rykiel outlet store? Step this way. The 14e is home to the **rue d'Alésia,** a street of several bargain shops, including the Sonia Rykiel outlet store. There's also a great flea market nearby (**place de Vanves**). Montparnasse—in all its high-rise glory—is here if it interests you. I use the tall skyscraper of Montparnasse as a beacon to guide me to **Inno** (see p. 197).

The 14e is large and has many districts—some are nice, others are not. The stock shops and the flea market should be your primary reasons to visit the 14e; although parts of the 6e do back right up to the 14e, so you can easily branch off to the Latin Quarter from here. Don't be afraid of the 14e or think it's too far away; it's worth knowing this part of Paris!

The Fifteenth (15e)

A piece of the 15e touches the back side of the Eiffel Tower, near the Paris Hilton. Rue de la Convention is a main drag. The Porte de Versailles is just beyond, and there are tons of commercial streets all around this portion of the neighborhood. See page 137 for some neighborhood shopping tips to this special part of town.

THE SHOPPING QUARTIERS

The Left Bank is not very large; there is much overlap between its neighborhoods, and only the sophisticated eye will catch the nuances between some of them. You can use the St-Germain-des-Prés métro stop for all of these areas and select a lunch or tea stop from any of the choices I give below. You will find, however, that it's a pretty long schlep from one end to the other; I certainly cannot do it in a day, and I would not want to pick a lunch spot that was 2 miles from my afternoon shopping choices.

If you have no particular plan, at least look at a map, pinpoint the suitable métro stops, and decide where you want to be around noon. Not to sound like a major princess, but I most frequently stay on the Right Bank with the Concorde métro stop as my home base. I often arrange my patterns of exploration so that I end up going out of the Left Bank at the end of the day either through the Sèvres-Babylone métro stop or the rue du Bac métro stop because then I don't have to change trains to reach Concorde. At the end of a hard day's shopping, especially if you are laden with packages, you might want to forgo a long, complicated journey on the métro.

If you prefer a taxi, it can be difficult to flag one down in this area. Go either to the Hôtel Lutétia or to the taxi rank in front of Emporio Armani on boulevard St-Germain. Note that the traffic on the boulevard St-Germain moves one way, uptown.

Many of the restaurants I recommend for lunch are places first introduced to me by fellow journalist Alexander Lobrano, who lives on the Left Bank and keeps up with the latest chefs and their newest dishes.

9|13|10 St-Germain-des-Prés, 6e

Métro: St-Germain-des-Prés.

Shopping Scene: Young, hip, and busy, but somewhat touristy.

Where to Have Lunch: Café Armani, Emporio Armani, blvd. St-Germain.

Where to Have Tea or Coffee: Les Deux Magots (if it was good enough for Hemingway . . .), 170 blvd. St-Germain; **Café de Flore** (ditto), 172 blvd. St-Germain.

What's new? More designer stores! This is still the main drag of the Left Bank and the center of the universe. Have a taxi drop you at the church (or take the métro, no sweat), and you'll have arrived at the center of all the action.

You can begin the day with breakfast (coffee and croissants) at any number of famous bistros, like **Les Deux Magots** or **Café de Flore**. Sure, a cup of coffee costs $5 and continental breakfast is $15, but you can sit for hours and watch the passing parade. Nothing is more French.

Those who can afford the rent on the boulevard have their stores clustered around here. In addition to Etro, Armani Emporio, and other big names, there's **Sonia Rykiel** at no. 175 and **Shu Uemura**, a fabulous Japanese cosmetics firm, at no. 176. More than anything, the big names have revitalized the area and made it even more important for you to know what's happening here. **Inès de la Fressange** may have closed shop in this part of town, but everyone else is moving in. Also, there are several bookstores, artsy postcard and poster shops, a number of cafes, even a small but packed *parapharmacie*. You'll certainly have no trouble finding a cafe for coffee or a meal. If you are headed for the most famous places, try to eat at early or odd hours, especially if you want a seat with a view.

Behind the Church, 6e

Métro: Odéon or St-Germain-des-Prés.

Shopping Scene: Busy locals; less touristy than the main areas.

Where to Have Lunch: **Allard** (a local bistro, with few tourists), 41 rue St-André-des-Arts, reservations suggested: ☎ 1/43-26-48-23.

Where to Have Tea: **À la Cour de Rohan**, cour du commerce St-André, 59–61 rue St-André-des-Arts, ☎ 1/43-25-79-67.

My favorite part of the 6e is located behind the church of St-Germain-des-Prés. Behind the church you'll find place de Furstemberg, rue de Buci, rue Jacob, rue Bonaparte, rue de Seine, rue du Bac, and quai Voltaire. Many of these streets house antiques and decorating shops, and, of course, the rue de Buci offers a street market (open Sundays!), where flowers and food are sold in profusion. This is a must-do Paris stop; let those who appreciate a visual scene come feast their eyes.

These streets are mostly filled with boutiques, bakeries, eateries, markets, and—the fame of the neighborhood—antiques and design showrooms. It is very quaint back here, and the stores feel different from the ones in the other parts of the Left Bank. This is one of the most charming areas in all of Paris.

9/13/00   great people watching

Rennes Central, 6e–14e

Métro: St-Germain-des-Prés, St-Sulpice, or Montparnasse/Bienvenue.

Shopping Scene: Real-people Montparnasse (14e) leads to touristy Left Bank.

At one of the major intersections of the Left Bank, two streets converge in a "V"—the rue de Rennes and the rue Bonaparte. Bonaparte runs behind the church as well; rue de Rennes does not. Rue de Rennes is the central drag of this trading area. It's a pretty big street with a lot of retail; the farther away it reaches from St-Germain, the less fancy the stores become. Rue Bonaparte, a very nice street for strolling, is sort of smaller and runs off at an angle. See page 134 for a description of this area, which feels neighborhoody and very different from rue de Rennes.

Rue de Rennes has a big-city feel, so it isn't exactly the charming Left Bank kind of place you were expecting. Closer to boulevard St-Germain, but on rue de Rennes, there are many big-name designer shops, from **Céline** to **Habitat,** as well as **Guy Laroche, Stefanel, Courrèges, Kenzo,** and **Burberrys.** A number of hot-shot boutiques, such as **Loft,** and new trendsetters like **Estéban** (for homestyle) at no. 49, are also here.

As you move away from the boulevard St-Germain, there's still plenty to enjoy, but fewer designer stores.

Teens can have **Morgan,** while I'll take **Geneviève Lethu** (no. 95) for tabletop and fresh fabric ideas.

Whatever you do, don't bail out until you've shopped at **Inno,** a place that always makes my heart sing—it's a dime store/grocery store.

9/13/00   Gail bought shoes here —

Little Dragons, 6e

Métro: Sèvres-Babylone or St-Germain-des-Prés.

Shopping Scene: Trendy.

Where to Have Lunch: Le Bamboche, see page 135.

Where to Have Tea: Lutétia.

To the right of Rennes Central (if your back is to the church) are several very small, narrow streets crammed with good things to eat and to wear. They are epitomized by the rue du Dragon, which is why I call this neighborhood Little Dragons. But you'll also want to check out rue de Grenelle and rue des Sts-Pères. This whole warren of tiny streets is crammed with great shops, many belonging to designers of fame and fortune (**Ferragamo, Sonia Rykiel Enfant, Philippe Model**).

This area is sandwiched between the Sèvres-Babylone métro stop and the neighborhood I call Rennes Central. To one side is **Le Bon Marché,** one of Paris's biggest and most famous department stores. You can also easily walk to St-Placide from here.

St-Sulpice, 6e

Métro: Mabillon or St-Sulpice.

Shopping Scene: Chic.

The core of this area is between rue Bonaparte and the place St-Sulpice. It comes complete with a gorgeous church, a park, several designer shops (**Christian Lacroix, Castelbajac**) and some picture-postcard places. But it stretches over to the rue Tournon and the rue de Seine, and even includes the newish American-style mall, **Marché St-Germain.** The side streets are full of small designer shops, some with names you've heard of—like **Souleiado** and **Les Olivades**—but many more with names that are largely unknown to Americans and exciting to discover.

Although I hated the mall when it first opened, I've now gotten used to it and even pop in there every now and then. There are several branch stores of English multiples, such as **Monsoon** and **The Body Shop**; there's **GAP** and a few French chain stores, including **Koba,** which sells nice underwear. There's a rather well-stocked *parfumerie* as well. *Note:* This is a great place to use the bathrooms or telephones. Bathrooms cost 1 F.

Along the rue St-Sulpice, before you get to the park, you'll find all the kinds of shops you came to Paris to visit. Among them are both a store run by the magazine *Elle* (no. 30), which features items they also sell by mail order from the United States, and **Maison de Famille** (no. 29), which is adorable inside, but does sell many items imported from the U.S. Both stores have upstairs levels to them, so don't miss any of the nooks or crannies.

Rue du Bac, 7e

Métro: Sèvres-Babylone or rue du Bac.

Shopping Scene: French Left Bank snob.

Where to Have Lunch: Le Bamboche, 15 rue de Babylone, reservations ☎ 1/45-49-14-40.

Where to Have Tea or Coffee: Hotel Lutétia.

As a residential neighborhood, you can't beat the 7e—not even in the 16e. As a shopping neighborhood, you can't beat the rue du Bac, especially if you like looking at the <u>lifestyles of the rich and Parisienne</u>.

You can get here two ways: the easy method or the longer, more complicated, but more fun method. For the former, take the métro to rue du Bac and walk away from the river on rue du Bac. (See, easy.) For the latter, begin on the Right Bank, cross the bridge at the Louvre (see that bright golden statue of Jeanne d'Arc?), and hit the quai at rue du Bac. Walk toward the métro stop rue du Bac and away from the river. You get 3 or 4 more blocks of shopping this way. While it's not the best part of the rue du Bac, it's great good fun. The street twists a bit, but just wonder and wander, following the street signs. You will quit rue du Bac only when you get to **Le Bon Marché**, so *bon marche* to you.

You'll note that I've stopped you off for tea or coffee in the department store. One of the things I often do is get a pastry from **Hédiard** and sit in the tiny residential park for a quick break. If you prefer chocolate to stimulate you through the late afternoon, **Christian Constant**'s store is at no. 26.

Secret Seven, 7e

Métro: Rue du Bac.

Shopping Scene: Privately chic. You came with the car and driver, didn't you?

I don't suggest places to stop for lunch or tea in this neighborhood because you will reenter the real world for these things; this is just a 2-block stroll in another world, a world inhabited by very rich and chic women.

You are going to walk along the rue du Pré-aux-Clercs, which is only a block or two in length. It lies between boulevard St-Germain and the river.

Quai to Heaven, 6e

Métro: St-Michel.

Shopping Scene: Insiderish, quiet, and private.

Where to Have Lunch: Les Bookinistes, 53 quai des Grands-Augustins, reservations ☎ 1/43-25-45-94.

Where to Have Tea: À la Cour de Rohan, see page 132.

Most of the serious antiques dealers on the Left Bank are nestled into the real estate between the river and the boulevard St-Germain. Many line the quai

Voltaire. If you continue along the river and just shop the quais, you will pass the stalls that sell old books, ephemera, and junk. This is a tourist scene, which is fun to do once or twice as you get to know Paris. The real antiques scene is much more hidden. It's best to make appointments in advance, even. While some browsing occurs, this is generally done by locals who continually visit the dealers, know them by name, poke around, chat, pat the dog, and then peek in the back room.

Paris Hilton, 15e

Métro: Champs-de-Mars.

Shopping Scene: Hidden, French, residential, upper-middle class.

Where to Have Lunch or Brunch: Paris Hilton's Pacific Eiffel or **Jules Verne** in the Eiffel Tower.

Where to Have Tea: Eiffel Tower.

For years I would have scoffed if you even mentioned the Paris Hilton to me. Sure, it's next door to the Eiffel Tower, but there's not much else for a shopper to do. But on Sundays, especially, there's shopping in the nearby Village Suisse and the brunch scene is energetic.

Aside from the obvious **Eiffel Tower** business (very little shopping, even in terms of souvenirs), none of the rest of the shopping here is immediately obvious. We come with the car; there really isn't that much of a métro connection. But the highlights are infectious: The **quai Branly** sometimes has an exhibition, be it an art show or an antiques show; the **Village Suisse**—a village of antiques shops—is 2 blocks from the Hilton. And 2 blocks from there is a very nice street market underneath the elevated rail track. I promise you, there are very few tourists here. It's on the rue Grenelle under the elevated railroad tracks of La Motte Picquet station. This market is held on Wednesday and Sunday only, from 8:30am until 1pm. Although it's mostly a food market, there are other vendors selling Provençal fabrics, olive oil, and the like.

Best of all, though, is the Sunday morning market on the **rue Cler,** where 2 blocks of the street celebrate French food. Yes, all the stores, even the ones that don't sell food, are open. Go early; everyone's gone by 1pm. Then have brunch at the **Hilton** or at the **Eiffel Tower.** Or, if you've saved up for it and reserved ahead, have lunch at the Michelin-starred **Jules Verne** restaurant in the Eiffel Tower.

DISCOUNT NEIGHBORHOODS

. . . .

Alésia, 14e

Métro: Alésia.

Pronounced "Aleeeza" by some and "heaven" by others, this is one of the major discount districts in Paris. Prices in some of these shops may not be the lowest possible, but there are a good half a dozen shops to choose from. Not every store in this area is a discount house, so ask if you are confused. Don't make any false assumptions! Most of the discount houses have the word *stock* in their name, which means they sell overruns.

Some of the shops have a designer's name plus the word *stock* in their name; others have store names, without alluding to what is inside, such as **Stock 2,** a spacious space at no. 92, that sells men's, women's, and kids' designer clothes at discount prices. Most of it is from **Daniel Hechter,** but there are other brands.

Don't miss **Cacharel Stock** (no. 114), with fabulous baby and kids' clothes as well as some men's and women's things, although I've never found anything worthwhile here that wasn't for children. **Fabrice Karel,** no. 105, makes terrific knits similar to those of Rodier and is just across from Cacharel.

Diapositive is a big, hip line in Paris; their stock shop is at no. 74. But the highlight of the block is undoubtedly **SR** (no. 64), which stands for, shout it out folks, **Sonia Rykiel**. The clothes here are old, but they are true-blue Sonia. Last visit I found a pair of pants I bought at Saks Fifth Avenue for $500 (don't tell my husband) for $125! My new favorite is called **Feel Good,** and they sell only bodysuits. Not only are they chic, they are machine washable.

When you shop this area, keep store hours in mind. Stores are generally closed Monday morning, but open at 2pm; many are closed for the entire month of August. Also remember that not all of the stores are discount; they just want you to think they are.

St-Placide, 7e

Métro: Sèvres-Babylone.

This is not particularly near Alésia (although you can walk from one area to the other), but mentally the two areas are sisters—homes of the discount shop, the stock shop, the great bargain. St-Placide is a side street that is right alongside **Le Bon Marché,** the department store on the Left Bank. Take the métro to St-Placide and walk toward Le Bon Marché and the rue des Sèvres. Pass Le Bon Marché then turn left onto rue St-Placide.

There are maybe 10 stock shops in this 1 block, but they never do much for me. Every time I visit, which is about once a year, I come away empty-handed. The best of the bunch is a group of shops owned by **Le Mouton à 5 Pattes.** There's a children's shop, a designer shop, as well as a real-people shop. There were plenty of big names, like Gaultier and Ferre, in bins, the last time I visited.

St-Placide feels a bit seedy and isn't as attractive as Alésia, but there's nothing wrong with the neighborhood, and it is safe. Walk along the street, choosing what interests you, until you come to the rue de

Sèvres, a main street of the neighborhood. Because Le Bon Marché is right here, many other retailers have come along with branch stores to catch the overflow department-store traffic. There's a **Guerlain,** a **Rodier,** and a **Dorothée Bis,** in addition to a lot of other nice stores. It is not fancy here, but it is quite serviceable. Zara just moved in, and there's a métro station in the square (Sèvres-Babylone). You can come and go from here, or take the rue de Sèvres for 1 block, and hit the really exciting, fancy, expensive stores of the neighborhood.

Chapter Nine

· · · · · · · ·

BASIC PARIS RESOURCES
FROM A TO Z

ANTIQUES

· ·

Paris is one of the world's capitals for antiques.
One of the pleasures of shopping here is browsing
the wide variety of antiques shops. Whether you're
buying real antiques or just some "old stuff," remember that U.S. Customs defines an "antique"
as something that is at least 100 years old. If a
piece you purchase does not come with provenance
papers, you must have a receipt or a bill of lading
from the dealer that says what the piece is and its
origin and age. The French government is rather
stringent about what can be taken out of the country; they are even trying to keep some designer *fripes*
(used clothes) in the country now.

Expensive museum-quality antiques are generally
sold in the tony shops along the rue du Faubourg
St-Honoré and in the 16e, although there are plenty
of high-end dealers on the Left Bank all congregated
in their own exclusive little zone of refinement. Mid-
priced antiques are predominantly found in antiques
shops on the Left Bank, in the antiques *"villages"*
(as they are called), and at the markets of St-Ouen.
Junk is mostly sold at street markets or fairs or flea
markets.

If you just want to browse and get the feel of the antiques scene, get to the Left Bank. There's a grouping of very important dealers between the river and the boulevard St-Germain. They may be a tad more expensive than the others in town, but they are the real guys with the real reputations who do not even look up from their newspapers when you walk in. They can tell from the questions you ask just how serious you are, what you know, and often, whom you know.

If you want to familiarize yourself with the notions and motions of French-style antiques shopping, get to a large news agent and look at the several magazines devoted to antiques and to *brocante.* The most popular is *Alladin,* but there are half a dozen magazines—all of which give the schedules of big shows, fairs, specialty antiques events, etc.

Should you be flexible on the dates of your visit to Paris and wanting to maximize your antiques shopping possibilities, you might want to call SADEMA, one of the leading organizers of shows. They have a ton of shows between February and June, so you may want to book your trip around their dates, ☎ 1/40-62-95-95. Some Web sites may also post the better shows.

Antiques *Villages*

A *village* in Paris is not a subdivision of an arrondissement but a place for good antiques. *Villages* are buildings that house many antiques dealers under one roof. If you need a rainy-day-in-Paris occupation, a trip to any *village* probably will do it; some are even open on Sunday.

VILLAGE ST-PAUL
Rue St-Paul, 4e (Métro: St-Paul).

This, a *village* that's also accompanied by a block or more of street stalls selling antiques, can be a little hard to find if you aren't patient. It's hidden in a medieval warren of streets between the Seine and the church of St. Paul, very close to Marais and Bastille. The village itself is between the rue St-Paul, the rue Charles V, the rue des Jardins St-Paul, and the rue Ave-Maria.

Get off the métro at St-Paul and walk toward the river. Or walk along the quai going toward the Bastille and take a left when you spy the first antiques shop on the corner of the rue St-Paul. If you are coming from the river, you have the advantage of being able to see the sign that spans the street across the rooftops: Village St. Paul.

Hours are generally Thursday to Monday, 11am to 7pm. There are many shops to visit. Prices can be steep, but the variety of the merchandise, combined with the charm of the neighborhood, makes this a delightful way to pass the time. A good stop to piggyback with your visit to Marais. Yes, there's life on Sunday afternoons.

LE LOUVRE DES ANTIQUAIRES
2 place du Palais-Royal, 1er
(Métro: Palais-Royal).

This is a virtual antiques department store of some 250 dealers. You may have more fun here than at the museum! At least you can shop here. Many mavens claim this is the single best one-stop source in Paris because quality is high and the dealers have reputations to protect. You can even bargain a little. There are enough affordable small pieces that you're bound to find something you like, without having to pound the pavement going from shop to shop. Indoors is a restaurant and a shipping agent. Very sophisticated, very civilized, nothing junky at all. Closed on Sunday in August; otherwise the Sunday scene is from a movie—the other shoppers alone are worth the time it takes to visit. Clean bathrooms.

LE VILLAGE SUISSE
54 ave. de la Motte-Picquet, 15e
(Métro: La Motte).

You won't find any gnomes making watches here, or handing out chocolate bars . . . just a lot of dealers in the mid- to high-price range, with some very respectable offerings. There are 150 shops in an area 1 block long and 2 blocks wide—it's sort of like a mall that rambles from building to building. A number of the shops are thematic.

The Village Suisse is near the Hilton, the Eiffel Tower and l'École Militaire; it is within walking distance of the Paris Hilton. Prices are not outrageous, but they aren't low, either; most stores offer shipping. There are no cute or funky stores here, but several shops are theme-oriented, selling nautical items or antique jewelry, for example. Sunday is a big day here.

LE BON MARCHÉ
38 rue de Sèvres, 6e (Métro: Sèvres-Babylone).

Le Bon Marché is indeed a department store, but it's really two stores in one. One portion is the full department store; the other is a grocery store with a flea market upstairs.

I can't tell you this is a must-do experience, but it can be fun. It's especially good if you are in the neighborhood or want a taste of a flea market without going to the trouble of getting to one. There's a place for coffee; closed on Sunday.

Auction Houses

For years, the big name in Paris's auction world was the Hôtel Drouot. But ever since Sotheby's gave up its Monaco offices and moved to Paris and the government allowed others to play in the big leagues, the scene's become much more competitive.

When an entire estate is auctioned off today, there is usually nothing "important" (as the dealers tend to say) for sale. Important works are being saved for major auctions. Such big-time auctions are held in the relatively new Hôtel Drouot. (The house took over an existing theater on the avenue Montaigne.) Humdrum and average estate sales (where you can still get bargains) are at the main house, not far from Galeries Lafayette.

When you read auction catalogs in Paris, note that Hôtel Drouot listings with an "R" after them (for Richelieu) refer to the old location, and an "M" refers to the avenue Montaigne location.

Hôtel Drouot
9 rue Drouot, 9e (Métro: Le Peletier); 15 ave. Montaigne, 8e (Métro: Alma-Marceau).

If you prefer your used furniture to come by way of an auction house, this is the place for a serious deal. For years, the Hôtel Drouot tightly controlled the auction business in Paris.

Some 90 auctioneers are in the main house, with several auctions going on simultaneously. The auctioneers are all shareholders—equal partners, in fact—in the business and, as a result, it's run much like a law firm. Speaking of lawyers, there are lawyers in France who specialize in auctions because this is a very, very different business from the one you know and love in the United States and the U.K.

Drouot is a weird and fascinating place. At the entrance, an information counter has catalogs and notices of future sales. Three TV sets on the ground floor show different parts of the building, and there is an appraiser who—free of charge—will tell you if an item you bring in is worthy of auction, and will appraise it for you on the spot. The estimate is done in a small private room. If you agree with the estimate, you can set a date for your auction. The seller pays an 8% to 10% commission to the house.

Auctions are held every day, except in summer, when they are not held on weekends. They always begin at 2pm and go until concluded, usually about 6:30pm. Previews are held on Wednesday until 11am. You can buy their magazine on newsstands and get an instant look at the auction of the month.

The auction rooms are various sizes; some can be divided or opened according to need. All the rooms are carpeted; art and/or tapestries are on the walls. The clients sit on chairs to watch the bidding; paddles are not used. Most of the clients are dealers; we have never noticed a very jazzy crowd here, even when we went to a Goya auction. All business is in French. If you are not fluent, please bring your own translator or expert, or book a translator ahead of time (☎ 1/42-46-17-11 to arrange for a translator).

You needn't register to bid; anyone can walk in, sit down, and bid. All auctions have catalogs, and the lots are numbered and defined in the catalog. You do not need a catalog to enter a preview or an auction, as you do in New York. The conditions of the sale are plainly printed inside the first page of the catalog (in French). You can pay in cash up to 10,000 F. French people may write local checks; Americans cannot write checks. If you have only American dollars on hand, there is an exchange bureau in the house. If you pay in cash, you can walk out with your item. Shills are occasionally used by some dealers to drive up the price. Auctioneers are familiar with all the dealers and could possibly choose to throw a piece their way. Dealers may even pool in on items.

You are responsible for shipping; there is no shipping office in the auction house. You start paying storage charges after 24 hours.

Brocante Shows

Brocante is the French word for junk; *brocante* and those who sell it are not antiquers—this is very strict in the French sense of things. An American might not notice the difference.

Brocante is sold everywhere in France, from local markets to fancy shoes. SADEMA is an organization that hosts *brocante* shows, as mentioned above. *Brocante* shows are annual events (or semiannual), most frequently held at the same time (more or less) and place each year. They are announced in the papers (check *Figaroscope*), or in the weekly guides such as *Pariscope* . . . or you can call, write, or fax for their schedule: Sadema, 86 rue de Lille, 75007 Paris, ☎ 1/40-62-95-95; fax 1/40-62-95-96. Some shows are weekend events; others last up to 2 weeks. Sadema charges admission to most of their fairs, usually about 25 F per person. They do have a registration service, so you can get on their mailing list. I'm waiting for the Web site!

Sadema is not the only game in town; there are other organizations that sponsor shows. Some are fancier and charge 40 F to 50 F admission. In fact, the admission charge is a direct indication of how tony the dealers are; the higher the gate fee, the more expensive are the dealers and their wares.

There is an exhibition venue almost directly across the street from the Paris Hilton, on the Quai de Branly, 7e, which is a tented space where they hold the Salon des Antiquaires. This space will be turned into a museum in a few years, but now it's still a venue for high-end shows. I attended an event here only once and found it way too fancy for me. Here is a list of the shows I adore:

- **Ferraille de Paris:** Held in the Parc Floral de Paris (Bois de Vincennes), this fair occurs toward the end of February every year. This is a good-sized indoor fair, with a lot of affordable merchandise and approachable merchants. Everything from empty perfume bottles to the kitchen sink. The French country kitchen sink. (Métro: Porte Dorée.)
- **Brocante de Printemps:** A March event that usually lasts 10 days; heralds the coming of spring, of course. (Métro: Porte Edgar-Quintet.)
- **Brocante à la Bastille:** An annual event that you can tell, from its title, does not take itself or its merchants too seriously. This fair is usually held on both sides of the canal. Pay near the place de la Bastille; there are bridges to the other side. Usually held for 10 days in April or May, this is

particularly fabulous in fine weather. I'd fly in just for this event. (Métro: Bastille.)

- **Brocante de Paris:**   This huge event is the talk of the town for those who hope to get a designer bargain. Held for 10 days in May. (Métro: Porte Brochant.)

AMERICAN DESIGNERS IN PARIS

. . . .

The second American liberation of Paris began quietly enough when Ralph Lauren opened a shop on the place de la Madeleine. Not so subtle was the arrival of GAP, which now has a store in every major shopping neighborhood in Paris, along with GAP Kids freestanding stores.

Now the American look is the latest thing in town, and even French designers are copying it. Or more accurately, even American designers are becoming French designers (Michael Kors, Marc Jacobs). You can see much American merchandise at home and pay less for it, but in France there's always the chance you may find your favorite items in shades you can't get at home. Still, I don't suggest you spend too much precious Paris time looking at American-based designers; these guys are out to win the local population, and they are selling status to locals, not merchandise that offers value for money.

There are also a few local scandals, on which I will not dwell, that may confuse American shoppers. Let me explain that many French designers who do not hit the big time in France move to America (or Canada), where they find it is easier to break into the business. Once they become rich and famous in America, their biggest need is to return to France, open some stores, be famous . . . and rub everyone's French nose in their success and glamour. Furthermore, most of these firms have French names, so that you may never even guess they are actually American businesses, available at your local mall for less money. Watch it!

Finally, if you want to really laugh, stop in at a store called **Colette**—which is the French interpretation of American concepts and is the latest thing in Paris despite the fact that it's 3 years old (and very boring). No American could get excited by this store, yet the French are gaga. Paris has many Colette wannabes drifting around.

More important, you'll find that American methods of merchandising and selling are creeping into the French lifestyle, so that even the big department stores are getting a little more American. In no time at all it will be very hard to find someone in France to be rude to you. Oh yes, everything is not coming up sweatshirts for all Americans in Paris—the Joan & David shop has quit the rue du Faubourg St-Honoré.

BCBG
412 rue St. Honoré, 8e (Métro: Concorde).

CALVIN KLEIN
56 & 45 ave. Montaigne, 8e (Métro: Alma Marceau).

CRABTREE & EVELYN
177 blvd. St-Germain, 7e (Métro: rue du Bac); Passy Plaza, 53 rue de Passy, 16e (Métro: La Muette).

ESPRIT
9 place des Victoires, 2e (Métro: Bourse).

GAP
Everywhere, including the Champs-Elysées.

JOSIE NATORI
7 place Vendôme, 1er (Métro: Tuileries).

OSHKOSH B'GOSH
32 rue de Passy, 16e (Métro: La Muette).

RALPH LAUREN/POLO
2 place de la Madeleine, 8e (Métro: Madeleine).

BARGAIN BASEMENTS

. . . .

The French are finally admitting that they've been far too snobby about paying full retail, and factory outlet malls are starting to pop up outside of Paris. Most are in Troyes and Lille, but a few are in Paris proper.

Because the pickings are hit-or-miss, you won't want to devote an entire trip to these sources, but there are more choices than ever before. Like the criminal who returns to the scene of the crime, I always manage to visit the "stock shops" where I have done well on previous trips. Bargains are addictive!

See page 240 for resale shops, which can offer bargains on pre-owned designer clothing, and the discount neighborhoods section of chapter 7, which lists two different streets in Paris where you can go from shop to shop in search of a bargain.

Paris has seen a lot of stock and so-called discount stores open in the last few years. Some even call themselves outlet stores. Mostly they are regular mom-and-pop stores that have chosen to carry name brands, but who have cut their profit in order to gain appeal with shoppers who are disgusted by the high prices on regular retail in France. Department stores are known to locals as being very expensive, so a store that has goods for 50 F less calls itself an outlet and becomes a "find" to many. We do the same thing in America, of course.

I don't need to give you the lecture about the nature of bargain shops, but I will say that on my last research trip I noticed two new addresses in popular tourist magazines (no names, please). I eagerly went off to these sources—each in the heart of Paris's best shopping district and convenient for any visitor. Maybe I hit a bad day; maybe I am too big a snob. I hated both of them so much that I refuse to list them in this book. On the other hand, that doesn't mean that the sources I have listed are going to be super on the day you visit. Bargain hunting in Paris is even harder than in America, so think about how much time you want to invest in this pursuit. Good luck.

Anna Lowe
104 rue du Faubourg St-Honoré 8e
(Métro: Miromesnil).

For more than a decade this has been a terrific store, and now people visit for clothes and pashmina. Aside from a few Chanel accessories, there were no name clothes but I still spent $500 on a no-name suit. Open Monday through Friday, 10:30am to 6pm.

L'Annexe des Créateurs
19 rue Godot-de-Mauroy, 9e (Métro: Madeleine).

This shop is crowded and lacks charm, but is crammed with clothes and bolts of fabric. It has all sizes up to 44 (American size 12). You won't have to make a special trip; the location is close to many places in every woman's journey through Paris—halfway between boulevard Madeleine and the big department stores on boulevard Haussmann.

It tries to specialize in younger and kickier designers, such as Moschino and Mugler; pieces are a season old and therefore are sold at 30% to 40% off regular French retail. Stop in to check out hats and accessories as well—the good stuff begins at $100.

Stock Griffes
17 rue Vielle-du-Temple, 4e (Métro: Hotel de Ville or St-Paul).

This is my new favorite stock shop in Paris; they have other branch stores around town. I like this one because you don't have to go out of your way to find it—it's part of anyone's visit to the Marais and the Picasso Museum—and there are other stock shops just a sneeze away, so if you strike out here, there's hope for you and your wallet.

Now then, despite the fact that this is a so-called stock shop and is supposed to offer bargains, I am a spoiled American shopper and I don't think that $150 for a dress is a bargain. But I happily paid that for an Irena Gregori dress partly because I adore her stuff and partly because the dress was gorgeous—and mostly because the dress was machine washable. None of the Irena merchandise here was currently in any of the department stores, so I imagine it was old—that doesn't upset me, I just wish that old equaled cheap in France. It doesn't.

You may not recognize the names on the labels here, and sometimes the labels are cut out, but the merchandise is often fashion forward and less money than in regular retail sources.

A few tacky things to round out this rave: They made fun of my French here by mimicking me in French (but they didn't speak English!). Also, I discovered when I got back to the U.S. that the electronic sensor was still on the garment I bought, and no American contraption could remove this sensor because I couldn't get a fit with the machinery. Pay attention to details (and practice your French) if you shop here.

LA BRADERIE
38 rue de Rivoli, corner rue Vielle-du-Temple, 4e (Métro: Hotel de Ville or St-Paul).

Although this small chain has almost a dozen discount shops in Paris and has separate shops for men and women, I have listed this one because it is half a block from the above listing. While I personally struck out when I last visited, they do carry some French brand names and have plenty of choices at very realistic prices. There's a men's shop a few stores away at 11 rue Vielle-du-Temple.

RIVOLI 44
44 rue de Rivoli, 4e (Métro: Hôtel de Ville).

While we're in the area, I thought I'd add this in here rather than in the shoe section. This is one of those really sweet little shops that doesn't look like much and the owner doesn't speak much English, but she's very sweet and will explain everything to you. The store carries only the Arche brand of shoes. I happen to wear this line, but I never pay $265 per pair at Nordstrom's. The prices here vary with the style, but they are current season and cost about 50 F less than in department stores.

MOUTON À CINQ PATTES
15 rue Vielle-du-Temple, 4e (Métro: Hôtel de Ville or St-Paul).

This is a small chain of stock shops; I know the one on St-Placide better and I hate that one. I have always called it "The Lamb Chops Store." This branch is much more civilized and worth looking at; I saw several items that were worth dreaming about at about $100 per dress. You will find big names.

LES COMPTOIRS DU TROCADÉRO
17 ave. Raymond Poincare, 16e (Métro: Trocadêro).

I found this by accident while I was leaving Alain Ducasse's restaurant, which is down the street; I'm not sure that I suggest a special trip here. Although I still regret the coat I didn't buy my son for 200 F (but it was my first day in Paris and what did I know?). This discounter sells men's and women's clothing; I saw no name brands that I recognized, nor did I see any special bargains except for the 200 F coat. Still, this location is so easy that you might want to pop in and try to get lucky.

L'ASTUCERIE
105 rue de Javel, 15e (Métro: Felix Faure).

Don't let this address throw you; the store is not too far from the Eiffel Tower and the Paris Hilton. This is a *dépôt-vent*, which means the clothes have been used, or at least worn, by models for photo shoots and on the runway. The house specialty:

designer clothes and accessories at basically half the regular retail price.

MI-PRIX

27 blvd. Victor, 15e (Métro: Porte de Versailles).

This store is far from fancy. It's also far from central Paris. You can be making a long trip for nothing, but that's life in the bargain fast lane.

But the bargains? Mi-Prix has a very weird combination of items—the junkiest of no-name merchandise, some very nice skiwear, a fabulous collection of Maud Frizon and Walter Steiger shoes (and boots), Bottega Veneta closeouts, and Philippe Model hats—at almost give-away prices. The store is packed with merchandise; much is current. The shoes are a different story. Some could be as current as last season, others as old as your grandmother.

If you are attending a trade show at the Porte de Versailles, this is a must. Also check the newspapers for *brocante* and antiques shows that may be held in this area, so you can combine agendas. It's hard to convince yourself to come all the way out here for one store, especially when it is a matter of hit-or-miss, but I've never been sorry I did. Walk from the convention center along boulevard Victor about 2 blocks; there are some other shops and discounters along here you may also want to check out.

BATH & BODY
. . . .

My favorite French bath suds and soaps come from Annick Goutal; I "steal" them regularly from Concorde hotels whenever I stay in France. But, I don't stop there—I also buy numerous bath products in every *parapharmacie* I hit in France; I've been testing slimming baths (stop snickering) and *thalossotherapie* for a few years now. I'm also big on testing unusual scents in soaps, such as the Roger & Gallet cherry-tomato! Although I personally adore fancy soap, I also think it makes a great gift, so load up for all your $5 friends!

Should you want to get into the swim of *thalossotherapie* (treatment through sea water and seaweed products), there are a few firms you'll want to know about. **Phytomer** is the most famous, but only **Louison Bobet** has limited U.S. distribution and a good name in France. You can buy both brands in department stores and drugstores in Paris.

Please don't neglect the section in this chapter on makeup and perfume, as many of the stores listed there carry wonderful bed and bath products as well.

Annick Goutal is one of the best examples, but **Sephora** has everything, including their own house line of bath products. **Roger & Gallet** is a very old French name; I actually remember when they had a shop near Hermès on the Faubourg St-Honoré, but I am old, old, old. Now they have scads of bath and soap products, including the old line that's been sold for over 100 years and several new lines and new products. I like their liquid soaps in a tube (great for travel) and their new candles, which cost less than many fancier brands. Sold just about everywhere, but the best selection is in department stores. (My favorite soap in a tube is cinnamon/orange.)

Below I have listed some of the cult brands (and a few of the little-known shops) that have their own stores; some of them also have U.S. distribution on their own or through sales and spas in America.

DARPHIN
97 rue du Bac, 7e (Métro: rue du Bac).

This is one of those very chic, almost secret beauty salons that do facials and treatments (hair is never done in a skin salon in France) and sell their own line of natural bath and beauty products, which have now made it to America in limited doses so that only the rich and with-it know about this line. They're big on body shaping, as are all French cures, but also have many hydroplus (water-added) products to moisturize and balance.

L'OCCITANE
1 rue du 29 Juillet, 1er (Métro: Tuileries).

This is a huge chain, so I have only listed one convenient address above (close to the Louvre). but there are many chances to shop this brand in Paris and at French department stores. L'Occitane is not only home of the best 15 F gift (package of scented soap) in France, but makes scented water to pour into your iron—truly the silliest item I have ever bought (and I loaded up!).

L'Occitane is a soap manufacturer from Provence that now has a million shops around France and is growing globally. Moreover, L'Occitane is not only a line, it's a mood and a statement. There are numerous scented products for men, women, and children and for body, bath, and home; they launched color makeup a year ago.

This is a must-do stop. There is a L'Occitane store in almost every trading area; the one at the place des Vosges (no. 18) is open on Sundays as is the one above. There's another branch inside the mall at Le Passage du Havre, a half block from Printemps.

OCTÉE
18 rue des Quatre-Vents, 6e (Métro: St-Germain-des-Prés).

Known for its fragrance line, this small shop also sells color-coded perfume and soap. The gimmick is that the colors you prefer (no names) indicate your personality type. Honest. Could I make this up? Note that the store has moved if you are a regular.

PERLIER
8 rue de Sèvres, 7e (Métro: Sèvres-Babylone).

This beauty line is made with honey and is widely sold in the U.S. In fact, sometimes I can buy it at Marshall's and save on French prices. The nicest thing about the line is its large number of small items that make adorable gifts (like the honey bath balls!). There's all sorts of beauty products, though—shampoos, bath gels, body lotions, night creams, morning creams—you're getting the idea. I'm addicted to the vanilla-scented line.

SAPONIFÈRE
16 rue Vignon, 8e (Métro: Madeleine); 59 rue Bonaparte, 6e (Métro: St-Germain-des-Prés).

This is a combination gift shop–towel shop–bath shop that sells tons of soaps. It has a chic, Provençal, yet beachy feel to it.

SANTA MARIA NOVELLA
2 rue Guisarde, 6e (Métro: Mabillon).

This is a very, very famous (to the point of cult worship for some) Italian pharmacy from Florence. It has begun to expand into international shopping cities only in the past few years. The Paris shop does not compare to the mother ship in a former convent in Florence, but if you can't get to Italy, stop in here. I buy the weekend soap, divided into three small bars for Friday, Saturday, and Sunday.

BRITISH BRANDS

If you want to buy British but can't make it through the Chunnel, you will have some opportunities in Paris. **Marks & Spencer** has had no trouble convincing French shoppers that it's an important brand—the firm seems to be doing better in France than they are in the U.K. these days. Other British clothing lines, especially the young and hip lines, are sold in Galeries Lafayette, which features everything from **Top Shop** to **Monsoon** and more.

British tailors and men's haberdasheries such as **Sulka, Hildtich & Key,** and **Dunhill** have stores in Paris.

There's **W.H. Smith** right on the rue de Rivoli. A few blocks away, at the mall inside the Louvre, there's a branch of **Virgin Megastore**—which has another branch on the Champs-Elysées.

Perhaps one of the most interesting stores in town sells a purely Brit look but in a French way, **Old England**—which is a small French chain with an enormous store right near Opéra. They do veddy, veddy British clothes, almost of the hunting and shooting category, but then twist them into French fashion by changing the colors—the duffle coats in a rainbow selection of solids is so brilliant you have to wonder why the British never came up with this idea.

For the Japanese twist on British retail, **Muji** has invaded Paris with several stores; the one on the Left Bank (27 rue St-Sulpice, 6e) is the easiest to shop because you don't have to go up and down stairs. The stores are standard Muji, so if you've seen them before, there's nothing new here. If not, check out this emporium and ode to minimalist chic in everything from clothes to toothbrushes.

Don't forget that every now and then you get a British brand that has actually turned French, such as the perfume house **Creed,** which made the switcheroo about a hundred years ago, so its probably official by now.

BODY SHOP
Le Carrousel du Louvre, 99 rue de Rivoli, 1er (Métro: Louvre).

This British icon, despite hard financial times, still has several stores all over Paris—look for them in major trading areas, especially where there are teen and tween fashions.

MARY QUANT
49 rue Bonaparte, 6e (Métro: St-Germain-des-Prés).

The woman who brought us the mod mode world back in the 1960s has several new shops in London and has freestanding stores in other shopping capitals, such as New York and Paris. Mostly she sells makeup, but there are some accessories.

CHILDREN'S CLOTHING

. . . .

If you're the kind of mom—or grandma—who likes to drop a bundle on a single outfit for your little darling, Paris welcomes you and your moolah. You'll have no trouble finding expensive shops where you can swoon from the high fashion and the high price. Don't forget about the department stores, all of which have rather famous children's departments and much more moderate prices.

If you like cheap, fun, throw-away things, try Monoprix or Inno. Each has a toy department, a good selection of inexpensive basics, and some great ready-to-wear clothing. But wait, sometimes you'll find prices at one of these "dime stores" are the same as at a department store. Still if you can get an outfit for $12 to $15, I think you're doin' good. Because Inno and Monoprix are owned by the same firm, you'll see a lot of the same clothes. I buy a lot for my 8-year-old niece Julia.

Note: Julia's mom tells me that French clothes fit differently from U.S. clothes—they are smaller and closer to the body. French kids' clothes are usually marked by the age in years just like American clothes, so 8A means 8 years (*8 ans*). There is a more complete size chart in the back of this book.

Some of the trendy, fashion-forward boutiques also have a kiddie division, such as H&M—I find the quality is not as good as at Monoprix, but some trendy pieces are just so adorable you have to snap them up.

Meanwhile, if you're looking for children's shoes, you will need a size chart (see the back of this book) and some luck. My favorite source is a cheapie chain called **André**, with branch stores everywhere—they have copies of all the hot styles that usually cost well under $20 a pair.

BONPOINT
15 rue Royale, 8e (Métro: Madeleine).

BONPOINT SOLDES
82 rue de Grenelle, 7e (Métro: rue du Bac).

For classic styles, you won't find better than Bonpoint and its perfectly crafted outfits. You've never seen anything so superbly made in your life. An adorable romper costs $50; a simple smocked dress starts at $100, but prices can go to $300 for the grander stuff. If your child is over age 5, go upstairs where the fashions for older children are displayed. Parisian women with money and style swear by this resource.

There are several Bonpoint shops around town, by the way. Some specialize in kids' shoes; one has furniture only. There are freestanding stores in New York, London, and Milan. The brand is a French tradition, although Americans may find it way too uptight.

If you're impressed with the clothing once you've seen the store, but can't hack the prices, perhaps you'd like to try the outlet store where last season's collection (or what's left of it) is sold for a fraction of the uptown price. Here you'll find that $300 little frock for a mere $60! They are closed on Saturday and Sunday. This outlet happens to be convenient to everything else on the Left Bank, so don't miss it.

DIPAKI
18 rue Vignon, 8e (Métro: Madeleine).

This is a chain with stores in just about every trading area in Paris, so you won't have trouble finding one wherever you are shopping. While there are plenty of folks who like the Bonpoint route, it's way too stiff and formal for me and Dipaki epitomizes what I want—bright colors and fun. The line is also affordable. There's boys' and girls' clothes and baby/ infant items, too. I think 200 F is the very most you'll pay, and most items are much less.

TARTINE ET CHOCOLAT
89 rue du Faubourg St-Honoré, 8e
(Métro: Concorde).

French-style maternity dresses and layettes, both classic and nouveau. My own fave: the big pink hippo in pink and white stripes sitting in a play-pen, just begging to be taken home to someone's child. There are Tartine et Chocolat boutiques in the major French department stores as well. Some duty-free shops (like Silver Moon) sell the children's toiletry line. Any one of the items makes a nice gift.

PETIT FAUNE
33 rue Jacob, 6e (Métro: St-Germain-des-Prés).

Very original baby clothes in the nouveau style. Some even have matching shoes and hats. Everything is very, very small—up to size 2. The clothes are very American, and even the fanciest isn't in the classic style.

Y. BLAYO
Carrousel du Louvre, 99 rue de Rivoli, 1er
(Métro: Louvre).

This is a small shop that sells the designs of an artist named Yvan Blayo, who does very graphic squiggles similar to the late Keith Haring. All sorts of products are sold here; I am charmed by the baby bottle which I find a fabulous gift—99 F.

UNE ÉTOILE EST NÉE
Passage du Havre, 9e (Métro: St-Lazare).

This is a small shop on the ground floor of this mall right next door to Printemps; they carry many designer lines, including Kenzo, Catimi, and Baby Dior. I bought Julia a cotton sweatshirt job here that cost an outrageous $60 but was the cutest thing I had ever seen. They offer a *fidelity* card to frequent shoppers. And yes, the name of this shop is "A Star Is Born."

CHOCOLATE

Who makes better chocolate, the French or the Belgians? You'll just have to keep tasting until you decide. Designer chocolate is not inexpensive. Expect to pay about $100 per kilo. Of course, no one could eat a kilo, could they? Hmmm.

CHRISTIAN CONSTANT
37 rue d'Assas, 6e (Métro: St-Placide);
26 rue du Bac, 6e (Métro: rue du Bac).

The more things change, the more they remain Constant, especially when you are considered one of the top *chocolatiers* in town. Constant also sells ice cream and other sweet treats. You'll pass it automatically as you shop the rue du Bac. Open Monday through Saturday, 8am to 8pm.

DEBEAUVE & GALLAIS
30 rue des Sts-Pères, 7e (Métro: Sèvres-Babylone).

This shop is on the part of Sts-Pères between the boulevard St-Germain and the river; many shoppers are more familiar with the other portion of this famous shopping street. This incredibly fancy chocolate shop sells unusual flavors. Note the chocolate postcards for $7.

LENÔTRE
49 ave. Victor Hugo, 16e (Métro: Victor-Hugo).

One of the older, more famous names in candy and sweets, Lenôtre is known for its chocolates and desserts, as well as its tearoom. A nice place to go for a gift for your hostess—Parisian prestige in a box.

LA MAISON DU CHOCOLAT

8 blvd. de la Madeleine, 9e (Métro: Madeleine);
19 rue de Sèvres, 6e (Métro: Sèvres-Babylone).

If you read American gourmet-food magazines, you'll find plenty of mentions of this boutique, which wraps its *chocolats* much as Hermès wraps its goodies. They are famous for their truffles, which are so rich you can't eat more than three a day (breakfast, lunch, dinner). Chocolates are handmade, a rarity these days, and mavens claim you can get no closer to heaven. They now have several branch stores so you shouldn't have trouble getting a fix.

MARQUISE DE SÉVIGNÉ

32 place de la Madeleine, 8e (Métro: Madeleine).

Since I like sweet chocolates, I send you here for the hazelnut praline. It has a picture of the marquise herself on the golden foil. There are other divine chocolates here; I'm just addicted to this one flavor. There is also candy for diabetics. Those who prefer dark chocolates and more heady stuff may pooh-pooh this as a source.

RICHART

258 blvd. St-Germain, 7e (Métro: Solférino).

This address is in the chic and tony part of the Left Bank. It serves the local wealthy residents with chocolates from Lyon. The most famous ones are filled with cremes of whiskey or champagne. They open Monday and Saturday, 11am to 7pm; Tuesday to Friday, 10am to 7pm.

COUTURE

Couture is considered the epitome of French style. It also has become an international statement of fashion and elegance. *Haute couture* translates as fancy seams; and when you're talking about couture and realize that you are talking about $30,000 garments, you'd better believe that you get very fancy seams.

Now then, about actually going to a couture house to shop. Some of them are very accessible; some of them are terrifying. Some of the houses have a retail boutique on the premises; others keep their couture business completely separate from their boutiques. If you are a true couture customer, you go in with an appointment and a letter of introduction (a fax will do) . . . or with Pamela Harriman at your side.

If you are just browsing, you might want to consider the houses on avenue Montaigne, all accessible to the public through their retail operations. It is more or less unheard of that madame should wander in off the street and want a couture fitting. If madame wants to see the earrings that are for sale, that's another matter entirely. This way, please.

ADELINE ANDRÉ
5 rue Villehardouin, 3e.
☎ 1/42-77-72-56.

BALENCIAGA
30 ave. d'Iena, 16e.
☎ 1/47-23-03-00.

BALMAIN
44 rue François-1er, 8e.
☎ 1/47-20-35-34.

CARVEN
6 Rond Point des Champs-Elysées, 8e.
☎ 1/42-25-66-52.

CHANEL
31 rue Cambon, 1er.
☎ 1/42-86-28-00.

CHRISTIAN DIOR
30 ave. Montaigne, 8e.
☎ 1/40-73-54-44.

CHRISTIAN LACROIX
73 rue du Faubourg St-Honoré, 8e.
☎ 1/42-68-79-00.

COURRÈGES
40 rue François-1er, 8e.
☎ 1/47-23-00-73.

DOMINIQUE SIROP
352 rue Saint-Honoré, 8e.
☎ 1/42-92-05-55.

EMANUEL UNGARO
2 ave. Montaigne, 8e.
☎ 1/53-57-00-00.

GIVENCHY
3 ave. George V, 8e.
☎ 1/44-31-50-00.

GUY LAROCHE
29 ave. Montaigne, 8e.
☎ 1/40-69-68-00.

HANAE MORI
9 rue du Faubourg St-Honoré, 8e.
☎ 1/47-23-52-03.

HERMÈS
24 rue du Faubourg St-Honoré, 8e.
☎ 1/42-65-21-68.

JEAN-LOUIS SCHERRER
51 ave. Montaigne, 8e.
☎ 1/42-99-05-79.

JEAN PATOU
7 rue St-Florentin, 8e.
☎ 1/42-60-70-10.

LOUIS FÉRAUD
88 rue de l'Arbre Sec, 1er.
☎ 1/42-86-00-00.

NINA RICCI
39 ave. Montaigne, 8e.
☎ 1/47-23-78-88.

PACO RABANNE
4 rue Cambon, 1er.
☎ 1/42-22-87-80.

PIERRE CARDIN
27 ave. de Marigny, 8e.
☎ 1/42-66-92-25.

SIDONIE LARIZZI
8 rue Marignan, 8e.
☎ 1/43-59-38-87.

TORRENTE
1 rond-point des Champs-Elysées, 8e.
☎ 1/42-56-14-14.

VALENTINO
8 place Vendôme, 1er.
☎ 1/55-35-16-21.

YVES SAINT LAURENT
5 ave. Marceau, 16e.
☎ 1/44-31-64-00.

CONTINENTAL BIG NAMES
. . . .

Despite the fact that the French think French fashion is the best in the world (many other people happen to agree), they have graciously allowed other designers to open up shop in Paris. Of course, the Italians have a good number of shops, representing some of the most famous names in fashion. Everyone knows a handful of the couturiers are British (John Alliano, Alexander McQueen, Stella McCartney) and many of the world's biggest fashion names come from other countries, yet show their lines in Paris (Valentino, Hanae Mori, Kenzo, Yohji, etc.) . . . so they have come to be considered French designers. In most cases, nationality doesn't matter—it's the clothes. The list that follows separates out the non-French brands by house not by designer.

AKRIS
54 rue du Faubourg St-Honoré, 8e (Métro: Concorde). Opening on avenue Montaigne soon.

ARMANI EMPORIO
25 place Vendôme, 1er (Métro: Tuileries); 149 blvd. St-Germain, 6e (Métro: St-Germain-des-Prés).

BORSALINO
368 rue St-Honoré, 1er (Métro: Concorde).

BOTTEGA VENETA
6 rue du Cherche-Midi, 6e (Métro: St-Germain-des-Prés).

BURBERRY
55 rue des Rennes, 6e (Métro: St-Germain-des-Prés).

CERRUTI 1881
15 place de la Madeleine, 8e (Métro: Madeleine).

DUNHILL
15 rue de la Paix, 2e (Métro: Opéra).

ERMENEGILDO ZEGNA
10 rue de la Paix, 1er (Métro: Opéra).

ESCADA
418 rue St-Honoré, 8e (Métro: Concorde); 51 ave. Montaigne, 8e (Métro: F-D-Roosevelt).

ETRO
66 rue du Faubourg St-Honoré, 8e (Métro: Concorde); 177 blvd. St-Germain, 6e (Métro: St-Germain-des-Prés).

FERRAGAMO
50 rue du Faubourg St-Honoré, 8e (Métro: Concorde); 68–70 rue Sts-Pères, 6e (Métro: Sèvres-Babylone).

GIANFRANCO FERRE
38 ave. George V, 8e (Métro: George V).

GIANNI VERSACE
62 rue du Faubourg St-Honoré, 8e (Métro: Concorde).

GIORGIO ARMANI
6 place Vendôme, 1er (Métro: Tuileries).

GUCCI
27 rue du Faubourg St-Honoré, 8e—this store is expanding (Métro: Concorde); 350 rue St-Honoré, 1er (Métro: Tuileries).

HOLLAND & HOLLAND
29 ave. Victor Hugo, 16e (Métro: Victor-Hugo).

ISSEY MIYAKE, PLEATS PLEASE
201 blvd. St-Germain, 7e (Métro: rue Bue).

JIL SANDER
52 ave. Montaigne, 8e (Métro: Alma Marceau).

JOSEPH
44 rue Étienne Marcel, 2e (Métro: Étienne-Marcel); 14 ave. Montaigne, 8e (Métro: F-D-Roosevelt).

KRIZIA
48 ave. Montaigne, 8e (Métro: Alma-Marceau).

LA MAISON SALON VERSACE
41 rue François-1er, 8e (Métro: F-D-Roosevelt).

LAURA ASHLEY
94 rue de Rennes, 6e (Métro: Rennes); 261 rue St-Honoré, 1er (Métro: Concorde); 95 ave. Raymond-Poincaré, 16e (Métro: Victor-Hugo).

LAUREL
402 rue St-Honoré, 8e (Métro: Tuileries); 52 rue Bonaparte, 6e (Métro: St-Germain-des-Prés).

LES COPAINS
4 rue du Faubourg St-Honoré, 8e (Métro: Concorde).

LOEWE
57 ave. Montaigne, 8e (Métro: F-D-Roosevelt or Alma-Marceau).

MARIELLA BURANI
412 rue St-Honoré, 8e (Métro: Concorde).

MAX MARA
*31 avenue Montaigne, 8e (Métro: Alma-Marceau);
265 rue St-Honoré, 1er (Métro: Concorde or
Tuileries); 100 ave. Paul-Doumer, 16e
(Métro: La Muette); 37 rue du Four, 6e
(Métro: St-Germain-des-Prés).*

MISSONI
*43 rue du Bac, 7e (Métro: rue du Bac); 1 rue du
Faubourg St-Honoré, 8e (Métro: Concorde).*

MIU MIU
*10 rue du Cherche-Midi, 6e
(Métro: St-Germain-des-Prés).*

MOSCHINO
*68 rue Bonaparte, 6e
(Métro: St-Germain-des-Prés).*

MULBERRY
*14 rue du Cherche Midi, 6e (Métro: St-Germain-
des-Prés); 45 rue Croix des Petits Champs, 1er
(Métro: Palais-Royal).*

PATRICK COX
*21 rue de Grenelle, 6e
(Métro: St Germain des Pres).*

PRADA
10 ave. Montaigne, 8e (Métro: Alma-Marceau).

SYBILLA
*62 rue Jean-Jacques Rousseau, 1er
(Métro: Musée-du-Louvre).*

TRUSSARDI
*21 rue du Faubourg St-Honoré, 8e
(Métro: Concorde).*

VERSACE JEANS
67 rue des Sts-Pères, 6e (Métro: Sèvres-Babylon).

COSTUME JEWELRY

. . . .

The essence of French fashion (aside from couture) is simplicity—consider the basic black skirt and white silk blouse—a staple of every stylish Frenchwoman's wardrobe. Of course, the way to spruce up these basics has always been accessories. Hence the importance of the Hermès silk scarf.

Should you care to go for something more glitzy, these sources offer some of Paris's boldest statements. Their specialty is either in making copies of more serious jewelry or in making originals that will have value in the marketplace for years to come, originals that reach beyond the basic definition of "costume jewelry."

BURMA
249 rue St-Honoré, 8e (Métro: Concorde).

If the real thing is beyond you, try Burma! There are a few Burma shops in Paris and one in Cannes, too—faux plays well to the local crowd.

LESAGE
21 place Vendôme, 1er (Métro: Tuileries).

Located in the Schiaparelli space on the place Vendôme, Lesage announces itself with discreet lettering in the window (just below the pink SCHIAPARELLI sign). You could easily walk by without ever noticing, but designer mavens have known for years that Lesage is the house that does all the beading for the couture houses.

This shop, with its shocking interior, offers a host of accessories at the highest retail prices in Paris. You sit at a little table and trays of costume jewelry, handbags, and even some heavily beaded or embroidered clothing are brought to you. The work is sublime, but the price tags are not. We're talking investment chic.

YVES SAINT LAURENT
*32 rue du Faubourg St-Honoré, 8e
(Métro: Concorde).*

Saint Laurent shows us what he's made of by having the good grace to open a razzle-dazzle shop that allows us to smell the refined air of couture but still come away with a trophy we can afford. His shop for accessories has two levels of goodies, many of which are made of crystal and are meant to make your friends very envious that you've been to Paris.

Go upstairs for the serious shopping. While the store sells more than jewelry (shoes, sweaters, scarves, ties, and more), it's the jewelry that you should be buying. I recently blew my whole travel budget on one piece; prices can be several hundred dollars for the smallest of items. But it does say Saint Laurent on it.

SWAROVSKI
7 rue Royale, 8e (Métro: Concorde).

Over the years, this crystal maker has provided much of the glitter to Lesage and Chanel. Now, it has its own shop on the rue Royale selling diamondlike jewels made from their top-of-the-line crystals, as well as accessories (handbags with crystal clasps) and glassware. The store—the company's first retail effort on the international scene—is owned by the people who run the Ciro stores (also famous for faux baubles).

ANEMONE
*7 rue de Castiglione, 1er (Métro: Tuileries or
Concorde).*

Resource for costume jewelry and earrings in Paris that has been reliable, year after year. Anemone is on the rue de Castiglione across from the Meurice and near Catherine, so you'll be right there. Earrings begin around $50 (this is Paris, you know), but may prove to be the best buy of your trip. Prices are not give-away, but sometimes you can find some good pieces; I bought a YSL gold-tone collar here that I still live in—it was worth every bit of its $350 price tag. Fun to look in the window even if you don't buy.

CLEOPATRE
1 rue du Renard, 4e (Métro: Hôtel de Ville).

Located across from BHV, this shop sells obviously fake jewelry and hot fashion looks for a few francs. I'm talking teen-time here—really low-end but fun. They have hair ornaments, bracelets, necklaces, pins, and more earrings than you can imagine.

GAS
44 rue Étienne Marcel, 2e (Métro: Étienne-Marcel).

This is a small store with very inventive pieces, often made from odds and ends. More fun than couture in terms of a look; possibly a good investment as a collectible. Mr. Gas has opened up next door with clothes, accessories, and things that are to swoon for. For some weird reason related to a legal technicality you cannot combine purchases made at the two stores for one détaxe deduction. I've liked this source for years; I'm now collecting their flashy bumble bees.

NEREIDES
23 rue du Four, 6e (Métro: St-Germain-des-Prés).

This shop sells a very south of France look, sort of casual and fashiony and resorty, but with bigger pieces than you might wear to work. You'll find various sizes and shapes and a touch of brushed gold and Etruscan influence.

MICHAELA FREY
9 rue Castiglione, 1er (Métro: Concorde).

A Viennese design firm with stores in most European capital cities, it has none in the U.S., so you may not know the brand. If you are familiar with the enamel bracelets that Hermès makes, then you are unwittingly familiar with Frey's work. Frey has been doing this enamel work long before Hermès put their own distinctive twist to it. Because the Frey shop is almost next door to the *parfumerie* Catherine, you may want to peer into the windows to see the look for yourself.

Frey is most famous for reproductions of artworks inspired by art history, from Claude Monet to William Morris to Egyptian hieroglyphics. There are bangle bracelets, earrings, and pendants; prices begin around $150. Unique.

LES CRÉATEURS

· ·

The French have an expression (don't they always?) for big-name designers who do not make couture. They are *Les Créateurs*, the Creators. Many are as rich and successful as the names who make couture; some more so.

The list below gives the address of each *créateur*'s studio (which may or may not have a store attached—roughly half have stores). If you study the list, you'll also note that the times they are a changin'. Case in point: Claude Montana began as a *créateur*, became a couturier for Lanvin, and then left couture and is once again a *créateur*. Some *créateurs* have such a large following (and major international advertising campaigns to match) that they can be considered big names. So check "French Big Names," later in this chapter, if you don't find your favorite French designer below. Note that not all of these designers are French. Italian Valentino shows in Paris as well as in Rome. Several Japanese designers are actually considered French designers because they show in Paris. More and more English and Italian designers choose to show in Paris; even Americans are trying to figure out who they are— Tom Ford is Italian? British, Dutch, and Spanish designers have all taken over the big design houses, to say nothing of what Marc Jacobs has done to

Louis Vuitton. It's a big vegetable soup in Paris, but God, is it chic.

For academic purposes, you may also want to know that *prêt-à-porter* (ready-to-wear) is made by the *créateurs*. They usually have various lines in order to cover multiple price points. Some of the designers below show with the couture; some show with ready-to-wear.

AZZEDINE ALAÏA
18 rue de la Verrerie, 4e.

CHANTAL THOMASS
100 rue du Cherche-Midi, 6e.

COMME DES GARÇONS (REI KAWAKABO)
16 place Vendôme, 1er.

DOROTHÉE BIS
17 rue de Sèvres, 6e.

EMMANUELLE KHANH
39 ave. Victor Hugo, 16e.

ISSEY MIYAKE
5 place des Vosges, 4e.

JEAN-PAUL GAULTIER
70 Galerie Vivienne, 2e.

JUNKO KOSHINO
5 rue de Rigny, 8e.

JUNKO SHIMADA
354 rue Étienne Marcel, 2e.

KENZO
3 place des Victoires, 1er.

SONIA RYKIEL
175 blvd. St-Germain, 6e.

THIERRY MUGLER
6 rue Boissy -d'Anglas, 8e.

YOHJI YAMAMOTO
47 Étienne Marcel, 2e.

DEPARTMENT STORES

. . . .

French department stores have been basically for French people for over 100 years. Recently, however, they have opened their arms to embrace international tourists; **Galeries Lafayette** and **Au Printemps** make a serious attempt to woo American and international tourists . . . **Bon Marché** is quickly joining this parade.

Few Americans even realize that there are plenty of other department stores in Paris—for example, there's a rather large branch of the British icon **Marks & Spencer** across the street from Au Printemps—or that boulevard Haussmann is virtually a mall of department stores. There's also the Dutch low-price giant **C&A** nearby.

The biggies offer a lot of bang for your time, but they get incredibly crowded on Saturdays, especially in summer. If your time in Paris is limited, go to these stores early and use them to your best advantage: Check out the designer fashions and all the ready-to-wear clothing floors of a good department store, and you will immediately know what's hot and what's not. Don't forget to tour the housewares floors (or building, in the case of Printemps) to see the latest ideas for the home and table.

Also note that there are commonsense reasons to shop at a department store—aside from the obvious time-saving trick—there are financial benefits. Go to many stores separately and you have many separate purchases; buy it all under one roof and you'll get a détaxe refund if you spend 1,200 F!

Galeries Lafayette has two different buildings and Printemps has three (this is a total of five buildings of department-store proportions!). There are also scads of street vendors (selling goods from the stores, by the way) outside these two stores as well as in a nearby alley. In short, this area is overwhelming. It's not an easy browse, so it won't be fun if you think you are going to tackle it all.

What you need is a plan. I suggest hitting Galeries Lafayette first for fashion, then moving on to the Galeries Lafayette supermarket (Lafayette Gourmet). Afterward, I'd move on to Printemps Maison (a really great store); do only the first two floors of Printemps and finally end up at Prisunic, which is behind Printemps. You can do all of this in 3 to 4 hours and have a ball; I think you need to limit your time here to best enjoy it.

However, if you are doing some very serious shopping, and it looks like you are going to be spending 1,200 F (about $200), do not divide your time between two different department stores. Buy everything from one store so you qualify for the détaxe refund.

Allow at least 15 minutes for the détaxe paperwork, which you must commence in the department store. Expect it to take longer if it's the middle of the tourist season.

Announcement: Before I get into the actual listings, it's time to announce that last year Galeries Lafayette hired me to write the English-language version of their store guide. It doesn't have a byline on it and it doesn't use the same tone as *Born to Shop,* but I wanted you to know this up front for reasons of honesty. This job has not affected how I view the store or what I write about in these pages. In fact, I actually think I know the stores in the area better than I did before because I needed to understand not only Galeries Lafayette but how it was different from other stores. In this text I make no attempt to try to persuade you to pick Galeries Lafayette over another choice.

GALERIES LAFAYETTE
40 blvd. Haussmann, 9e (Métro: Chausée-d'Antin); Commercial Centre Montparnasse, 14e (Métro: Montparnasse/Bienvenue).

I have come to love Galeries Lafayette in my middle age, mostly because it's easy. They sell everything here. If it's raining or you are in a hurry, you are in good hands. If you want an overview of Paris retail before you begin to shop the streets and small boutiques, this is a good place to educate your eye. If you have kids with you, this place is great—there's a kiddie entertainment center! There isn't a more complete department store in France.

Come early in the day and take notes, if need be. Before I learned to love the store, I hated it because I got lost in it and never learned my way around. Don't be intimidated. Trust me, it pays to take some time to familiarize yourself with a reconnaissance trip or by studying the free store maps given out on the ground floor. This is one of the largest stores in the world; it is not square, so you need help in learning where everything is and how to get found, not lost.

If you are planning on buying a lot, a lipstick here, some pantyhose there, a top or two, and a toy and maybe a handbag . . . and the thought of writing up all those sales slips on an individual basis makes you nuts, you can use a "shopper's card," available at the Welcome Desk.

This is how it works: Each purchase is rung up on a cash register and held at the desk, while your card is marked with the amount. You go around shopping all day, clutching your card in your hand. When you are finished, you pay for the grand total. This means you don't have to keep opening and closing your wallet and signing multiple sales receipts. It's also one of the easiest ways to get your détaxe, since you pay and claim the credit all at once.

There's only one problem: After you have paid, you must collect all of your packages. It helps if you have marked on the map where you left them.

Foreign visitors get a flat 10% discount on most purchases (except food and red-dot items) with a discount card that can be obtained for free from the Welcome Desk. (Be sure to present yours before the sales clerk rings you up.) You can also receive a coupon for this 10% discount from your U.S. travel agent or hotel. The export discount is 13% after an expenditure of 1,200 F; do not confuse the flat 10% discount with the 13% détaxe discount—we are really looking at 10% plus 13%!

When you use the discount card, don't be surprised if you are sent to a main cash register; there are several on each floor, so it's no big deal. It's just annoying if you don't know about it.

GL is open until 9pm on Thursday. I don't know about you, but this is my idea of heaven: Shop all day, have tea, and then shop into the night. Collapse back at your hotel for room service, or, better yet, go to GL's grocery store for a gourmet take-out *pique-nique*.

Galeries Lafayette offers a free fashion show on Wednesday throughout the year, and on Wednesday and Friday from April through October. Make reservations by calling ☎ 1/48-74-02-30. The show is in the Salon Opéra. Use the store's Auber entrance, then the Mogador escalator and head to the 7th floor. The fashion show is actually quite jazzy and good and has no commentary, so there's no language problem; free refreshments are served. It's really worth doing and gives you a preview not only of what's available in the store but also of ongoing hot looks and trends.

Now then, the store also has numerous other services too amazing to mention or explain; there are so many of these services that many people in the store don't know about them. The store doesn't do a great job of telling you all the ways it will take care of you, so ask a lot of questions or just trust me—whatever you need, they have thought of it and provide it; you just have to find where.

Some of my favorite secrets include the Internet center (it's hidden, so ask) where you can send out e-mail for a very low price. On the 5th floor is a telephone center where the salespeople speak English. This isn't for too many tourists, but if you have bought one of the new pay-as-you-go mobile telephones but don't know how to use it very well, you can stop here and get lessons; they are very nice about it. You can also buy here.

The kids department is one of the best in the world, both kids' clothes and kids' toys. The kids' book selection isn't that great on the 4th floor because there is a full bookstore in the basement. There is a play area where you can leave your children for a while or you can just plop down and rest in a chair while they do arts and crafts or play with others.

The store is very big on philosophy, which explains some of the unusual things hidden within the store—they are truly a full-service department store—meaning GL is really a small city. There's a post office, a shoe repair kiosk, a bank (and an ATM machine that takes U.S. cards is outside on the wall on rue de Chausée-d'Antin), a penny candy store, two souvenir departments, an exposition space, and a separate museum with real exhibits that have to do with culture, not shopping. As for the expo space, it's on the 3rd floor. The store has been famous for these giant expo's for the past century—they may or may not amuse you. There are beauty salons, there's a mini spa, there's everything. When I am asked to categorize this store in terms of an American point of reference all I can say is: It's Macy's.

Open Monday through Saturday, 9:30am to 6:45pm; Thursday, 9:30am to 9pm. Open on the Sundays prior to Christmas and a few other exceptional openings. Closed on French holidays.

Note: The Galeries Lafayette on the Left Bank is a small store catering to locals who work in the area. Its best feature: It opens early in the morning on weekdays. Its second-best feature: It's across the street from **Inno,** my dime-store supermarket. I suggest forgetting it.

AU PRINTEMPS *OVERwhelming —*

64 blvd. Haussmann, 9e (Métro: Chausée-d'Antin).

PRINTEMPS NATION
25 cours de Vincennes, 20e (Métro: Porte-de-Vincennes).

PRINTEMPS ITALIE
30 ave. d'Italie, 13e (Métro: Italie).

PRINTEMPS RÉPUBLIQUE
*10 place de la République, 11e
(Métro: République).*

Most people call it merely *Printemps,* which means spring. The store is much smaller than Galeries Lafayette, so you really cannot compare the two. I'd say Printemps was trying to be Saks; I say trying, because only the first two floors of the store have been redone. They are fabulous and very Saks-like. The rest of the floors are exactly like Galeries Lafayette only smaller, with fewer brands.

The Maison Store, however, is fabulous—really worth visiting and no, it doesn't carry only items for the home. It has a huge perfume department on the ground floor and a children's department upstairs. The basement paper goods and crafts are excellent; the store launched this department called *Esprit Libre* (free spirit) that is sensational.

Just like Galeries Lafayette, Printemps has a coupon that entitles foreign visitors to a 10% discount. Mine was in a stack of coupons at the concierge desk at my hotel; while I got the coupon during the winter season, it was valid for a full year. You present the card and your passport at the Welcome Service desk on the street floor of the main fashion store, and you will be given something resembling a credit card.

The 10% discount offer does not apply to food, books, or already discounted merchandise. This has nothing to do with the détaxe refund; if you qualify for détaxe, you get an additional 13% off.

The main store is divided into three separate stores: **Brummell,** the men's store, which is behind the main store; the home store (**Printemps de la Maison**); and the fashion store, **Printemps de la Mode.** Brummell has just been renovated and is sensational.

Printemps hosts a free fashion show on Tuesday every week of the year, and on Tuesday and Friday from March through October. The show is held at 10am on the 7th floor, under the cupola. Commentary is in English and French; the show lasts 45 minutes.

If this sounds enormously like what you just read about Galeries Lafayette, don't be shocked. I find the stores are like two neighbors who are out to show off to each other. One gets Angelina so the other gets Ladurée; they are always out to have the same but different ideas, although Printemps does have a few exclusive brands that Galeries Lafayette cannot get. Although the rivalry is intense, to me, the stores are not competitive—they are very different.

Open Monday through Saturday, 9:35am to 7pm. On Thursday nights the store is open until 10pm! Open on the Sundays prior to Christmas and some other exceptional openings.

[handwritten: 9/15/00 Everything you could ask for,]

BAZAR DE L'HÔTEL DE VILLE (BHV)
52–56 rue de Rivoli, 1er (Métro: Hôtel-de-Ville).

If you think this is a funny name for a store, you can call it BHV (pronounced *Bay*-H-Vay in French), or remember that the full name of the store tells you just where it is—directly across from the Hôtel de Ville. The store is famous for its do-it-yourself attitude and housewares. You owe it to yourself to go to the basement (SS) level. If you are at all interested in household gadgets or interior design, you will go nuts.

The upper floors are ordinary enough, and even the basement level can be ordinary (I assure you—I am not sending you to Paris to buy a lawn mower), but there are little nooks and crannies that will delight the most creative shoppers among you. I buy the brass lock pieces and string them on necklaces for gifts.

The store has been redone lately and I like it; it's sort of like a nice Kmart in terms of fashion and style statements. Also note that now that the gift-with-purchase idea is getting to be hot in France, if you miss the gift at Galeries Lafayette it may be here at BHV.

Open Monday, Tuesday, Thursday, Friday, and Saturday, 9:30am to 6:30pm; Wednesday, 9:30am to 10pm.

LE BON MARCHÉ
5 rue de Babylone, 6e (Métro: Sèvres-Babylone).

Be still my heart. I move into dead heat and get hot flashes when I ponder the changes at Bon Marché and the remarkable *joie de vie* that now permeates this store. If I were sending retailing students to Paris to learn anything about remaking a store, I'd send them straight away to Bon Marché. Goodbye old lady; hello Barney's!

There is also a Welcome Desk so you can get a discount coupon, the store is small and easy to handle, and the display is so visually exciting that you will just walk around with your mouth open. Even if you buy nothing, you have to see the true meaning of *oh la la*.

They also have a sensational gourmet grocery store (**Grand Epicerie**) next door; look for me there.

Bon Marché is the connecting point between two fabulous neighborhoods—of the Left Bank, the rue du Bac and the part of town I call "Little Dragons" (see p. 134). It's convenient not only to enticing little boutiques, but also to a collection of discount stores on rue St-Placide (see p. 139).

Open Monday through Saturday, 9:30am to 6:30pm.

FRANCK ET FILS
80 rue de Passy, 16e (Métro: La Muette).

Franck et Fils is a specialty store. The store is elegant, easy to shop, uncrowded, and relatively undiscovered by tourists.

You can find respectable, classical fashions in a well-bought atmosphere geared for madame. You'll feel very French if you browse, although you may get bored if you were expecting something hot or hip. I buy my Chanel-style camellias here; $10 is all each costs!

Open Monday through Saturday, 10am to 5:30pm.

MARKS & SPENCER
33–45 blvd. Haussmann, 9e (Métro: Chausée-d'Antin); 88 rue du Rivoli, 4e (Métro: Hôtel-de-Ville).

From boulevard Haussmann, you can zigzag into the Garnier Opéra or go immediately into Marks & Spencer. Which would you rather do, really? The Marks & Spencer in Paris is amazingly like the flagship Oxford Street store near Selfridges in London. Locals depend on it, especially the fabulous grocery store on the first level. Go there not only for English snack foods but for picnic supplies and sandwiches and ready-made foods to cut down on your dining costs in Paris.

Marks & Spencer is still a good place for underwear (try the private-label brand, St. Michael) and for good, sturdy, inexpensive kids' clothes. It seems more elite to the French than to American tourists, but is not a must-do experience if your time is limited.

Open Monday, Tuesday, Thursday, Friday, and Saturday, 9:30am to 6:30pm; Wednesday, 10am to 6:30pm.

0\11\00

SAMARITAINE
67 rue de Rivoli, 1er (Métro: Châtelet or Pont-Neuf).

It can be confusing to find your way around the separate stores and interconnecting basement here, but Samaritaine offers a distinctively French atmosphere to shoppers. Of the four buildings that make up the store, only one of them is even called Samaritaine. The most important shop is Store 2, which is behind Store 4. Store 4 has recordings, books, and art supplies. The sports department is in Store 3.

In recent years, though, Samaritaine has made a concerted effort to take its image upscale. The best examples of this is the newly installed Inès de la Fressange home furnishings department and the *trés chic* new perfume department. Samaritaine is not the obvious choice, but it makes you feel so much more French.

There is also a roof garden with a great view. I often eat at the restaurant Toupary, which has a view of the Seine and is open for dinner even when the store is closed.

Open Monday, Wednesday, Thursday, and Saturday, 9:30am to 7pm; Tuesday and Friday, 9:30am to 8:30pm.

9/12/to *Good day!*

FABRICS, NOTIONS & CRAFTS

. . . .

For those who sew, Paris, the home of fancy seams, offers plenty to get creative with. While fabric may not be less expensive than at home, the selection in Paris is so incredible that you are unable to think about price at all. Besides couture fabrics, you'll find the trendy fabrics—imitations of the hottest looks that Americans are still reading about in *Women's Wear Daily.* When the Gianni Versace–style prints went crazy a while back, I was able to buy a washable polyester with a silky hand to make a skirt. The total cost of the project was $25. No one in the U.S. had anything to compete.

Should you be somewhat interested in fabric, but not interested enough to spend much time tracking it down, stop by **Bouchara.** It's moving around a little bit in the next few months due to construction in the area, but you'll find it somewhere near all the big department stores in the 9e. Try no. 35 blvd.

Haussman. The store has every imaginable fabric and notion—for reupholstering chairs or making your own clothing. Most items are moderately priced. I like this store a lot.

If you want a taste of the world of couture, or just a silly adventure, you may want to spend a few hours in the Marché St-Pierre area in the 18e arrondissement, a neighborhood that sells fabrics and notions almost exclusively. Couture ends are sold; shopkeepers are friendly. Some working knowledge of French will be helpful, and lots of cash. Take the métro to Anvers, or hail a taxi (a pricey ride), and go directly to **Sympa**. It has three locations—two on rue d'Orsel and one directly across from the Anvers métro stop, on the corner of boulevard de Rochechouart and rue du Steinkerque—you can't miss it; there are bins in the street.

For a few other couture fabric resources, try the following (all are famous for their fabric selections—Chanel, YSL, Dior): **Artisanat** in the Sentier, which also sells wool and yarn goods; **Sevilla,** right off Passy, which can be fabulous if you hit it right. Please remember that couture fabrics are not inexpensive—often they are $100 a yard for a silk that may not even be very wide. **Bouchara** carries the good stuff, but is more famous for its wide range of copycat fabrics at good prices. **Le Stand des Tissus** is a small shop in the heart of the textile markets. Pascale-Agnés has seen couture fabrics here; there were none when we looked last time. However, there were absolutely gorgeous English wools for about $20 a meter.

For some reasons, the French are not that into crafts, so you will have a hard time finding the basics you crave. There are two bead stores near Les Halles, and Printemps has added a fabulous department, **Esprit Libre,** to the basement level of their Maison store where you'll find more craft items (and beads) than just about anywhere else in Paris. They also sell beads and a few kiddie craft kits on Galeries

Lafayette's 4th floor. But don't be expecting Michael's in France. Also check out **La Drougerie** (9 rue du Jour, 1er—right near Forum Les Halles) for trimmings and some beads and crafts fixings.

ARTISANAT TEXTILE
21 rue des Jeûneurs, 2e (Métro: Sentier).

BOUCHARA
54 blvd. Haussmann, 9e (Métro: Chausée-d'Antin).

This store has moved down the block but may return to its original site.

LA SOIE DE PARIS
14 rue d'Uzès, 2e (Métro: Rue Montmartre).

LE STAND DES TISSUS
11 rue de Steinkerque, 18e (Métro: Anvers).

RODIN
36 ave. des Champs-Elysées, 8e (Métro: F-D-Roosevelt).

SEVILLA
38 rue de l'Annonciation, 16e (Métro: La Muette).

TISSROY
97 ave. Victor Hugo, 16e (Métro: Victor-Hugo).

FLEA MARKETS

Paris is famous for its flea markets, although I think only two of them are worth getting hot and bothered over. I have found that many people think of the markets in St-Ouen as the only game in town, when, in fact, I think Vanves is better.

PUCES DE VANVES
(Métro: Porte de Vanves).

When people tell me they are headed to the flea market in Paris, I always ask "which one?" They look at me like I am an idiot, then they stammer and finally say it's "the big one" or "the famous one." That means they are headed to St-Ouen, which is a lot of fun.

However, I personally think the number one flea market in Paris is Puces des Vanves. This market is not like any other; it's more like a bunch of neighbors who all went in together for one of those big five-family garage sales. The garage sale just happens to stretch for a mile or so. The market is L-shaped: On the main part of the street are the licensed vendors who pay taxes to the city; on the branch part are the illegal, tag-sale vendors, who are, of course, the most fun.

The tag-sale people's goods are of lesser quality than those of the pros, but together they make for wonderful strolling and browsing. If you don't have much time or can't stand the strain of St-Ouen, this is a neighborhood affair that is perfect for a Sunday or a Saturday. In fact, Saturday is considered the best day to shop Vanves. Early birds get the worms, of course; I'm there at 9:30am.

The main part of the market is on the avenue Georges-Lafenestre. With the legal and the illegal guys, there are almost 200 vendors here. Prices are the best in town: I bought a plaster virgin for 10 F, an old postcard album (empty) for 50 F, and numerous *fèves,* all for 10 F each. I splurged on a green glass necklace from the 1960s for 150 F. I make *découpage* baskets and bought lots of old hotel luggage labels and French ephemera items for not much money.

There's a *crêpe* stand at the bend in the road; the street market on Sunday enhances the experience. *Note:* The basic part of the market closes up at noon, but there are dealers who stay on. In the afternoon (around 1–2pm), a new bunch of dealers moves in to sell new (and cheap) ready-to-wear, shoes, socks, towels, etc.

THE MARKETS OF ST-OUEN
(Métro: Porte de Clingnancourt).

Also known simply as the Marché aux Puces, or the famous flea market, St-Ouen comprises several different markets, each with its own kind of dealers and each with its own special feel. Before I get into the complexities of the market, I might add that unless your French is good, you may not be properly pronouncing this venue and may have difficulty getting directions or help. Get a lesson from your concierge before you set out, or use my idiot's guide to speaking French: It's pronounced "San-Twan." Honest.

The St-Ouen markets grew from a series of little streets and alleys. Today, over 75 acres of flea market sprawl through this suburb. The market most frequently bears the name of the street on which it rests—even though you may be hard pressed to find the original street sign. The markets themselves are usually well marked; they often have doors on two different streets.

Usually the stalls open onto the street or a walkway but have some covered parts; these are not street vendors set up garage-sale style. Even the informal markets are sheltered. There is some amount of street action and selling off makeshift tables, but not a lot. There is, however, plenty of street action in terms of stalls, candy stands, and blue jeans dealers as you walk from the métro to the flea market. This is not the flea market you are looking for; these dealers should all be ignored.

Do remember there are plenty of places to eat on the premises, not as many places to go to the bathroom as you might like, and more pickpockets and rowdy boys than the French government would like to admit. I was once terrorized with lighted cigarettes and burning matches held by teenage boys who

Rossiers - Rue du

wanted to chase me. While they did burn holes in my clothes, I refused to run—or to surrender my packages. I mention it because if it happened to me it could happen to you. But it hopefully will not.

If you feel like you need to have a system for working this vast amount of space, try mine. Start with the big guns (Biron, Cambo) and the markets in that area, and walk your way back, so that Malik becomes one of your last stops. In fact, if you like Marché Malik as little as I do, you'll be happy to run out of there and call it a day.

To do it my way, you'll turn into the market streets on the rue des Rosiers (if your back is to the métro station you came from, you'll turn left). You'll work this street until the good stuff peters out, and cut to the left by shopping your way through the Marché Paul Bert. Then you'll go right on the rue Vallès until you've shopped it thoroughly. At that point, retrace your steps by cutting through Malassis. Note that there are freestanding antiques stores as well as the big (and small) markets.

Marché Antica
99 rue des Rossiers.

Just a little-bitty building refinished in the Memphis Milano teal-blue-and-crème look. This market is filled with cute shops selling small collectibles of good quality at pretty good prices. Actually a corner of the Marché Vernaison at the corner of rue des Rosiers and rue Voltaire.

Marché le Biron
85 rue des Rossiers.

This is the single fanciest market in the place; it's one of the first markets you'll come to on rue des Rosiers. This should be the first stop for dealers who are looking for serious stuff. If you come here first and you are looking for fleas, you may be turned off. It's quite hoity-toity.

MARCHÉ CAMBO
75 rue des Rossiers.

Another serious market, but a little less refined—
the dealers are usually busy hobnobbing with each
other and may ignore you totally. You'll see furnishings in various states of refinish and find dealers in
various states of mind—some know what they have
and are very hard-nosed about it; others want to
move out the merchandise and will deal with you.
They are particularly responsive to genuine dealers
who know their stuff and speak some French. The
selection is less formal and more eclectic than at
Biron, and there are rows of stalls along lanes or
aisles. Next door to Biron.

MARCHÉ DAUPHINE
140 rue des Rossiers.

[handwritten: Great street shops wonderful shops]

A newer village of some 300 shops opposite the
Marché Vernaison on the rue des Rossiers, making
it one of the first places you want to hit when you
get to the market area. It's enclosed with a balcony
and a factory-like high-tech atmosphere under a glass
rooftop and industrial lighting. There is a shipping
agency on hand. Some of the dealers are affordable
here; I found a button dealer to buy from and a
specialist in vintage designer clothing that flipped
me out for *fripes*.

MARCHÉ DES ROSSIERS
3 rue Paul Bert.

A very small market specializing in the period between 1900 and 1930. There are about 13 small
stalls in an enclosed U-shaped building; fronts on
the rue Paul-Bert.

MARCHÉ JULES-VALLÈS
7 rue Jules Vallès.

I like this one, although it's small and junky; it's got
reproduction brass items for the home mixed in with

real antiques and real repro everything else. Cheap, cheap, cheap.

Marché Malik
Ugh! It may be famous for its *fripes*—used clothes— but I find it seedy, disgusting, expensive, and dangerous. Need I say more?

Marché Paul-Bert
96 rue des Rossiers.

I saved the best for last. Are we having fun yet? If not, send the husband and the kids to the pizza place and go for it on your own—this is too good to not enjoy. This is the market that is more outdoorsy than the rest; it surrounds the Marché Serpette in three alleys forming a U. This market is both outside and inside, with lower-end merchandise, including art deco, moderne, and country furniture. Most of the items here have not been repaired or refinished. There could be some great buys here, but you need to have a good eye and know your stuff. Piles of suitcases, carts, dolls, and buttons in bins. Yummy. If you do only one market or want to start with the very best, or you think the weather may turn on you, start here please.

Marché Serpette
110 rue des Rossiers.

This market is in a real building, not a Quonset hut. There is carpet on the floor, and each vendor has a stall number and a closing metal door. There also are nice, clean bathrooms on the second floor. It's on the edge of the Marché Paul-Bert, but you can tell the difference because this one is totally indoors and is sort of dark and fancy.

Marché Vernaison
I like this market a lot, although the new building puts me off a bit. There isn't that much I want to buy; I just like to prowl the various teeny showrooms.

There are a few fabrics, textiles, trim, and needle-works mavens who always have things I covet. It sprawls to quite an extent, and you may not at first realize that this market alone rather constitutes a village with its own streets and byways, all with stalls, of course. This is a good first stop because it has a lot of natural charm and many affordable places; it's also first if you follow my walking path.

PUCES DE MONTREUIL
(Métro: Porte de Montreuil).

I have included this market because I want you to know that I know it exists and that I've been here. But it's really only for die-hard flea market shoppers. It's a junk fair of sorts, so there are very few diamonds here—and those that exist are artfully hidden. You could hunt for hours before throwing up your hands in disgust, having found nothing.

This immense market has absorbed three other nearby markets and has a huge path of illegal vendors that stretches from the nearest métro station all the way across a bridge to the beginning of the market proper. There's a good selection of *fripes* (used clothes), Victorian bed linens, old hats, new perfumes (look, Mom, who needs détaxe?), work clothes, cheap clothes, records, dishes, junk, junk, and more junk. Did I mention there is a lot of junk? This is a really low-end market without any charm whatsoever. Dealers work this market very thoroughly—it runs a good 10% to 20% cheaper than St-Ouen. But it is 50% harder to find anything good. This is for those with a strong heart and a good eye; princesses and blue bloods need not apply.

FOOD MARKETS

One of the difficulties of shopping in Paris is deciding which markets to visit and which to pass up. Unlike most other cities, which usually have one or two good markets, Paris is crawling with them. There are dozens, and it's impossible to get to them all unless you spend a month doing little else.

Most food markets are closed on Monday mornings; anything that is more or less open on a Sunday is not open on a Monday. The rue du Buci gets a slow start on Monday, but the action builds quickly. *Note:* With the exception of the Sunday market at Porte de Vanves and the *brocante* offerings at the place d'Aligre, most flea markets do not have food markets attached to them.

Years ago, the major wholesale food markets were in Les Halles; they have since moved to Rungis. This is a wholesale market, and tourists are not particularly welcome; you can go, but you should speak some French and know how to stay out of the way. It's best to sign up for a tour given by a professional, as the market really is "to the trade."

Markets selling organically grown vegetables and fruits are one of the newer trends in Paris; these are called *marché biologique* or simply "bio." There's one at the intersection of rue de Rennes and boulevard Raspail on Sunday on the Left Bank. I was not impressed.

When shopping markets, remember:

- Dress simply; the richer you look, the higher the price you'll pay. If you wear an engagement ring or have one of those wedding bands that spells "rich American" in pavé diamonds, leave it in the hotel safe. I like to wear blue jeans and try to fit in with the crowd; I also have a pair of French eyeglasses to complete my costume. Even though my French is atrocious, I speak French or mime my way through it.
- Ask your hotel's concierge about the neighborhood where the market is located. It may not be considered safe for a woman to go there alone or after dark. I don't want to be paranoid, but crime in market areas can be higher than in tourist areas.

- Have a lot of change with you.
- Don't touch the food, especially in the wholesale market. Ask for a taste or let the vendor choose for you. (Try flirting first for a better choice.)
- Food prices are usually fixed; you don't bargain as you might at a flea market. If the vendor likes you, he may throw in something extra after you've weighed in.

In Paris, many market areas are so famous that they have no specific street address. Usually it's enough to give the name of a market to a cabbie. Buses usually service market areas; but the métro goes everywhere and is usually your best bet. Food markets can be held any or every day of the week; flea markets are usually weekend events. Food markets alternate in various neighborhoods; you can often find a good one any day of the week. All of the food markets listed below are open on Sunday!

RUE DE BUCI — *great street*
(Métro: St-Germain-des-Prés).

The rue de Buci is behind the church of St-Germain-des-Prés. This is a flower and food market that is colorful and quaint; the market is on rue de Buci and also on rue de Seine. Although it's located in a neighborhood with a number of antiques shops, the market does not sell *brocante*. If you go to only one street market in Paris, this should be the one. This is everyone's fantasy of Paris.

There are fresh fruits and vegetables piled high on tables, buckets and buckets of brightly colored flowers, rotisserie chickens, even seashells and sponges. There are a few grocery stores and takeout food joints as well. Come hungry; leave very satisfied. Avoid Monday mornings, if possible, since not very much is open. Sundays are a special treat here.

RUE CLER *6/17/00*   *Gail & jack →*
(Métro: Latour-Maubourg).

My last visit to rue Cler was very upsetting. Although the weather was gorgeous and I was in a happy mood, I was dumbfounded by the number of Americans here. Furthermore, these Americans had the nerve to be speaking English! Still, the rue Cler is a lot more sophisticated than the rue de Buci and is a very special way to spend a Sunday morning. I can't blame all those Americans for visiting; I just want the area to stay French in its soul.

This is in a residential part of the Left Bank, not that far from the Paris Hilton and the Eiffel Tower, but not the kind of place you would find on your own without knowing about it.

The rue Cler is only about 2 blocks long, and it is jammed with the things that delight foodies. There are two local supermarkets; many small vendors who set up on the street; several branches of famous *chocolatiers*, including **Leonidas** (no. 39); and two famous cheese shops. **Tarte Julie** (no. 28) is a great little place for dessert, tea or coffee, or Sunday brunch; they also have takeout. I'm addicted to the quiche Julie; there are branches of this food chain around town.

Almost every store on the 2-block stretch is open on Sunday (closed all day Monday), so you can buy many things, not just food items. This is a fabulous "we are French" adventure. Stores open early Sunday—anywhere from 8:30 to 9am, and then close at 1pm for the day. Obviously, this is a morning excursion.

If it's a Sunday and you are looking for a nice stroll, you can leave the rue Cler via the rue St-Dominique, window-shopping as you stroll (sorry, the shops in and around here will be closed), and find yourself at the Eiffel Tower in no time at all.

RASPAIL
Boulevard Raspail, 6e (Métro: Sèvres Babylone).

While the rue Cler and the rue de Buci are small and closed-in affairs, this is a wide street and a very open market, much more hustle and bustle. The regular market days are Tuesday and Friday morning; there is a *bio* market on Sunday mornings. I'm not that wild for the *bio* market, but the Friday street market is worth doing.

PLACE D'ALIGRE
(Métro: Ledru-Rollin or Gare de Lyon).

I read this column in the magazine *L'Officiel* wherein they ask a famous person to name his or her favorite shopping venues. I can't tell you how many celebrities name the *marché* d'Aligre. Frankly, it's not one of my faves, although I am now heading back there to figure out what I've missed. I often go on a Sunday, but there is market every day.

The place d'Aligre has a covered indoor meat market, an open flower and vegetable market, several tables devoted to *brocante* dealers, and even a few shops along the way. Furthermore, few tourists come here, so you are really getting a true picture of real life Paris, as there is a lot of ethnic diversity in the shoppers and some of the wares.

Betty, a discount source that hasn't impressed me for a few years, is right here (open on Sunday); so if you're curious, you can stop by. This used to be a great place to buy Léonard at discount; lately it has a lot of career clothes that don't do much for me.

The *brocante* is yard-sale quality; you may be annoyed you came so far if you expect much more. This market is open every day except Monday, but closes at about 1pm. While ready-to-wear is sold here, it is exactly what Grandma Jessie would call dreck, if you'll pardon her French. The yard goods are worthy buys from nearby factories. This market has a real-people Paris feel to it that will make you feel like an insider.

Please note that this area used to be in the boonies. Now, thanks to **Le Viaduc des Arts,** a new shopping attraction only a block and a half away, this is no longer the case. However, the stores here are not open on Sunday, which is a big mistake. The two can be combined on other days of the week, except for Monday.

PRESIDENT WILSON
Avenue du President Wilson, 16e (Métro: Iena or Trocadéro).

This is my new favorite market; it's not small and intimate like some of the others. While it's held in the street, it doesn't so much feel like a street market because it's so dignified. This is a very upmarket street market; the Museum of Modern Art is across the way. The market is on Wednesday and Saturday mornings. It is long and quite complete, which means there's even cooked foods. Once before you die.

FOODSTUFFS
· ·

If you are looking for an inexpensive gift to bring home, consider taking a small but tasty treat or even putting together your own food basket. Foodstuffs are not necessarily easy to pack or lightweight, but they can be rather cheap and look like a lot once you get home and put them in your own basket or wrap them up in a clever fashion.

My single best gift in this category is a jar of Maille's Provençale mustard. You can purchase a selection of four Maille's mustards (total cost in France, $6), which makes a great hostess or housewarming gift.

The easiest place to do foodstuff shopping, and probably the cheapest, is at **Monoprix**. I've become an **Inno** convert and usually go there (place Juin 18, in the 14e) immediately after checking into my hotel. It's a direct shot on the métro and a good job for someone with jet lag. There's a **Monoprix** on the Champs-Elysées, another behind Printemps on boulevard Haussmann, and yet another at St-Augustin;

all of these locations are central to most hotels on the Right Bank.

If your palate or your pocketbook is advanced, Paris has no shortage of food palaces. As far as I'm concerned, the grocery store next to Le Bon Marché (**Le Grande Epicerie**) and on boulevard Haussmann (**Lafayette Gourmet**) are more reasonably priced than the more famous houses and more fun to shop. Don't forget the entire rue du Buci, with two grocery stores and many small shops, including a branch of **O & Co.**, an olive oil specialty shop.

The entire circle of stores surrounding the place Madeleine is almost entirely food specialty shops, including **Maille** and **Maison de la Truffe** as well as some of the food palaces such as **Fauchon** and **Hédiard.** One block over on rue Vignon, there's the **Maison de Miel,** the honey shop. You will not starve in Paris nor lack for gifts to bring home.

You cannot bring back any fresh foods; processed hard cheeses are legal, all others are not. Dried items (such as mushrooms) are legal; fresh fruits and vegetables are not. Foie gras in a tin is legal; fresh is not.

If you plan on buying foodstuffs, save your plastic bags from your shopping adventures or bring a boxful of plastic bags with you. Wrap each jar or bottle in plastic and tie the top of the bag with a twist tie before you pack the item. If the cushion provided by your clothes doesn't protect the jar, at least you won't get mustard all over your new suede shoes. Many of the big food stores will ship for you, but beware: Foodstuffs usually are very heavy.

Augé
116 blvd. Haussmann, 8e (Métro: Madeleine).

It's not hard to find a great wine shop in Paris, but this one is unique and special, so try to pop in. This immediate neighborhood has enough of interest that it's worth a trip over here; see the Boulangerie St-Ouen listing below.

Barthélemy
51 rue de Grenelle, 7e (Métro: Sèvres-Babylone).

This is a shop the size of a large closet, but it smells like cheese heaven and is one of the most famous cheesemongers in France. Everything is fresh and ready to go; if you love cheeses, you will be so happy here you'll never want to leave.

Boulangerie Saint-Ouen
111 blvd. Haussmann, 8e (Métro: Madeleine).

Okay, Paris has plenty of bread shops where the bread is delish and you wonder what is wrong with me to send you to one very specific address and an address that is slightly off center. Well guys, do you trust me? This shop makes bread in shapes, including the Eiffel Tower! Furthermore, you can get it with an egg wash, which preserves it. They will ask you in the shop if you want the bread for eating or for display, so we're really talking about a super souvenir for under $10.

The store is only about 2 blocks past Madeleine and is also near the new Monoprix flagship store, so you're going to like it here. Oh yes, it's also near Augé, so look at that listing above. Finally, a pronunciation lesson—if your French isn't that great, you may not know how to pronounce the name of this shop. It's just like the flea market in Clingancourt: San-Twan. Trust me on this.

Fauchon
26 place de la Madeleine, 8e (Métro: Madeleine).

Prices are high here, and many of these items are available elsewhere (have you been to a Monoprix or Inno lately?), but it's a privilege just to stare in the windows or check out the renovation and all the new ideas. The salespeople also are extraordinarily nice. There are three parts to the store: Fruits and dry goods are in a mini-department store of many floors, prepared foods are next door, and the cafeteria is across the street. You buy a ticket, then pick up your purchases. Don't forget to check out the new tearoom.

FOUQUET
22 rue François-1er, 8e (Métro: F-D-Roosevelt).

If asked to pick the single best gift item in Paris, I just might say it's a Fouquet gift box. As heavy as they are famous, they are nonetheless wonderful. Too heavy to carry home with you? Not to worry: The store will ship for you. There's no problem finding lovely gifts in the $25 to $50 range; just bear in mind that the cost of shipping may double the price. Still, the boxes are so extravagant that it does seem worth it. Jars are filled with chocolates, jams, gingered fruits, nuts, and other assorted edibles.

GARGANTUA
284 rue St-Honoré, 1er (Métro: Tuileries).

Another of my regulars between the Hôtel du Louvre and Hôtel Meurice, Gargantua has cooked foods, wines, jars, and cans of fine eats. It's only a block from the Tuileries, so you can picnic in the garden if you like. This is a full-line shop, so you can get everything at one stop. They'll happily throw in free plastic knives and forks.

HÉDIARD
21 place de la Madeleine, 8e (Métro: Madeleine).

Conveniently located around the bend from Fauchon and Marquise de Sévigné (my favorite chocolate candies are bought here), Hédiard competes handily with Paris's other world-class food stores. It's been in the food biz since the mid-1800s, and there is little you cannot buy in this shop. They will also deliver, but room service may not be amused.

LA BOUTIQUE LAYRAC TRAITEUR
29 rue de Buci, 6e (Métro: St-Germain-des-Prés or Mabillon).

Here you can pick up anything from boeuf bour-
guignonne to pommes de terre au gratin dished out
in a container for your picnic. Few items are over
$15. Who needs Tour d'Argent?

LENÔTRE
*44 rue d'Auteuil, 16e (Métro: Michel-Ange
Auteuil); 49 ave. Victor Hugo, 16e
(Métro: Victor-Hugo); 5 rue du Havre, 8e
(Métro: Havre-Caumartin).*

Lenôtre will always mean chocolate and dessert to
me, but the store is a full-fledged *charcuterie*. Pick
up a picnic here. They're open on Sunday (quite
unusual) and will gladly guide you through any pig-
out. For a price, they will deliver to your hotel.

O & Co. 9/11/00 *Wonderful—
one of my favorite*
*28 rue de Buci (Métro: St-Germain-des-Prés);
81 rue St-Louis en l'Isle, 4e (Métro: St. Michel,
then walk across bridges).*

This is a small chain which will no doubt become a
famous chain; it was begun by the people who created L'Occitane, which they sold and went on into
the olive business. The store in Cannes is actually
better than either of the Paris stores because it's
larger, but never mind; either one of these stores will
do the trick, and both are open on Sundays.

The firm specializes in olive products, selling
everything from designer tapenade (an olive spread)
to assorted olive oils from different parts of the
Mediterranean basin. There are French, Spanish,
Italian, and even Greek oils—all of which can be
tasted. The small can of oil costs about 100 F, but
some cost a little more, and every now and then one
is special—there was a big sale on Serbian olive oil
last time I was in the store, no joke.

If you are looking for a great $5 gift, there's a
25 F bottle of flavored olive oil that will do the
trick. Be sure it doesn't leak into your clothes
though.

There are also soaps, beauty treatments, olive wood products, and much more. One of the best new stores in France.

Pierre Champion
30 blvd. Haussmann, 9e (Métro: Chausée-d'Antin).

This is a chain of foie gras specialists with a Paris branch store right between Galeries Lafayette and the Ambassador Hotel. I pass it several times a day when I am in Paris and often wander in. They sell all sorts of regional foodstuffs from Périgord and will show you which foie gras can be taken into the U.S. legally and which kind must be eaten then and there.

Tchin-Tchin
9 rue Montorgueil, 1er (Métro: Halles).

I've included this shop partly because I adore it and think it's special, but also because I love the entire block that it's located on and also because it's in a convenient part of Paris where you will undoubtedly be prowling. This is a wine and champagne shop, but they specialize in small and unknown labels and specialty champagnes.

FRENCH BRAND NAMES

It's impossible to write a dictionary of every French brand, just as it's impossible to get to shops in all these stores, especially if you are in Paris for less than a month. The easiest way to see a lot of designer lines is to go to one of the big department stores. Of the big ones, Galeries Lafayette, has the most brands. However, there is a huge rivalry between Galeries Lafayette and Printemps, and Printemps has several exclusives, so it pays to visit both stores, or at least the lower floors of Printemps where they have the good clothes (floors one and two).

Also note that Galeries Lafayette in particular makes it a point to carry many international brands so that there are Spanish, German, and Italian brands mixed into their selection. This can be very confusing when you are not familiar with any of the brands.

The list that follows includes only French brands but covers a wide range of price categories.

AGNÈS B.
3 and 6 rue de Jour, 1er (Métro: Étienne-Marcel).

An international chain of ready-to-wear shops selling casual clothes with enough of a fashion look to make them appropriate for big-city wearing. Jazzier than the Ann Taylor look. Near the Forum des Halles with other branch stores here and there; also department store sales. Now makes makeup and travel gear, too.

ANDRÉ COURRÈGES
46 rue du Faubourg St-Honoré, 8e
(Métro: Concorde); 40 rue François-1er, 8e
(Métro: F-D-Roosevelt); 49 rue de Rennes, 6e
(Métro: St-Germain-des-Prés); 50 ave. Victor
Hugo, 16e (Métro: Victor-Hugo).

ANDRÉ COURRÈGES STOCK
7 rue de Turbigo, 1er (first floor) (Métro: Étienne-Marcel).

Courrèges invented the mini-skirt and gave us all white patent leather boots. Despite his excesses of the past, Courrèges actually has a very traditional basic line, some dynamite skiwear, and very little that is weird or wacky. You still can find some stuff that is so reminiscent of the 1970s that you don't know if it's new or old merchandise.

The upstairs stock outlet is closed on Monday and opens at 10:15am otherwise.

AZZEDINE ALAÏA
7 rue de Moussy, 4e (Métro: St-Paul).

ALAÏA STOCK
18 rue de la Verrerie, 4e (Métro: Hôtel-de-Ville).

Tunisian-born Alaïa shocked Paris fashion with his skin-tight high-fashion clothes and his first boutique in the then up-and-coming Marais neighborhood. Now people expect the unusual from him; get a look at the architecture of this place and you know he'll never disappoint.

The clothes are only for the young, or those with figures like movie stars, but the man is on the cutting edge of fashion and retail. Like many shops in the Marais, this one opens at 11am.

The outlet shop is in the headquarters of the firm and not inconvenient to touristic haunts. You'll find end-of-season clothing, samples, pieces of this and that, all at 50% to 60% off regular retail. Even with last season's garments, you're looking at prices that begin around $200.

BARBARA BUI
50 ave. Montaigne, 8e (Métro: Alma-Marceau).

Barbara Bui is not too well known to Americans, but has done so well in Paris lately that she now has four shops. There is also a store in Soho in New York and one in Milan. The stores are sparse in design and chic in simplicity; there's a cafe in her Étienne Marcel shop (no. 23). If you like Prada, test the waters.

CACHAREL
5 place des Victoires, 1er (Métro: Bourse).

CACHAREL STOCK
114 rue d'Alésia, 14e (Métro: Alésia).

Jean Cacharel made his name in America when he introduced charming clothes in precious prints. Thankfully, he has graduated from sweet along with the rest of us and now does a wide line of separates that are moderately priced. I prefer Cacharel for children's clothes rather than for adult fashion; there is a discount/stock shop that sells the whole shebang.

CÉLINE

38 ave. Montaigne, 8e (Métro: F-D-Roosevelt or Alma-Marceau); 24 rue François-1er, 8e (Métro: F-D-Roosevelt); 26 rue Cambon, 1er (Métro: Tuileries); 58 rue de Rennes, 6e (Métro: St-Germain-des-Prés).

An old French name that was actually born right after World War II and reborn last year when Michael Kors took over the design of the line. Céline makes clothes and leather goods; nothing smacks of hot more than this current line; the stores truly sell out of many of the models. There are already 83 stores around the world.

Céline has pretty much lost the horsey motif and the idea of going after Hermès; now it's all very sleek and sophisticated and casual, yet rich, rich, rich—scarves, bags, and ready-to-wear are the specialty with an emphasis on creativity in materials, such as string knits. Prices are lower than Hermès, but they are not modest; the cowl-neck sleeveless cashmere shell costs $650 (after détaxe!); a ribbon knit cardigan costs $1,200.

CHACOK

Les Trois Quartiers, place de la Madeleine (Métro: Madeleine).

This is a French sportswear line with boutiques all over France; I have no idea why they haven't conquered the rest of the world. The clothes are usually bright and fun filled, with a slight ethnic edge. For designer sportswear, the prices are moderate. I was tempted by a sweater coat for $400, but decided to wait for the sale. I love these clothes for restful weekends in the south of France. I don't know who wears them in Paris.

CHANEL
*31 rue Cambon, 1er (Métro: Tuileries); 42 ave.
Montaigne, 8e (Métro: F-D-Roosevelt or Alma-
Marceau).*

What becomes a legend most? The mother house, as it's known in French, which holds both couture and a boutique at this famed rue Cambon address, tucked behind the Ritz.

Two smaller boutiques are open across town on the tony avenue Montaigne; they are expanding since rue Cambon is mobbed with tourists. Meanwhile there are also specialty boutiques, such as one that sells only fine jewelry and another that sells only shoes.

There aren't a lot of bargains here, even on sale. You may be hard pressed to find sales help that is pleasant. But prices are less than regular retail in the U.S., and you will undoubtedly qualify for détaxe if you are a serious shopper. Sale prices in the U.S. may be surprisingly competitive.

A lot of the accessories—which are the only things that mortals can hope to embrace—are put away in black cases, so you have to ask to be shown the earrings and chains, which is no fun and puts a lot of pressure on you. However, the sales help is usually nice, and the selection is fun. I try to treat myself to a pair of earrings whenever I am flush and find that at $150 per pair (simple ones), I have a lasting souvenir of Paris.

If you're game, try a used Chanel suit. A classic is a classic is a classic, no? Check with **Réciproque, Dépôts-vent de Passy,** or **Didier Ludot.** Used suits are not cheap, since this is not a new trick; you'll pay around $2,500 to $3,000. Usually the blouse is sold with the suit at Ludot, but it brings the price of the suit up; at Chanel the blouse is another purchase. Expect to pay $3,500 or more for a new suit at Chanel. (*Note:* Used Chanel is less expensive in New York and in London.)

If by any chance you expect to find faux Chanel in French flea markets, you can forget it right now.

France is very strict about copyright laws; Chanel is even stricter. You want a pair of imitation earrings for $20? Go to Manhattan.

CHARVET
8 place Vendôme, 1er (Métro: Opéra or Tuileries).

Although Charvet sells both men's and women's clothing, this is known as one of the grandest resources for men in continental Europe. Elegant men have been having shirts tailored here for centuries. You may buy off-the-rack or bespoke. Off-the-rack comes with only one sleeve length, so big American men may need bespoke. The look is Brooks Brothers meets the Continent: traditional yet sophisticated. American men like to come here for status appeal. The mini-department store of the shop is filled with *boiserie* and the look of old money. A man's shirt, like all quality men's shirts these days, costs well over $100.

CHRISTIAN DIOR
30 ave. Montaigne, 8e (Métro: Alma-Marceau).

Oh la la, totally renovated and rejuvenated to make room for all that Dior has become since its reinvention with John Galliano, this is a showplace that you just have to visit, if only to *lechez les vitrines.* This large house has many floors for shopping—you can get ready-to-wear, costume jewelry, cosmetics, scarves, menswear, baby items, and wedding gifts, as well as the couture. In fact, several little shops are clustered around the main "house," and you merely wander as if you were in Bergdorf's.

I give Dior high marks for merchandising their famous name to make everyone happy; I give their salespeople high marks for carrying out the stereotypical haughty behavior that offends many. Okay, I give the $1,000 necklace I loved high marks, too—for high prices. And that was costume jewelry; imagine the new line with precious gemstones!

CHRISTIAN LACROIX

26 ave. Montaigne, 8e (Métro: Alma-Marceau);
73 rue du Faubourg St-Honoré, 8e
(Métro: Concorde).

You no longer need to be a couture customer to buy a little something from Christian Lacroix. I found a pin for under $100 worth writing home about. The Bazaar line is less expensive than the regular line, although I did pay $450 for a skirt—so we are not talking bargains here. Clothes may be dramatic and expensive, but the accessories are wearable and affordable. Walk in to examine everything; the Montaigne space is a visual feast. For color and sheer delight, this place should be on everyone's must-see list. They've just launched their new frangrance.

DEVERNOIS

255 rue St-Honoré, 1er (Métro: Tuileries).

This is an extremely French line that I can't imagine any American would know much about yet. It's somewhat similar to Rodier in that there are great knits that travel well, but much of it will appear a tad old lady-ish to a young American eye. There are shops everywhere. These are clothes that work well if you must mix with a European crowd and don't want to look too American.

DOROTHÉE BIS

46 rue Étienne Marcel, 2e (Métro: Étienne-Marcel); 33 rue de Sèvres, 6e (Métro: Sèvres-Babylone).

The woman responsible for getting this business off the ground was none other than the duchess of Windsor. Sweaters and knits always have been the house specialty and continue as such. Prices are moderate to those of us used to outrageously high designer prices. There are several retail outlets: for men, for women, for sportswear, for discount.

EMANUEL UNGARO
2 ave. Montaigne, 8e (Métro: Alma-Marceau);
2 rue Gribeauval, 7e (Métro: Rue du Bac).

If you were to translate the colors of the rainbow through the eyes of a resident of Provence, you'd get the palette Ungaro is famous for. The couture house is a series of three chambers that connect on the rue Montaigne, so you can see many aspects of the line in one larger space. Don't be afraid to walk in and take a look.

Ungaro is now owned by the Ferragamo family; the shoes are made in their factories in Italy.

FAÇONNABLE
9 rue du Faubourg St-Honoré, 8e
(Métro: Concorde).

Façonnable has taken over the high street of every French city and moved into vacant space on the Faubourg St-Honoré. Under the auspices of Nordstrom, they have also come to the U.S. and even opened a store on Fifth Avenue in New York.

The clothes are simply preppy menswear. Navy blazers. Navy and white stripes for summer. Khaki trousers. Gray flannel trousers. Topsider shoes. You get the picture. The Faubourg store is sort of like a fancy version of "GAP goes BCBG"; the stores in Nice are nicer, if you'll excuse the expression. Maybe preppy just plays better at the beach.

GERARD DAREL
22 rue Royale, 8e (Métro: Concorde).

This is a mid-level designer with numerous free-standing stores all over France and representation in major department stores; he also advertises heavily in women's magazines, so you may fall for the ads before you find the clothes. The clothes are simple and tasteful; the ads are very evocative of Jacqueline Kennedy Onassis and actually have more flair to them than the current collection. Still, the clothes are tailored, excellent for the office, and not outrageously expensive. I paid $125 for a pair of silk trousers. Many branch stores in assorted trading areas all over France.

GIVENCHY
3 ave. George V, 8e (Métro: George V);
66 ave. Victor Hugo, 16e (Métro: Victor-Hugo).

Hubert de Givenchy retired, and his couture is now designed by brash British upstart Alexander McQueen, who moved in when John Galliano was switched over to the House of Dior. The couture house is upstairs at 29–31. The men's store takes up three floors and sells everything. Women's accessories and ready-to-wear are housed in two separate shops.

HERMÈS
24 rue du Faubourg St-Honoré, 8e
(Métro: Concorde); Hermès Hilton Hotel,
18 ave. de Suffren, 15e (Métro: Bir-Hakeim).

Perhaps the single best-known French luxury status symbol comes from Hermès. The Hermès scarf is universally known and coveted; the handbags often have waiting lists. I've personally gone nuts for the enamel bangle bracelets that are much less expensive in Paris than elsewhere in the world. Since they cost about the same as a scarf, you may want to reprogram your mind for a new collectible. And the tie? Well, it's a power tie with a sense of humor; that's all I can say.

Remember, in order to get the best price at Hermès, you need to qualify for the détaxe refund. Plan to buy at least two of anything (or four ties). Unless, of course, you buy a saddle.

If you can't buy anything but want the thrill of your life, wander the store to educate your eye and then show your copy of this book at the scarf counter, where they will give you a free copy of a gorgeous booklet called *Comment Nouer Un Carré*

Hermès—"How to Tie an Hermès Scarf," if they have the booklet in stock (which sometimes they do not). It's all pictures, so don't worry if you can't read French. As I just mentioned, they often run out of this book, so don't pout (or write me a nasty letter).

There are thousands and thousands of choices in this store, from the traditional to the downright silly. The ready-to-wear collection is so hot it will leave you panting. You'll also have trouble breathing as you battle your way through the throngs who gather at the scarf counter and the tie racks. If you are claustrophobic, go to the Paris Hilton and shop for Hermès in peace.

Final Tips: Don't forget to see if your airline sells Hermès scarves and ties in their on-plane shop; these usually cost slightly less than at Hermès (although the selection is often limited). If you want used Hermès, **Didier Ludot** is the most famous specialist (see p. 242). *Warning:* I recently flew both Air France and Delta and Hermès was less money on Air France than Delta. Go figure!

JEAN-CHARLES DE CASTELBAJAC
6 place St-Sulpice, 6e (Métro: St-Germain-des-Prés).

Castelbajac may be too wild and too expensive for you to make a special trip to this off-the-beaten-path location (a new address). His creative mind continues to produce original works of art for when you want the world to notice you. Not for the shy or the short. His mother has a shop near the Marché St-Honoré.

JEAN-PAUL GAULTIER
6 rue Vivienne, 2e (Métro: Bourse or Palais-Royal).

JUNIOR GAULTIER
7 rue du Jour, 1er (Métro: Les Halles).

Gaultier fans can use Paris as an excuse to find the Galerie Vivienne. The boutique is the cornerstone of the Galerie Vivienne, a landmark *passage* near Victoire. Soak up the pleasures of the *galerie* itself, while you take in the high-tech shock appeal of Gaultier's unique mix of videotech, fashion, and architecture. The younger line (Junior) is less expensive and not appropriate for anyone over age 40. Make that 30. It is sometimes sold at discount shops on rue St-Placide.

KENZO

3 place des Victoires, 1er (Métro: Bourse); 23 rue de la Madeleine, 8e (Métro: Concorde); 18 ave. George V, 8e (Métro: George V); 99 rue de Passy, 16e (Métro: La Muette); Kenzo Studio (Espace Nouvel), 60–62 rue de Rennes, 6e (Métro: St-Germain-des-Prés).

Yes, Kenzo does have a last name; it's Takada. Yes, Kenzo is Japanese, but he's a French designer. Yes, Kenzo has retired, but the line lives on. The clothes are showcased in big, high-tech stores designed to knock your socks off. The line isn't inexpensive—but there are great sales. If you're looking to make one moderate designer purchase, you can get a T-shirt for $30 that will make you feel like a million.

LACOSTE

372 rue St-Honoré, 8e (Métro: Concorde).

Lacoste, often called *le crocodile* in France, which is confusing for those of us who consider it an alligator! This is one of those tricky status symbols that you assume will be cheaper here—after all, it is a French brand. But it isn't. You can pay $85 for a short-sleeve shirt in France, when the same shirt costs $65 at Saks Fifth Avenue in the U.S.

LANVIN

15 rue du Faubourg St-Honoré, 8e (Métro: Concorde).

The House of Lanvin is one of the oldest and best known of French couturiers, due mostly to its successful American advertising campaigns for the fragrances My Sin and Arpége ("promise her anything . . . "). In recent years, the line has been in transition as the house tries to find its place in the modern world. I have no idea how they have stayed in business.

The men's store has a fabulous cafe on the basement level that is a must-do for any weary shopper. You can get a burger for less than $10, and some of the best scrambled eggs I've ever eaten were consumed right here.

Léonard
48 rue du Faubourg St-Honoré, 8e
(Métro: Concorde); 36 ave. Pierre 1er de
Serbie, 16e (Métro: Iena).

Léonard is a design house that makes clothes but is perhaps more famous for the prints the clothes are made of. Many pieces are made from a knitted silk; the prints are sophisticated, often floral, and incorporated in ties and dresses. A men's tie will cost about $100, but it makes a subtle statement to those who recognize the print. I can get it for you cheaper if you come to Italy with me; I've been to the factory shop.

The last time I was in Paris, Pascale-Agnés and I were walking past Léonard and admitted a terrible secret to each other: We now like Léonard. I don't know if we're getting older or the line is getting better (or both), but I do think this is a very chic, very French way to spend some money making a splashy entrance at just the right place.

Lolita Lempicka
14 rue du Faubourg St-Honoré, 8e
(Métro: Concorde); 3 bis, rue des Rosiers, 4e
(Métro: St-Paul).

Although she sounds like a Polish union leader straight from the docks, she is the darling of the hot set in Paris—and has been for several years.

The Lolita Bis line is sold in the Marais; it's a less expensive (and less wacky) line than her signature collection (jackets in the $350 range). Accessories are extremely affordable and may even come in around $25. Anything from this designer has to be considered collectible by fashion mavens. Fashions are sexy, sometimes suggestive, and always close to the body.

LOUIS VUITTON

101 ave. des Champs-Elysées, 8e (Métro: George V); 6 place St-Germain, 6e (Métro: St-Germain-des-Prés); 57 ave. Montaigne, 8e (Métro: Alma-Marceau or F.D-Roosevelt).

Mama Mia, what has Bernard Arnault brought to us? Paris is totally changed and the Champs-Elysées is energized by this new shop, this new push, and the arrival of Marc Jacobs. Bravo Bernie!

Louis Vuitton himself opened his first shop in 1854 and didn't become famous for his initials until 1896, when his son came out with a new line of trunks. Things haven't been the same since.

Nor will you ever be the same after you've seen what's been going on for the last 5 or so years: The Left Bank store, designed by Anoushka Hemphill and the newer Champs-Elysées store, built to showcase the ready-to-wear line designed by Marc Jacobs, are two of the most impressive new additions to Parisian style.

On the Left Bank, the front door alone is worthy of a half hour of silent, stunned appreciation. The store is on different levels, and you sort of weave up and down and around. Toward the front of the store is the house collection of restored but older LV luggage and steamer trunks; these are for sale. You may also bring in your old ones for repair or renovation.

The avenue Montaigne shop is brash, cold, and unfriendly. The Vuitton staff is there to take you by the hand and guide you to a purchase or two or three. There are set limits on how much you may buy. Worship on the Left Bank.

The Champs-Elysées store is so large it has entrances on two different streets and levels to explore. It's minimalist and luxe all at the same time.

MARITHE ET FRANÇOIS GIRBAUD
38 rue Étienne Marcel, 1er (Métro: Étienne-Marcel).

Masters of the unisex look, the Girbauds are still making the only clothes that make sense on either sex with equal style. While they have many lines, and you may never see everything these designers can do, their main store is a must because of the architecture. Discounted jeans can sometimes be found at **Le Mouton à 5 Pattes.**

NINA RICCI
39 ave. Montaigne, 8e (Métro: Alma-Marceau).

I think we can cut to the chase here. I mean, we all know Nina Ricci is a couture house. Let's go straight to the good stuff. Downstairs is where the samples are sold. There is a large and incredible selection of evening gowns and a few day dresses and suits. If you don't need a ball gown but are looking for a gift to give someone you want to impress, consider the Ricci gift department, which is small enough to consider with one big glance. This store is closed all day Saturday and from 1 to 2pm every day for lunch.

PHILLIPE MODEL
79 rue des Sts-Pères, 6e (Métro: Sèvres-Babylone).

Have you ever looked at those pictures of the fashion showings (couture and *prêt*) in your *WWD* or *W* and fallen in love with the hats that have been teamed with the clothes? If so, you'll be pleased to find Model, who makes many of the hats and is famous for his inventive, slightly crazy, and very stylish *chapeaux*. There are also shoes. This shop happens to be behind the Hôtel Meurice; there is a more accessible shop in Little Dragons on the Left Bank. Prices on sale are over $100 for a simple hat, but these are the things whimsy is made of. Pascale-Agnés's mother saw a bunch of out-of-season hats at Mi-Prix, the discounter, for reasonable prices. You just never know. Model has been expanding past hats recently.

RODIER

*Rodier Étoile, 15 ave. Victor Hugo, 16e
(Métro: Victor-Hugo); Rodier Rive-Gauche,
35 rue de Sèvres, 6e (Métro: Sèvres-Babylone);
Rodier Forum des Halles, 1er (Métro: Châtelet);
Rodier Passy, 75 rue de Passy, 16e
(Métro: La Muette); Rodier Kasha, 27 rue
Tronchet, 8e (Métro: Madeleine).*

Rodier makes knits that are ideal for travel. I wear a lot of their clothes on the road. Regular retail prices in Paris are no bargain, but can be good during sales. However, prices at French sales may not be as good as U.S. sale prices! Know your stuff before you pounce. Also note that some pieces in France are not available in the U.S.

There are 16 boutiques in Paris; the big news is the new home for their Kasha line. It's near place de la Madeleine, so take a look.

SONIA RYKIEL

*70 rue du Faubourg St-Honoré, 8e
(Métro: Concorde); 175 blvd. St-Germain, 6e
(Métro: St-Germain-des-Prés). Sonia Rykiel Enfant,
4 rue de Grenelle, 6e (Métro: Sévres-Babylone).
SR Stock, 64 rue d'Alésia, 14e (Métro: Alésia).*

Sonia Rykiel began rewriting fashion history when she was pregnant and couldn't find a thing to wear; her children's line was born when she became a grandmother. I say forget the expensive kiddie things and save up for the expensive grown-up clothes. Also visit the outlet if you are a true fan because you might get lucky. I've been there when it was great and when it was lonely; you simply never know. Sonia's things are unique—they are classics and stay

in style forever; in fact, there's a cult following for
20- and 30-year-old sweaters.

TEHEN
*Les Trois Quartiers, place de la Madeleine, 8e
(Métro: Madeleine).*

Tehen is designed by Maria Cornejo, who made her
name in the British fashion scene as the other half of
the Richmond-Cornejo duo. She's now in Paris doing knits, short skirts, and Lycra jerseys that retail
from $100 to $400. There are branch stores here and
there; the most convenient address appears above.

THIERRY MUGLER
*49 ave. Montaigne, 8e (Métro: Alma-Marceau);
10 place des Victoires, 2e (Métro: Bourse); 6 rue
Boissy d'Anglas, 83 (Métro: Concorde).*

Count on Mugler for a certain look—both pure and
outrageous. The shops offer selling space that could
put a museum to shame. Walk down a longish entry
after you are inside and into a salon of selling space.
Along the way you'll pass blue lights, modern art,
and a few spare articles of clothing.

VALENTINO
*17–19 ave. Montaigne, 8e (Métro: Alma-
Marceau); 27 rue du Faubourg St-Honoré, 8e
(Métro: Concorde). Valentino Homme, 376 rue
St-Honoré, 1er (Métro: Concorde).*

Valentino shows in Paris and takes his fashion very
seriously here. He renovated the shop rather recently
in order to hold his place of esteem among his couture neighbors. The Oliver line is also sold here, but
you won't find V or Night in this palace of beige
marble and glass.

VENTILO
267 rue St-Honoré, 1er (Métro: Concorde)

This is actually one of half a dozen Ventilo shops in
Paris; I have been to most of them, and for some

reason each one feels different. It's a good lesson in the use of space and how it reflects the customers reaction to the clothes. My favorite shop is at 2 rue Louvre; this has a tearoom and the home furnishings line.

Ventilo was once a famed name in couture; now it's a bridge line with slightly exotic touches and some ethnic inspirations that make it fashionable and yet memorable. I'm a huge fan, although the last 2 years have not driven me as wild as the collections before that. I also like the fragrances.

YVES SAINT LAURENT

Rive Gauche, 19–21 ave. Victor Hugo, 16e (Métro: Victor-Hugo); 38 rue du Faubourg St-Honoré, 8e (Métro: Concorde). YSL Couture, 43 ave. Marceau, 16e (Métro: Alma-Marceau). YSL Couture Accessories, 32 rue du Faubourg St-Honoré, 8e (Métro: Concorde). L'Institut Beauté Yves Saint Laurent, 32 rue du Faubourg St-Honoré, 8e (Métro: Concorde).

What becomes a legend most? This past year YSL brought in Alber Elbaz to create the Rive Gauche line. He may eventually succeed to the entire empire. Stay tuned because Tom Ford from Gucci is also in the running. Don't forget that Saint Laurent is also in the beauty biz. There is a beauty institute that does skin care (but not hair) next to the accessories shop on the Faubourg. More affordable than clothes. If you must be up on the newest, shop nowhere else but the Victor Hugo store, which is the model for the way all branch stores will be renovated in coming years. I didn't find it so shockingly different, but *tout Paris* is impressed.

HAIRSTYLISTS

I now have a hairstyle I can "do" myself, but for years I was slave to someone clever enough to take the curly kink out and give me a coif of merit. So I have been to just about all the major salons in Paris and many of the not-so-major ones.

Going to the hairstylist in Paris is fun if you have the time and the patience; usually there is someone who speaks English, so don't worry about language problems. While it's expensive to go to the fanciest salons, it's not only a chance to pamper yourself but you get a social history lesson and a look at a way of life that you can't be part of on any other level unless you marry into it. For me, I'd give up a few hours in the Louvre in order to visit Carita.

CARITA
11 rue du Faubourg St-Honoré, 8e
(Métro: Concorde).

Perhaps the most famous name in beauty in all of Paris, Carita offers an entire town house devoted to putting madame's best foot forward. The entrance is on the Faubourg, but off the street and inset a little bit, therefore slightly hard to find.

The great thing about this place, aside from the fact that the staff at reception speaks English, is that it's so organized you can be assured you'll be taken care of. Just walk to the appointment clerk (on street level to your left once you've parted the waves) and make an appointment. You can, of course, ask for a particular stylist, but if you don't, not to worry. You'll be in good hands, regardless.

The stylists are all dressed in white uniforms; the patrons are wearing expensive clothes and carrying the best handbags in Paris. You are given a paper number when you check in; don't lose it. This is your client number, which stays with you until you pay the bill.

Note: You receive your number when you check your coat and/or belongings and pick up your smock. Patrons do not take off their clothes here; the smock is put directly over what you are wearing.

The cost of the pampering is the going rate for ultra-fancy in Paris; you can do better price-wise, but never experience-wise. I consider each trip to Carita a souvenir for myself. I come away with a memory and a good do. A shampoo and blow-dry, which includes service, costs about $60 . . . or more if you add on products in the hair care choices. Yes, in France you pay for each ingredient they put in your hair when they wash it.

More beauty products and accessories are sold at the back desk at street level. Call or fax ahead for an appointment if you wish: ☎ 1/44-94-11-00; fax 1/47-42-94-98. Carita has expanded recently, so there are salons outside of Paris if you are traveling around France.

ALEXANDRE DE PARIS
3 ave. Matignon, 8e (Métro: Matignon),
☎ *1/43-59-40-09; Les Trois Quartiers,*
place de la Madeleine, 1er (Métro: Madeleine).

Alexandre is legend. The aura lives on within the house; there is cachet attached to just who at Alexandre does your hair. Indeed, Alexandre may be the most famous of the old-school hairdressers. The name is so well known that there's a separate hair accessories business, with shops all over the world and products sold in major department stores. ☎ 1/49-26-04-59.

Charlie, the most famous stylist in the house in recent history, has set up her own shop (see below), and the accessories are so expensive that you could faint—still, how could I leave out this famous name and not tell you the skinny? And puh-leeze, *chère*, you must know that Charlie is a woman or you aren't in the swim at all.

CHARLIE EN PARTICULIER
1 rue Goethe, 16 e (Métro: Alma-Marceau).

There is only one Charlie in Paris and she's a she—the hair stylist who rose to fame doing celebrated locks at Alexandre and is now off on her own. Rumor has it she charges $400 for a haircut. I've even heard that she's worth it. I hear that regulars fly in from Geneva just for a trim. I hear so much that I'm saving up. For an appointment call ☎ 1/47-20-94-01. I have also heard that on Wednesdays you can get a junior cut for 150 F; ask!

JACQUES DESSANGE
37 blvd. Franklin D. Roosevelt, 8e (Métro: F-D-Roosevelt).

Still famous after all these years, Dessange has a number of shops in Paris and other locations. Not as fancy as Carita, but with a big-time reputation nonetheless, Dessange attracts a younger client than Carita. Hollywood's Jose Eber started here. Sometimes you can run into a promotional package where the shampoo, cut, and dry costs 195 F! They may also give you a free makeup consultation. There is a beauty and makeup line, which is sold at the salon and at pharmacies. Call ☎ 1/43-59-31-31 for the salon nearest you. There are literally hundreds of salons in France; they are expanding throughout the U.S. If you want a cut at a training session, you'll pay a mere 40 F—sessions are offered 3 days a week, you must make a reservation at least 1 week in advance, call ☎ 1/44-70-08-08.

L'ORÉAL CENTRE TECHNIQUE
14 rue Royale, 1er (Métro: Tuileries or Concorde).

It can't get easier than this; right in the heart of things the L'Oreal offices plus their technical center, which is reserved for testing models and VIPs. If you are in Paris and feel like a hair fling but are watching your budget, you can volunteer and sometimes they will take you—it costs about $25 for color or a cut. They are closed for lunch from noon to 2pm, but otherwise you can drop in or simply phone to ask. The location couldn't be better. Call ☎ 1/40-20-97-30.

JEAN-MARE MANIATIS
35 rue de Sèvres, 6e (Métro: Sèvres-Babylone),
☎ *1/45-44-16-39; 18 rue Marbeuf, 8e*
(Métro: F-D-Roosevelt), 1/47-23-30-14.

Still one of the hot shops for models and runway stars, Maniatis has salons in Paris (one is in Galeries Lafayette) and a beauty school. The beauty school, at the Forum des Halles, has a service that offers free haircuts to those clients who are willing to let a student practice on them. To get information about the training sessions, which offer free haircuts and makeovers, call ☎ 1/47-20-00-05. Men, women, and teens may participate; the stylists makes all the choices—you are the guinea pig.

If you want to go for a regular Maniatis session, pay attention to your location and the day of the week. The Right Bank salon is open on Monday; the Left Bank salon is not. If you are doing this up proper, forget about going to GL. I mean, really. On the other hand, if your time is limited and you must do a shopping and beauty combo, thank GL for the good sense to put the salon here.

Hair Salon Chains

Jacques Dessange is a chain of salons with shops all over France; there is a trend now for even less expensive and less formal chains—many of them do not require appointments, and some of them have salons in the U.S. Check out **Jean Louis David** (known in the U.S.), **Camille Albane,** and **Jean Claude Biguine.** All three of these major brands have convenient salons; your hotel concierge will tell you which is nearest you. They are all relatively inexpensive (by Paris standards), but do not expect the same quality of work or service that you get at a major name salon. If you are having a number of services performed and price is an issue, go over a price list with someone who speaks English before you begin, as most Paris salons charge à la carte, which means you can be charged for each sham-pooing. Service is included in the price; only regulars top off the bill.

Note: Most of the chains have training sessions when you can get a free do or a very cheap one (usually for under $10). For **Camille Albane,** call ☎ 1/48-59-31-32. Sessions are available on Monday, Tuesday, and Wednesday—and here's the bad news: 45 years of age and over and you do not qualify. Dessange also does training sessions; similar age restrictions; call ☎ 1/44-70-08-08.

HANDBAGS & LEATHER GOODS

. . . .

No one does handbags like the French; *non,* not even the Italians. If you want to splurge on only one thing, a handbag is a great notion—especially a brand that isn't well known in the U.S., so you can get a style that few others will have. Also note that the banana war could very well raise the price of French hand-bags made with plastic in the U.S., making them an excellent purchase when in France.

Most of the department stores have enormous handbag departments, usually on the ground floor. It makes more sense to buy a handbag at a depart-ment store if you can use the tourist discount card.

Didier Lamarthe
219 rue St-Honoré, 1er (Métro: Tuileries);
19 rue Danou, 2e (Métro: Opéra).

This line has been uneven in the past few years, so I can't rave the same way I used to—still, Lamarthe is worth knowing about. If you are looking for some-thing drop-dead French—elegant and sportif and totally different from the other big names sold in duty-free shops and American department stores—head for one of this designer's shops. Lamarthe sells luggage, handbags, and small leather goods (wal-lets and much more) at high but not top-of-the-line prices to those who buy only the best and crave fabulous color. I now buy mine at a department store with the discount card.

HERVÉ CHAPELIER
1 bis, rue du Vieux-Colombier, 6e
(Métro: St-Germain-des-Prés); rue St-Honore, 8e
(Métro: Concorde).

Right smack in the middle of the great shopping on the Left Bank is the mother shop of designer Hervé Chapelier who made his mark on the Paris handbag scene almost 10 years ago, but is just beginning to be known in America. I suggest you make a beeline as soon as possible and maybe go back every day. This could be the stock-up gift and indulgence resource of your trip. While I have not been especially moved by Kate Spade's work, I have gone nuts for Hervé—who is not even as clever as Kate Spade and yet has a very similar look, although always in nylon.

I'm not the only one who is impressed; these bags are a cult status symbol and the must-have accessory in Paris, especially in summer as a weekend tote or beach bag or travel carry-on. While a few bags are sold at both Printemps and Galeries Lafayette, ignore that fact and go only to one of the stores, so you can see the wide range of yummy colors—that's what does you in. The design lines are sleek and sturdy and sometimes boxy, just like, uh, Kate Spade.

For some reason, there are also cashmere sweaters: Forget that. You came for the tote bags. Almost all styles cost less than $100; the average price you will pay is $40 to $50, and you will be chic for years to come. There are two other shops, but they aren't in as high-traffic shopping districts for tourists, so this is the must-do address of your trip.

LONGCHAMP
404 rue St-Honoré, 1er (Métro: Concorde).

Totally renovated and rejuvenated new flagship with tons of fabulous bags, totes, and luggage. Many leather items are coated to withstand rain or snow.

LANCEL
8 place de la Opéra, 9e (Métro: Opéra) and many other locations.

Another French brand that many Americans don't know too well; again they make an excellent travel bag because it's not real leather, and some models have an outside flap-pocket doodle that is perfect for the plane ticket and passport. I have five versions of the same bag in assorted colors and sizes. Again, buy at a department store so you can use the discount card.

MAKEUP & PERFUME

. . . .

For tips on buying strategies, see page 68. Please don't be fooled into paying high prices for American goods with French names—for example, François Nars is indeed a Frenchman, but he's American now and his makeup is an American brand. Frederic Fekkai is also French; his firm is technically a division of Chanel—but he, too, has an American brand.

ANNICK GOUTAL
14 rue de Castiglione, 1er (Métro: Tuileries or Concorde); and other shops around town.

The tiny shop on the rue de Castiglione is a Paris landmark, but there are actually a number of outlets for Annick Goutal in Paris and elsewhere in the world. For example, it's sold at Bergdorf's in New York and Harrods in London. So what's so special? Just step into the belle epoque–style salon and sniff the house brands, which include perfumes, lotions, and house scents.

If you are looking for a special gift for someone who understands the meaning of the word *sublime,*

About Bourjois

You've heard of Chanel, but Bourjois? Bourjois is the name of the company that owns the Chanel line of makeup and perfume; it makes a lower-priced line of makeup under the Bourjois name—at the same factories where Chanel is manufactured! This doesn't mean that the two lines are identical, but if you can't afford Chanel and want to give this line a whirl, you may be pleased with the investment (about 50% to 75% less than Chanel).

Bourjois is hard to find in the U.S., but it's not hard to find in Paris—if you know where to look. You can buy Bourjois at any branch of **Monoprix** or **Sephora,** or at any big French department store. Prices are the same in all retail outlets; it's 2 F less at a duty-free store.

What makes the line so special? For starters: many, many, many shades of eyeshadow sold in big containers that can last you forever. The nail polishes and lipsticks are also good. Their rouge colors are excellent.

search no further. Be sure to look at the firm's logo, which is spelled out in a mosaic on the sidewalk in front of the store. I'm addicted to the soap called l'Hadrien, which happens to be the house soap for hotels in the Concorde chain. I like it so much I've been known to pay cash for it. *Zut!*

BY TERRY
21 Galerie Vérot-Dodat, 1er (Métro: Palais Royale)

Makeup addicts, search no more, this is the new "in" place to visit and test and swoon for—Terry has an itsy bitsy salon not too far from the place des Victoires and the Palais Royale in an old *passage.* Terry herself gained fame as the woman who created all the colors and makeup for Yves Saint Laurent's beauty line, for which she still consults.

After years in the big-time beauty biz, Terry de Gunzberg created her own line that is known for the density of the pigment: It is a color story. Because she uses so much pigment, the color is said to last longer than normal makeup.

You get "made over" while in the salon and then pick the choices for your palette—a small plastic container that is fitted to hold assorted color pots. The palette is given for free if you fill it but you can also buy à la carte.

Absolutely great item for someone who travels. Fluent English.

GUERLAIN
68 ave. des Champs-Elysées, 8e (Métro: F-D-Roosevelt); 2 place Vendôme, 1er (Métro: Opéra); 93 rue de Passy, 16e (Métro: La Muette); 29 rue de Sèvres, 6e (Métro: Sèvres-Babylone); 35 rue Tronchet, 8e (Métro: Madeleine).

GUERLAIN INSTITUTS DE BEAUTÉ
68 ave. des Champs-Elysées, 8e (Métro: F-D-Roosevelt); 29 rue de Sèvres, 6e (Métro: Sèvres-Babylone).

Perhaps the most famous name in fragrance in France, Guerlain has two different types of boutiques in Paris: Some sell products only, while others have salons on the premises.

Perfumes are sold only through Guerlain stores and are not discounted; the brand is rarely found at a duty-free store. If you see it at a duty free, chances are there is no discount. Some of the Guerlain fragrances you'll see in France are not sold in the U.S.

PATRICIA DE NICOLAI
80 rue Grenelle, 7e (Métro: Rue du Bac).

A nose is a nose is a nose; this is the granddaughter of the Guerlain family, out on her own. Fragrance, candles, potpourri, and more. Note the odd hours: It's closed for lunch every day from 2 to 2:30pm.

POUDRE LECLERC
10 rue Vignon, 1er (Métro: Madeleine).

Barney's helped establish this old-timey French loose face powder as the hottest thing in America; trendies can buy theirs in many shops in Paris, at several *parapharmacies,* or at this, the brand headquarters, a block from place de la Madeleine. There are assorted pale colors to even out skin tone as well as many neutrals.

SALON SHISEIDO
142 Galerie de Valois, Jardin du Palais-Royal, 1er (Métro: Palais-Royal).

If you think this is one of those stores that caters to Japanese tourists, you can forget it right now. This happens to be not only one of Paris's best-kept secrets, but one of the must-do addresses any serious shopper (I mean, sociologist) should seek, merely from an academic standpoint.

First, a quick history lesson. Shiseido is a Japanese makeup firm, true. A million years ago they hired the most famous makeup artist in Paris, Serge Lutens, and let him explore his creativity. This tiny shop, with the most glorious decor in Paris, sells the private inventions and designs of Mr. Lutens and is best known for his custom-made perfumes. And note that everything is a perfume—there are no derivatives. A bottle of scent costs about 550 F. Beware the stopper; it's not set in too well, so you must pack your fragrance carefully or hand-carry it onto the plane.

Now then, about the location. The location is simple and easy for all; it's the address that may confuse. Pay no attention to the address and follow my directions. Get yourself to the Comèdie-Française (next to the Palais-Royal métro); walk behind it and into the garden of the Palais-Royal. First you'll see creative modern sculpture that will make you think you are at a métro station on Mars. Then you will see the many-centuries-old gardens. On both sides of the gardens there is an arcade, crammed with shops.

Each arcade has a name. Ignore the names. The Shiseido salon is in the far arcade across the garden.

SEPHORA *9/14 Great fun here!*

70 ave. des Champs-Elysées, 8e (Metro: F-D-Roosevelt); Forum des Halles, 2e (Métro: Châtelet or Les Halles); 50 rue de Passy, 16e (Métro: La Muette); 66 rue de la Chausée d'Antin, 9e (Métro: Trinité); 38 ave. du Général Leclerc, 14e (Métro: Alésia).

This is a chain of cosmetics shops with stores all over France, in most major Euro capital cities, and now in the U.S. as well. The Champs-Elysées store, which is the flagship, is open 7 days a week.

Sephora gives only the détaxe, which means that they do not discount and are therefore much more expensive than need be. Still the stores are so much fun to visit that you might not care about prices. Note that Sephora has a new Web site in the U.S. (www.sephora.com) and they have e-commerce.

SHU UEMURA
176 blvd. St-Germain, 6e (Métro: St-Germain-des-Prés).

He's one of the most famous makeup artists in the world, and you can buy his makeup products in every world capital. He's a cult hero in his native Japan. Color is the name of the game here. The hues are spectacular. If you consider yourself an aficionado of cosmetics, to be in Paris and not go to Shu Uemura is a sin. Yes, it's even better than Bourjois; more expensive, too. A single square of color costs about $16. Splurge. This high-tech shop is filled with samples and mirrors and brushes, just encouraging you to come in and make up your face again and again. You can also book a private appointment to be made over in their professional studio; this is not far from Galeries Lafayette at 12 rue de la Paix; call ☎ 1/53-59-52-00 for an appointment. This is not a store, it is the makeup *atelier*.

Makeup & Perfume Discounters

Remember, *discount* is a dirty word in France and duty free has become a bit confusing. Even a source that discounts, and has done so for years, suddenly is now terrified of consumer mix-ups. So here's the deal: Discount is one thing, détaxe is another, and duty free is still another. Duty free when sold at the airport is a flat 13% off—you qualify to buy duty free when you are departing the EU only. Discounting is not approved of by the big beauty firms, nonetheless they tolerate it up to 15% or 20%—this varies by brand, so when you go to an honest store, they will explain that the amount of the discount varies with the brand. Détaxe is the tax refund that any non-EU passport holder qualifies for after spending 1,200 F at any one store in 1 day.

So, in a quick overview:

- When you buy at Sephora you get no discount, but you get détaxe if you qualify;
- When you buy at a major specialty *maison*, such as Guerlain, Creed, or Caron, you get no discount but you do get détaxe if you qualify;
- When you buy at a major department store you get a 10% discount with their tourist discount card (you obtain it free at the store's Welcome Desk), and you also get détaxe when and if you qualify for it;
- When you buy at the airport you pay exactly 13% less than the department store full price;
- If you shop at one of the few so-called "duty-free shops" in central Paris, you get the maximum discount that they allow, which ranges from 13% to 20%, plus the détaxe refund if and when you qualify for it. If you do not spend enough to get the détaxe refund, you get the upfront discount— even if you only buy one mascara.

CATHERINE
7 rue de Castiglione, 1er (Métro: Concorde or Tuileries).

If you've never been to Paris before, listen up. Catherine is my duty-free shop of choice. Believe me, this is where I do the bulk of my shopping because of their selection and the way they do their discounting and détaxe.

Catherine is one of the few duty-free shops that will not only give you the discount but also will advance you the détaxe upfront. It works this way: Let's say you have had no trouble at all spending 1,200 F (I have no trouble doing it; I think I can count on you). Now you qualify for a 20% + 20%. Your credit card will be charged with the discount in place! This is highly unusual. A second imprint is made with the tax difference written on it. Should you fail to file the proper papers, you will be charged the détaxe amount. If you do file the papers as you leave the EU, Catherine will destroy your second chit-ship when your paperwork is received.

Please note: To be exactly accurate we are not talking about a 40% discount but 20% + 20%, which because they are taken at separate times, comes out to be a micron shy of 40%.

A few other details about Catherine:

- The store moved about a year and a half ago; the new store is bigger.
- I always work with Patricia, but the store is run by the Levy family; Patricia is one of the sisters. She and her sister Fanny and their mother, Madame Levy, all speak perfect English. Monsieur Levy makes me speak French so he can laugh.
- If you do not buy 1,200 F worth of goods at first, but later return and buy more items, as long as the period is within the 6 months required by law, Catherine will let you tally up all the receipts and get the détaxe when you reach 1,200 F.
- There is a flat 15–20% discount if you don't reach the 1,200 F level on all brands except Chanel and Christian Dior, which allow only a 15% discount. If you show your copy of *Born to Shop*, you will get a 20% discount on those two big names.

- Mail orders are taken by fax or phone, but require a $100 minimum purchase. The store's fax number is 1/42-61-02-35; or call ☎ 1/42-61-02-89. The store also carries some accessories; most are brands but some are not. I got one of the best handbags of my life there for about $125—it's a copy of an Hermès bag, sort of a drawstring feed pouch with Kelly straps.

Parfumerie du Havre
9 place de la Madeleine, 8e (Métro; Madeleine);
15 place du Havre, 8e (Métro: St-Lazare).

The Madeleine store is larger and more attractive than its sister; both have many brands and some accessories. I bought some Christian Lacroix earrings here, which were slightly less money than in a Lacroix boutique. Their discounts vary with the brand, which they tell you up front. However, they give you the total price rather than the before and after price, so I never know if I'm really getting a good deal or not. Still, the shops have an excellent reputation among locals.

Parfumerie Rayon d'Or
94 rue St-Lazare, 8e (Métro: St-Lazare)

I recently got an angry letter form a reader who said she made a special trip to Catherine when it wasn't convenient for her and that there are plenty of other discounters in town and why didn't I mention them. Well, the ones I have found aren't as good. However, I found a store with very low prices and a large selection that may strike your fancy. I must also say that the saleswomen were more than a little rude here. Still, selection and price are excellent. This is a small chain; I visited this branch since it's a block from the Concorde St-Lazare Hotel where I often stay. They also have a Web site: www.aurayondor.fr. Good luck.

Silver Moon-Liz
Trois Quartiers, 23 blvd. Madeleine, 1er
(Métro: Madeleine).

I can't help but be attracted to Silver Moon, even though I'm not sure why. Essentially it's no different from any other place in town, yet the mere fact that it's spacious makes an American feel at home. They offer only a 10% discount and a *fidelity* card (star card). This location, in the mini-mall Trois Quartiers, gives you a reason to see the mall, although Silver Moon is a large chain with stores all over town. You can easily go from one to the next and use your star card to run up another 5% discount.

They sell big names in fragrances but also lots of treatment lines, skin and hair care products, and some dime-store makeup, including Bourjois. They also publish a very nice magazine with prices that makes an excellent reference guide if you want to compare French prices to U.S. prices.

MALLS & SHOPPING CENTERS

Slowly, Paris has been going mall mad. The shopping center of your teen years does not exist in great abundance in Europe, but Paris is trying out every kind of mall you can imagine. The larger mall structures are often called "commercial centers." The success of **Les Trois Quartiers** has brought about the *intime* mall—sort of American in feel, but smaller and therefore less intimidating. There are new entries constantly, all with very good addresses. Don't forget that the French had the original version of the mall, 150 years ago, with their *passages* and *galeries* (see "*Passages*," below).

FORUM DES HALLES
11 bis, rue de l'Arc-en-Ciel, 1er (Métro: Les Halles or Châtelet).

The Forum des Halles was built to rejuvenate a slum and serves as an exciting monument to youth, style, and shopping. It's a huge square with a courtyard. The atmosphere is rather American and sterile, and it's easy to get lost once you are inside. You'll find it conveniently located directly above a métro stop, Les Halles, and down the street from the YSL discount store, Mendès. It's also a stone's throw from the Beaubourg, which you may want to visit. There are fast-food joints in the métro part of the complex and real restaurants among the shops in the regular complex.

A series of escalators zigzags between the floors; there are master maps throughout the mall to help you find your way. Although a number of designers and upper-priced bridge lines have stores here, the stores are often not as charming as the boutiques on the street can be. The Forum was built in stages; be sure to see the newest part of the mall, which stretches underground. Most of the stores in the Forum des Halles open Tuesday through Saturday between 10 and 10:30am and close between 7 and 7:30pm. All stores are closed all day Sunday and Monday morning, opening for business again at noon on Monday. All stores take credit cards.

LES TROIS QUARTIERS
23 blvd. de la Madeleine, 1er (Métro: Madeleine).

This is what I'd call a mini-mall. It's nothing to write home about, despite the fact that locals love it and find it very American. The stores are small (with the exception of **Silver Moon**) and well integrated. I like the mix of designers and upscale suppliers. This is a good way to see a lot of shops fast. Designer shops range from **Kenzo** to **Chacok**; there's a little of everything thrown in, including **The Body Shop** and a few English chains. Also, the famed hairdresser **Alexandre** has a branch salon here.

The success of this mall has made the surrounding area one of the hottest in Paris retail; there's a new mall-like structure next door, Le Cedre Rouge, and a rehabbed passage across the place de la Madeleine.

LE CARROUSEL DU LOUVRE
99 rue de Rivoli, 1er (Métro: Palais-Royal).

This is an American-style shopping mall. While it isn't very big, its construction revolutionized Paris retail and brought on a new surge of mall building within landmark sites. The mall is attached to the Louvre and has many entrances and exits.

For the easiest access, enter from the rue de Rivoli, where there is a small banner announcing the space. This entrance is not particularly prominent, so you may have trouble finding it. The mall itself is on two subterranean levels; enter and take the escalator down one flight to the food court. Go down another level and you are in a mall like any other in your neighborhood, except that this one has **Lalique, The Body Shop, Esprit,** and **Virgin Megastore.** There are just over a dozen stores down here as well as a branch of the French Government Tourist Office.

I can't tell you that any of these shops are fabulous or that there's something here you haven't seen before (most of the stores are branches of famous French, American, or British chains), but it's still fun to see what our increasingly homogeneous culture has come to. This is also a great way to shop on Sunday, since everything is open then.

Through one of the mall walkways, you connect to the basement of the Louvre (underneath the I.M. Pei pyramid) and many artsy gift shops, including one that sells items from museum stores all over the world.

PLAZA PASSY
53 rue du Passy, 16e (Métro: La Muette).

It sort of looks like a redone deco-style apartment complex in South Beach, without the blue stucco, but this new mall helps you get a lot done in one neighborhood and has a very upper-class feel to it, especially when you glance around at your fellow shoppers. It's not a big mall or a very special one. It's just that it's easy and still French. Many of the retail tenants are French chains . . . or American ones, including GAP.

I am not embarrassed to tell you that I think it's super here; it's not terribly French, but it is very much a part of the new French retail scene—global, man, global! I also love the grocery store, **Champion,** on the lower level. Boutiques are open daily, 10am to 7:30pm; the grocery store is open Monday through Saturday, 8:30am to 8:30pm.

MUSEUM SHOPS

Almost all Paris museums have gift shops; and since there are about 50 museums in Paris, that's a lot of museum gift shops. Some are even organized into their own chains with branches in various museums; the Louvre has its own special shopping bags for all its gift shops. Some shops just sell slides, prints, and a few high-minded books or postcards. But several are really with it.

MUSÉE DES ARTS DÉCORATIFS
107 rue de Rivoli, 1er (Métro: Musée-du-Louvre).

The shop has been changed around a tad, so don't miss the salon in the far rear, which has books. The store sells a mix of books and gift items, all with a wonderful eye toward design. Prices aren't low, but you'll find unique gift items, even a copy of the very first scarf Hermès ever created. Some of the merchandise is tied to traveling exhibits and therefore changes regularly. There are books on design in several different languages.

Closed Monday and Tuesday. Sunday shoppers, note: Hours are noon to 5pm.

MUSÉE DU LOUVRE
Palais du Louvre, 1er (Métro: Musée-du-Louvre).

There's a gift shop under that glass pyramid, and it is a beauty, with two levels of shopping space. The store sells books, postcards, and repro gifts. Beaucoup fun! You do not have to pay admission to the museum to gain entrance. After walking into the pyramid, take the escalator down, and you will be in a lobby reminiscent of a train station. Glance around, read a few signs, and you'll soon see the gift shop—it's straight ahead.

MUSÉE D'ORSAY
Gare d'Orsay, 7e (Métro: Orsay).

The gift shop isn't as wonderful as the architecture, but it's damn good; you can buy prints and some reproductions, as well as a scarf or two. Good selection of postcards and gifts for kids. There are also small gift selling areas near specialty exhibits. I have bought wonderful art books for kids here.

CENTRE GEORGES POMPIDOU
Centre Georges Pompidou, 4e (Métro: Châtelet).

The gift shop takes up much of the first floor and is a wonderful source for posters, books, and postcards.

MUSÉE CARNAVALET
29 rue de Sévigné, 3e (Métro: St-Paul).

This museum is in the heart of the Marais and documents the history of the city of Paris; the gift shop sells reproductions of antique items, many of which are owned by famous people. I have the Georges Sand stemware. Closed on Monday.

MUSIC

· ·

I've gone nuts for Johnny Hallyday and have bought a number of his tapes and CDs. There are zillions of them (the man's career spans decades), but they can be pricey. I've paid 99 F, considered a bargain price, and I've paid 350 F for a multi-CD pack (it was worth it).

Jean-Louis Ginibre's Jazz Picks

Paris is my friend Jean-Louis's hometown. He's American now, but he still goes to Paris to buy jazz. His fave, for LPs and secondhand jazz and blues recordings, is **Paris Jazz Corner.** He also suggests that fans check out the stalls at the **Marché Malik** in the flea markets at St-Ouen (see p. 191), which are open only Saturday, Sunday, and Monday.

CROCODISC
64 rue de la Montagne Ste-Geneviève, 5e (Métro: Luxembourg); ☎ *1/46-34-78-38.*

LIBRARIE GILDA
36 rue des Bourdonnais, 1er (Métro: Châtelet); ☎ *1/42-33-60-00.*

PARIS JAZZ CORNER
5 rue de Navarre, 5e (Métro: Monge); ☎ *1/ 43-36-78-92.*

For the most part, music is not a good buy in France, but if you like French artists, you have little choice. I shop at any branch of **FNAC** I happen to pass (usually the one on rue de Rennes or the Champs-Elysées) or at the **Virgin Megastore** (again, ave. des Champs-Elysées—or the one at Le Carrousel du Louvre). There are also small music stores at all the Paris airports.

PARAPHARMACIES

· ·

These uniquely French places—essentially fancy drugstores selling everything from aromatherapy essences to products made with retin-A—all carry virtually the same lines of goods, but I haven't found one I could resist. These are great places to purchase bath and beauty gifts for friends back home and to try new French cures and beauty products.

Paris Santé Beauté
161 blvd. St-Germain, 6e
(Métro: St-Germain-des-Prés);
23 rue Tronchet, 8e (Métro: Madeleine).

The Right Bank shop opens Monday through Saturday at 9:30am; the Left Bank shop opens at 10am—both shops are open until 7:30pm, so there's no excuse to miss out. Not the largest, but chock-full of goodies. The Left Bank store has a location that you can't miss.

Euro Santé Beauté
37 rue de la Boetie, 8e (Métro: St-Augustin), etc.

This is a rather large chain of stores; there is also one next door to Hôtel Concorde St-Lazare. I love this chain; I visit one in every French city that has one. Most of the stores are relatively large by French standards. They also publish a price list, which you can pocket and use to comparison-shop. There are over 200 brands on sale here; I consider it one of the better *parapharmacies* in town.

Select Beauté Santé
4 rue Duphot, 1er (Métro: Madeleine).

This happens to be my regular *parapharmacie,* mostly because of the location—it's not that far from the Hôtel de Crillon. The store is large; I have a *fidelity* card that entitles me to 200 F off once I spend 2,000 F.

PASSAGES
. . . .

A *passage* (it rhymes with "massage") is a shopping area, exactly like an arcade in London. Today, *passages* are the French equivalent of American mini-malls and are cut into a building's lobby like a throughway. In the early 1800s, new buildings were large, often taking up a block. To get from one side of a building to another, a *passage* was built. Since it's inside the building, it's totally covered. Doorways lead through the original structure.

There are lots of *passages* all over Paris. One of the most famous is the **Galerie Vivienne.** One doorway is on the rue Vivienne; the other is on the rue des Petits-Champs. The passage is not surrounded by a greater building but is directly across from the National Library and near the Palais-Royal; it has a number of cute shops, a **Gaultier** boutique, and a lost-world ambience that makes it very much worth exploring.

The shop owners in a *passage* usually organize themselves, at least informally. Together they will decide if their shops will be open or closed during lunchtime. (The Galerie Vivienne is open during lunchtime.) *Passages* have cheaper rent than regular commercial space, so usually you'll find relatively mundane enterprises (like a printer or bakery) or young designers who are just starting out but may be moving fast.

Also check out **Cour du Commerce St-Anne** (59–61 rue St-André-des-Arts, 6e; Métro: St-Germain-des-Prés or Odéon), which is nestled into the Left Bank. The famous restaurant Le Procope is located in this tiny alley, but there's also a tea salon that I suggest for shoppers, called **Cour de Rohan,** and a few shops. It's not that the shopping is so great; it's that the charm is heart stopping.

Others to check out, if only for the architecture and not the actual stores within: **Galerie Véro-Dodat,** 19 rue Jean-Jacques Rousseau; **Passage des Panorama,** rue St-Marc; and **Passage Verdeau,** 31 bis, rue du Faubourg Montmartre. **Le Passage du Havre,** 109 rue St-Lazare, is a modern *passage.*

RESALE & VINTAGE

The French pride themselves on being a practical people. They rarely throw anything away; they buy only the best quality and use it forever; they hate waste of any sort. But if someone in the family dies or if someone falls on hard times, he can sell his fine possessions at a *dépôts-vent*. Or, knowing that good merchandise is being sold, he will frequent a *dépôts-vent*. No one in Paris is ever ashamed to be seen buying used items. They think it's smart. I do, too.

Do note that designer clothing that you may not consider purchasing at regular retail can be sale priced at the end of a season at virtually the same price you might pay at a *dépôts-vent*. *Dépôts-ventes* traditionally sell used clothing of current styles, while vintage shops sell older clothing. These days, with so many retro looks in vogue, it's hard to tell one from the other anyway. The two big flea markets, St-Ouen and Vanves, each have dealers who sell vintage clothing. The term *fripes* generally refers to nondesigner used clothing from the 1970s—not vintage Chanel or Balenciaga.

RÉCIPROQUE
89, 95, 97, 101, and 123 rue de la Pompe, 16e (Métro: Pompe).

Réciproque has grown at an alarming rate—there are now more storefronts bearing this store's name along rue de la Pompe than ever before. The main shop, no. 89, has two floors, so don't forget to go downstairs. There are racks and racks of clothes, all of which are clean. You'll find separates, shoes, evening clothes, and complete ensembles. You must look through the racks carefully and know your merchandise, although the labels are always in the clothes. Not everything is used or seriously used—many designers sell samples here. Every big name is represented; this is the best single resource for used couture clothing. A Chanel suit will cost over $2,500—so prices are not dirt cheap.

DÉPÔTS-VENT PASSY
14 and 25 rue de la Tour, 16e (Métro: Passy).

Another contender in the used-designer-clothing wars, Catherine Baril has two shops with top-drawer stuff—YSL, Chanel, the works. One shop is for women, the other for men. They are a few yards from each other. There is a fair amount of samples. On my last visit, I found tons of Chanel straight from the runway. The prices were generally high, but I found a few bargains. A Chanel suit (summer weight) for $1,500 seemed like a good buy, whereas a Chanel camisole for $200 was overpriced, at least to me.

The best part about this shop is its location. You can easily combine a stroll along the rue de Passy with a shopping spree here and have a fabulous time. Open Tuesday to Saturday, 10am to 7pm; Monday, 2 to 7pm. In July, Monday to Saturday, 2 to 7pm.

Didier Ludot

24 passage de la Galerie Montpensier, Palais-Royal, 1er (Métro: Palais-Royal).

Kind of vintage, Ludot has a new shop at Palais Royal selling only black dresses. He's also got a boutique in Printemps.

This shop is not easy to find, so have patience and remember that it is on the gallery side of the building, not the street side. Ludot tries to sell only top-of-the-line used designer goods, specializing in Hermès, Céline, and Chanel. You may find old Hermès bags from the 1930s, as well as vintage Vuitton luggage. This store is a standout for old-clothes junkies. Prices are high for quality items, but not unfair: a Pucci in perfect condition, just over $1,000; a wool Chanel suit (no blouse), $2,000.

The easiest way to get here is via the Palais-Royal métro. Zig to the right into the open arcade, then hug the left-hand side of the arcade (where it is covered). Shops line the walkway. Ludot is among them.

SHOES

Shoe freaks will find the Little Dragons neighborhood on the Left Bank (see p. 134) a treasure trove of little shoe stores belonging to famous designers and hoping-to-be-famous designers. Weave along these streets and you can't go wrong. Be sure to stop at the many shoe shops on the rue des Sts-Pères (there's even a branch of **Ferragamo** here), and then make your way onto rue du Four, where there are more shops for the teens. Don't forget to shop rue de Grenelle as well. For something truly French, try some of these resources.

CHRISTIAN LOUBOUTIN
Vero-Dodat (arcade), 19 rue Jean-Jacques Rousseau, 1er (Métro: Musée-du-Louvre).

One of the important shoe darlings for those with diamonds on the souls (or soles of their feet), Louboutin has made his mark with sophisticated and sometimes wacky designs all finished off with a bright red undersole—think heels that look like hand-carved trees. Prices begin at $300; many celebrity clients.

FRANÇOIS VILLON
58 rue Bonaparte, 6e (Métro: St-Germain-des-Prés).

This store is on the corner. The number is not well marked, and the store looks rather ordinary from the outset. Very little prepares you for the fact that this local shoemaker fits the stars, from Brigitte Bardot to Catherine Deneuve. I got the address from Princess Grace. (Honest.) Aside from the custom work, there are regular shoes in classical styles.

KARENA SCHUESSLER
264 rue St-Honoré, 1er (Métro: Concorde).

This is a German shoe designer who worked her way up through many big brands, including Stephan Kelian and Maud Frizon to have her own line. Very trendy.

WESTON
1 blvd. de la Madeleine, 1er (Metro: Madeleine).

Weston has been known for ages for their men's shoes, now the first women's boutique—very classical styles, needless to say; also handbags.

HAREL
7 rue Tournon, Paris 6e (Métro: Odeon);
8 avenue Montaigne, 16e (Métro: Alma-Marceau);
64 rue Françoise 1er, 8e (Métro: F-D-Roosevelt)

These are among the most exquisite shoes I have ever seen in my life, in terms of style, color, skins, and workmanship. The prices match. Flats begin around $500, while heels are more like $700. Still, press your nose to the glass just to understand all that Paris can be.

REPETTO
22 rue de la Paix, 2e (Métro: Opéra).

This is basically a supply house for ballerinas, but it offers much in terms of fashion, including dresses that would be great for black-tie events. This is the firm that introduced "le ballet" into fashion as a shoe rather than a dance item.

SOUVENIRS

Paris is loaded with souvenir shops, I often call them TT's (Tourist Traps). They congregate around the obvious tourist haunts (Notre-Dame, Champs-Elysées, etc.) and line the rue de Rivoli from Concorde all the way up to the front gate of the Louvre. They all sell more or less the same junk at exactly the same prices. Yes, folks, those prices are non-negotiable. The only way you can get a break is to deal on the amount you buy. If you buy a few T-shirts, you might get a few francs knocked off.

The price of T-shirts fluctuates, by the way, with the dollar: The price in francs varies (note the handwritten signs), so the T-shirts always cost $10. No dummies here. Naturally, there are T-shirts that cost more, but you'll have no trouble finding acceptable gifts for $10.

Some of my favorite things to buy at a souvenir stand include: a toothbrush with your (or some similar) name in French; a breakfast bowl sponged in blue and white, also with your name in French; boxer shorts with various Parisian motifs; T-shirts from French universities; key chains with all kinds of possibilities—miniature Eiffel Towers, street signs, Napoleon, and more; scarves with kitschy tourist-haunt designs that are so bad they are fabulous. For some reason, none of the department store souvenir departments are very good. Nonetheless Galeries Lafayette has two different souvenir departments, and the one on the sixth floor is better than the one on the street level.

SPANISH BRANDS

. . . .

Zara
2 rue Halevy, 9e (Métro: Opéra); 44 ave. des Champs-Elysées, 8e (Métro: F-D-Roosevelt).

Zara makes well-priced, chic, and fashionable clothes for work and weekend without being silly and cheap. They copycat the latest jacket shape or skirt silhouette or whatever fashion gimmick is cutting edge, so you can look on-the-minute without going broke.

Mango
6 blvd. des Capucines, 9e (Métro: Madeleine).

Mango has many shops around town; they are a low-cost brand of affordable fashions mostly for teens and tweens. Very popular with the French.

SPECIALTY LOOKS
. . . .

ANNE FONTAINE
66 rue des Sts-Pères, 6e (Métro: St-Germain-des-Prés).

This is a chain of stores with about a dozen shops in Paris alone—I simply chose the first address on their business card above. You can go online for more info and addresses (www.annefontaine.com) for this firm that sells only white shirts for women. Most cost less than $50.

COMPAGNIE FRANÇAISE DE L'ORIENT ET DE LA CHINE
*163 & 167 blvd. St-Germain, 6e
(Métro: St-Germain-des-Prés).*

Again, a large chain with stores all over, even in Brussels. There are some branches that carry the entire line and some that are divided into just clothes or just home style. Ignore the boutique in Galeries Lafayette; it doesn't do the line or the look justice.

As you can guess from the name, the clothes are inspired by the Orient. I have a jacket made of Scottish tweed in a Chinese style that is such a brilliant combination of ideas that I wear it all the time and love it. While the clothes are somewhat ethnic, they are not costumey.

ERES
2 rue Tronchet, 8e (Métro: Madeleine).

Eres is perhaps the most famous name in bathing suits in France—we're talking high end, almost couture bathing suits. They have since branched into lingerie. The line is also sold in some department stores; it is extremely chic and expensive. And wonderful. There are few boutiques around town, but this is the main shop and it's next door to Fauchon on the place de la Madeleine.

LE PHARE DE LA BALEINE
Passage du Havre, 8e (Métro: St-Lazare).

There are only a few of these shops, but they are
unique and very French—they specialize in the sea-
side inspirations of Brittany. The name means
"Lighthouse of the Whale" (I think). This is where
you can buy the blue and white stripe T-shirts and
tops that are so popular in summer and are a very
distinct French look—just ask Pablo Picasso.

TEENS & TWEENS

Teens will have no trouble spending their allowances,
and all future allowances, when they come to Paris.
Many will like the tourist traps along the rue de Rivoli,
with sweatshirts and boxer shorts; others will go for
the *fripes* and vintage clothing sold in markets.

Any young woman over the age of 11 will be
mad for any branch store of **Monoprix,** the big
French dime store—all have tons of fashion at pretty
fair prices, but are actually best for accessories,
grooming items, and small things. Local teens adore
GAP, so ignore that influence on French fashion.
Spanish brands (see above) and even English brands
are also big with teens—the big department stores
have the English franchises for names like **Top Shop**
and **Monsoon,** etc.

Most of the Left Bank is awash with stores that
cater to students, some more fashionable than others. American-style clothes are in vogue with the
French, so be careful . . . those Levis could cost
twice the price. For hot, body-revealing looks,
check out **Kookai** at 1 rue St-Denis, 8–10 place St-
Opportune, and 15 rue St-Placide; and **Morgan** at
165 rue des Rennes on the Left Bank and 81 rue
de Passy on the Right Bank. **H&M** is my best sug-
gestion—this is one of my favorite stores in the
world.

Many mothers prefer to take their teenage kids to the major department stores because the *grands magasins* carry so many different lines in one place. *Note:* They pronounce major brands with a French accent, so GAP is still GAP, but Zara is "Zah-rah"— it took me forever to figure this out. I went to a department store with a girlfriend and her teenage daughter and had no idea what they were talking about for an hour until I discovered that the usual names were being pronounced in a manner totally foreign to me.

Le Shop
3 rue d'Argout, 2e (Métro: Étienne-Marcel).

Don't let the address frighten you, this is easy to find and worth doing, possibly right after you check into your hotel. The store is huge, has loud music blaring at all hours, and hosts quite the teen scene. The clothes are cutting edge; this is where you'll find what's coming up next as well as the crowd that wears it. Plenty of giveaways about clubs and concerts as well. This is one of the most important stores in French fashion; I swear it.

Kiliwatch
84 rue Tiquetonne, 2e (Métro: Étienne-Marcel or Les Halles).

Located near all the hottest shops on rue Étienne Marcel and not far from the Forum Les Halles mall, this store is very deep and stocked with the most amazing combination of new clothes and vintage. The whole look is pulled together for you under one roof and you finally understand what being a teen is all about, at least, fashion wise. A marvelous mix which includes jeans, shoes, outerwear—everything you need to be trendy. Just do it.

Pro Mod
67 rue de Sevrès, 6e (Métro: Sevrès-Babylone).

This French chain is somewhere between GAP and Ann Taylor. It is not that teen-oriented unless your look is BCBG; it's for all female members of the family. In summer, the clothes are perfect for any beach destination. In fall, they are more serious and businesslike, copies of current styles. Everything is priced so you can wear it one season and forget about it the next year. Many branches.

Au Vrai Chic Parisien
8–10 rue Montmartre, 1er; 47 rue du Four, 6e
(Métro: St-Germain-des-Prés).

The Left Bank shop is tiny, but exactly what you want in a Left Bank store: small and cozy, with great stuff at moderate prices. On sale, you'll want to buy armloads of these quasi-teen/quasi-adult fashions.

VESTS
. . . .

There is a certain look going around Paris, mostly for dress-up, but I've also spotted it on waiters at chi-chi restaurants: a brocade vest made from jacquard silk that would make Marie Antoinette feel right at home.

L'Escalier d'Argent
42 Galerie de Montpensier, Jardin du Palais-Royal, 1er (Métro: Palais-Royal).

I found this shop because it's very close to the vintage clothing store Didier Ludot; it's also close spiritually—this store specializes in textiles that were made in the 18th century. They mostly make ties and vests; ties cost about $60. The location only reinforces the magic of the goods in the store; this is Paris at its best.

Favourbrook
Le Village Royal, 25 rue Royale
(Métro: Madeleine).

This is actually an English firm that has moved into the French fabric trend and gone wild for Regency this and that, including men's vests, but also accessories for men and women and all sorts of sumptuous creations. With a business suit, one of these ties would make a very powerful statement.

Chapter Ten

· · · · · · ·

PARIS HOME STYLE

FRENCH STYLE

· ·

Over the years, American home design has been tremendously influenced by French style. Guess what? Now French style is being influenced by Americans! If (when) GAP made bed linen, every teen in France would be on the GAP-wagon. But don't fret, there's still plenty of French-iness to bring home and there's even lots of other international resources to round out the look. In fact, last year Yves Saint Laurent launched several patterns of china.

While country French is now considered classic, my grandmother's idea of decorating had to do with draped silk swags, watered silk, and reproduction Louis. Maybe she knew which Louis it was; surely I did not. Today I live with a jumble of her Louis and my Souleiado mixed with flea market finds from all over France. I'm not alone.

Those going to Paris in search of home furnishings and accessories not only can choose between these two styles but also can check out the newer French designs—everything from the sleek modern designs inspired by Philippe Starck's work to Jacques Grange's modern Shaker look. "Paris in the Thirties" and oceanliner chic are popular modern sleek looks in Paris these days, but there's plenty of everything in a country where a new sofa can cost

$5,000 at a department store, so you might as well know what you are doing.

When shopping for the home in Paris, you can choose French antiques, *brocante,* table linens, or merely candles (wait till you see what the French can do with candles!). For listings of antiques shops, antiques events, *brocante* fairs, and even flea markets, see chapter 9. For everything else, flip this way. You need not do over the house or change your personal style, but please, make room for one lasting souvenir.

SMELLING FRENCH STYLE

Just before a trip to Paris a few years ago, I asked four different girlfriends, as I often do, "Is there anything you need from Paris?" All four of them asked for the same thing—a home scent. Despite all the aromatherapy available in the United States, each woman wanted a different French brand.

Since homescents are such affordable gifts, I think you'll want to know about them, too. Jill wanted **Guerlain** liquid potpourri, which is sold in all Guerlain shops but is not available in the U.S. Michele wanted the most interesting item of all—a lamp with scent from **Lampes Berger.** They have their own small store (14 rue Duphot, 1er; métro: Madeleine) but are also sold in department stores. Another woman wanted a linen spray from a small shop on the rue du Bac, and yet another wanted **Diptyque** candles, which cost about 30% less in France than the U.S. If I asked the same question today, undoubtedly there would be an even longer list. My favorite new product? **L'Occitane** makes a scented liquid that you put in the iron so that whatever you iron takes on the scent of the product—there's lavender and another, apple I think. I tested the lavender and didn't find that it worked great in the iron; it's better in a spritzer as a room spray. However, its such a silly gift that if you are willing to carry it home, spend the $10 and laugh yourself silly.

Even the Hôtel de Crillon has their own room spritz these days; they sell it in the hotel gift shop!

Home Scent Resources

LAMPES BERGER
14 rue Duphot, 9e (Métro: Opera).

Lampes Berger makes oil-burning lanterns, not unlike fashionable genie lamps. They come in dozens of styles and range from $40 to approximately $100. You buy the scented liquid oil separately for approximately $15 per bottle. There are over a dozen different scents. The process of using this product is more complicated than lighting a simple aromatherapy candle, but then, this one works.

If you smoke, look into this product immediately. Your colleagues at work will be much more fond of you after you set one up in your office. Now then, it is technically illegal to carry flammable goods on airplanes, so you may need to get the toll-free number in the U.S. for the liquid. It is totally legal to bring home the lamp itself on a plane.

ESTÈBAN
49 rue de Rennes, 6e (Métro: St-Germain-des-Prés).

One of my favorite suppliers is a firm called Estèban, which now has its own retail shop as well as international distribution all over Europe. Head over to the Left Bank to check their freestanding beauty; the store is organized by the type of scent and in each group all the different methods of scent distribution through diffusers, burners, incense, sprays, scented rocks, and so on. I am sad to report that the firm has discontinued their scented vacuum cleaner powder.

DIPTYQUE
34 blvd. St-Germain, 5e (Métro: Maubert).

As you can possibly tell from this métro stop, the shop is not in the heart of the Left Bank shopping where you think it is. In fact, it's in the 5e, not the 6e, and is not very far from boulevard St-Michel. In short, it's sort of in the middle of nowhere, and you must make a special trip here. If you are not seriously into Diptyque, you can buy the candles at Printemps and save yourself a trip. Otherwise, taxi right here and giggle right back to your hotel with a suitcase filled with gifts and goodies. The tiny store sells the candles, the soaps, and the scents. Candles are a deal at $25 each! Closed on Mondays.

MARIAGE FRÈRES
30 rue du Bourg-Tibourg, 4e (Métro: St-Paul);
13 rue des Grands-Augustins, 6e (Métro: Grands Augustins).

Mariage Frères is one of the most sophisticated and expensive tea houses in Paris; they have developed their own line of tea-scented candles, which are in demand by those willing to spend about $50 for a candle. Also sold in department stores. Very chic gift.

CHRISTIAN TORTU
17 rue des Quatre-Vents, 6e (Métro: Odeon)

Tortu is one of the most famous florists in Paris, sort of the Robert Isabell of the City of Light. He has gone the product route, which makes sense in his line of work, with a wide range of candles and home scents. His brand does not have very good distribution, but the shop is in the Left Bank very close to Souleiado.

SMART SHOPPERS' HOME STYLE

Let's face it, very few people with any smarts at all go to Paris to buy fine and formal antiques. Okay, maybe you're Lord Rothschild and you go to Paris for a few finishing touches for Spencer House. If you're playing in the big leagues, ignore this paragraph. There's no question that Paris has top-of-the-line resources;

but the truth is, if you have ever cast a wary eye at the bottom line, you know that Paris has top-of-the-line prices as well. Even Parisians leave town to buy antiques.

People who have price in mind work the wide network of antiques shows, *brocante* fairs, auctions, flea markets, and weekends in the country that provide not only wonderful entertainment but also far better prices than you'll ever find on the Faubourg St-Honoré. Note that there are a number of annual events that charge an admission price of about 40 F. Don't be turned off by the admission fee; it's usually the sign of a worthwhile event.

While Paris has very serious antiques, real joy—even for those who are shopping to ship—is found in flea markets and alternative retail. Do note, however, that prices may be no lower than at big-time dealers—especially if you don't know what you are doing. People who really want to save money buy their antiques in Belgium (a train ticket to Brussels costs $50).

If you're a serious shopper and plan on doing some big-time buying, keep the following tips in mind:

- Buy from a dealer with an international reputation.
- Prices are usually quoted in dollars once the sales tag is over $5,000.
- There is now a value-added tax on antiques; ask for a détaxe form.
- Make sure you are provided with the appropriate paperwork so that your purchase can leave the country. The French are not going to let any national treasures slip through their fingers.
- Insure for replacement value, not cost.

LE LOOK

Paris has its share of home-style shops that are similar to Pottery Barn—they sell a Euro look at a fair price, and it includes bed linens, textiles for the home, dinnerware, foodstuffs, and tabletop. Prices might not be any better than at home (in fact, they could be higher), but you'll find style galore, not to mention items you can't find elsewhere. I am constantly amazed by this Euro look because it was first mastered by the Englishman Sir Terence Conran (who has done so well in Paris that he has opened a restaurant and another branch of Conran's—these are two different places!).

9/14/00

LE CEDRE ROUGE   ☆ ☆ ☆ ☆ ☆ fabulous

5 rue de Médicis, 6e (Métro: Odéon);
25 rue Duphot, 8e (Métro: Madeleine).

A chain with shops outside Paris, Le Cedre Rouge tends to focus on a country garden look. Affordable style for the masses, but quite classy. Everything is beautifully displayed. There's enough here in terms of tote bags and small items that you may find items for yourself or gifts to take home; this is not just for those who are looking to stock the house.

MIS EN DEMEURE

27 rue du Cherche-Midi, 6e (Métro: St-Germain-des-Prés); 66 ave. Victor Hugo, 16e (Métro: Victor-Hugo).

Sort of a hipper, more French Conran's. On my last visit, there were lots of country tabletop looks (items made with twigs) and papier-mâché Christmas ornaments. Some items border on the fabulous; others are rather ordinary. But when you first step inside and see all the glassware, linens, furniture, and lamps displayed together, you will think it's quite extraordinaire.

GENEVIÈVE LETHU

95 rue de Rennes, 6e (Métro: St-Germain-des-Prés); 12 rue de Passy, 16e (Métro: La Muette).

This designer has a boutique in Printemps Maison, Galeries Lafayette, and Bon Marché, or you can check out any of her several freestanding stores in

Paris. Did I say several? There are about a dozen shops in Paris and maybe 50 scattered across France. There are also shops in the Far East and much of Italy. As of yet, there's only one in North America, and it's in Montreal. So shop in Paris or buy a franchise to this tabletop and kitchen shop and bring her to America.

Lethu does what I consider to be some of the most refreshing (and affordable) tabletop in Paris: Her use of color is bold and extravagant, and her prints are exotic, without being beyond the pale. She mixes contemporary tabletop and country looks so elegantly, that even a formal setting will work. The tablecloths are my favorite, but there's much more to choose from.

THE CONRAN SHOP
8 blvd. Madeleine, 2e (Métro: Madeleine);
117 rue du Bac, 7e (Métro: Sèvres-Babylone).

Despite the fact that this is a British shop, Sir Terence Conran is an expert on French design. The new store is even more exciting than the Left Bank store, partly because it's new but also because it has a cafe. Both stores are filled with tons of whimsy and charm. Just browse and breathe the magic: There are books, luggage, foodstuffs, gifts, home style, housewares, pens, and paper goods, etc.

HABITAT
8 rue pont de Neuf, 1er (Métro: Pont Neuf); 45 rue de Rennes, 6e (Métro: St-Germain-des-Prés); 12 blvd. de la Madeleine, 9e (Métro: Madeleine); CC Montparnasse, 14e (Métro: Montparnasse); 35 avenue Wagram, 17e (Métro: Wagram).

Although both were developed by Sir Terence Conran, Conran and Habitat are not the same store. In fact, these days they are no longer even similar. Still, there's a new flagship right near the department store Samaritaine, so have a look for yourself.

Habitat sells lower-end goods and is not my idea of something you'll want to plan your trip to Paris around.

SPECIALTY LOOKS

. . . .

There are a number of chicer-than-thou shops that are so unique and so fabulously French, you have to visit them, if only to browse.

TERRITOIRE
30 rue Boissy d'Anglas, 8e (Métro: Madeleine).

I'm not at all certain how to categorize this shop. It sells a look that evokes English breeziness, lighthouses along the French Atlantic coast, and American summer cottages with Adirondack chairs on the lawn. Many Parisians summer on the French Atlantic coast. This is their shop. There are books and gifts and some tabletop. It's a terrific store in a great part of town. Enjoy it.

MAISON DE FAMILLE
29 rue St-Sulpice, 6e (Métro: St-Sulpice
or Mabillon); place Madeleine, 8e
(Métro: Madeleine).

This is almost a multiple, since there are now a few stores in Paris and several in the provinces. And why not?! This is a terrific store with a wonderful look and a soothing blend of English and Euro and *chinoiserie* that will seduce you.

What I love about these stores is what they look like and what they feel like. What I don't like is that a shopper might pay high prices for British, American, or imported from elsewhere. I can easily find similar goods at home for less. But put it all together and you have a serious browse with some drooling.

LA TUILE LOUP
35 rue Daubenton, 5e (Métro: Cencier Daubenton).

Just trust me on this one. This shop is brimming with country French charm. It's worth the slightly out-of-the-way location, since you can easily wander into the 6e arrondissement from here. You may wish to call first to be sure they're open before making the trek. ☎ 1/47-07-28-90.

ROSEMARIE SCHULTZ ✸✸✸ *Outstanding*
30 rue Boissy d'Anglas, 8e (Métro: Madeleine).

This shop is quite close to Territoire, so be sure to see them both. Emotionally, however, the two shops are worlds apart. Schultz is a German designer and possibly a florist—her shop sells fabrics, pillows, sachets, and flowers. This is one of the most imaginative and truly special shops I've ever been in. Once I found this little gold string tied with shells and paper flowers, which may sound silly as I describe it, but is the most beautiful piece of whimsy I've ever seen. I hang it from my front door every spring.

There are "dream pillows," which are silken and almost medieval in look and feel; they cost between $30 to $50 apiece. Everything in the shop has texture and can be experienced through multiple senses: touch, smell, and sight. There are even items for under $10. If you check out only one new address this trip, this is it.

AGNÉS COMAR
7 ave. George V, 8e (Métro: Alma-Marceau or George V).

This is another perfect shop with much to see and touch, although its location is sort of off by itself and should be combined with a visit to this part of town. The shop is small and chic and very "in" with local ladies.

CATHERINE MEMMI
32 rue St-Sulpice, 6e (Métro: Odéon).

OK, who says I won't cave and bow to pressure? Every maven I know loves this store. I am not impressed, but since you will pass it anyway, perhaps a look-see will make you feel that you've properly "done" the scene. The look is very minimalist, which isn't my personal thing. There are clean lines, luxury fabrics, and neutral tones galore.

FABRIC SHOWROOMS

If you are a member of the trade or simply want to view showrooms, you are welcome to browse in decorator showrooms to get ideas. Don't be surprised if many of the home furnishings fabric suppliers want nothing to do with you unless you quickly brandish a business card that proves you are a designer. Most showrooms have U.S. representatives or distributors, and they do not want to undercut their own agents.

This leads to an even bigger point to bear in mind: You may find these same items are the same price (or even less) in the U.S. Mom, who ran a design firm in Manhattan, always traveled with business cards, which she presented—not when browsing but during final negotiations on price or when the bill was presented. In flawless French, she then asked for a 10% trade discount. It usually worked.

You may also want to negotiate for the détaxe refund, for which you must qualify when you arrange to ship outside the country. Many firms will not ship to the U.S. at the risk of offending their American agents. Ask when you are talking turkey. Finally, remember that a huge amount of "French style" is actually British. Some of the best fabric showrooms in Paris showcase British goods! If you discover that your favorite item is British, save money by buying it in the U.K.

PASSEMENTERIE & RIBBON

I buy bits of *passementerie*—fringe and braid—at the flea markets, but if you are decorating your home and willing to splurge on the best, Paris has several serious sources.

Passementerie de l'Ile de France
11 rue Trousseau, 4e (Métro: Ledru-Rollin).

This is just past Bastille, but right on Napoleon in terms of style. They open at 9am but are closed Saturday and Sunday.

Au Bon Gout
1 rue Guisarde, 16e (Métro: La Muette).

This store's name means "With Good Taste"; they aren't kidding. They sell braids and buttons and all the things I love. You'll find them at the low end of the Passy district, so combine a visit here with a trip to the neighborhood. Couture buttons are sold here, but there are no CC buttons.

Claude Declerq
15 rue Étienne Marcel, 2e (Métro: Étienne-Marcel).

This designer makes new *passementerie* following old color schemes and methods; he will do custom work to match.

Marie-Pierre Boitard
8 place du Palais-Bourbon, 7e (Métro: Invalides).

A good resource for simple *passementerie* in a chic, totally Parisian environment.

TABLETOP & GIFTS
. . . .

Every place you look in Paris, there's another adorable shop selling gifts or tabletop. No one sets a table like the French. The department stores often have exhibits or even classes in table arts; you can take notes—or pictures.

MURIEL GRATEAU
Galerie de Valois, Jardins du Palais-Royal, 1er (Métro: Palais-Royal).

Muriel once designed ready-to-wear for Charles Jourdan; now she's nestled into her own place. There are linens in more colors than the rainbow and beautiful textiles. Her linen napkins come in 36 different colors!

EN ATTENDANT LES BARBARES
50 rue Étienne Marcel, 2e (Métro: Étienne-Marcel or Palais-Royal).

Great shop for cutting-edge chic gifts. I'm most impressed with the items (especially candlesticks) made from resin. Stop by if only to gawk. At Victoires.

DINERS EN VILLE
27 rue de Varenne, 7e (Métro: Rue du Bac).

If you take my advice and stroll the rue du Bac, you will find this store on your own and congratulate yourself for being such a clever bunny. This is a small, cramped, crowded two-room store filled with the kind of French tabletop you and I adore. There isn't anything in this store I wouldn't buy. The address shouldn't throw you. It's on the corner of rue de Varenne and rue du Bac.

ART DOMESTIQUE ANCIEN
231 rue St-Honoré, 1er (Métro: Tuileries).

This is an antiques store specializing in kitchen and household items—it's fabulous. It's also a little bit hidden; you must walk into the courtyard in order to find it. It's worth doing.

LA DAME BLANCHE
186 rue de Rivoli, 1er (Métro: Tuileries).

Nestled between the tourist traps on the rue de Rivoli is this tiny shop selling reproduction faience, Limoges boxes, and Louis-style porcelains.

LAURE JAPY
34 rue du Bac, 7e (Métro: rue du Bac).

The first time I saw this shop I mentally wrote it off as another Geneviève Lethu shop. Don't make that mistake! Just because the store specializes in color, it's not the same as Lethu! This shop is more up-scale, more sophisticated, and, *mais oui,* more expensive. The porcelains are made by Ginori in Italy.

SIÈCLE
24 rue du Bac, 7e (Métro: Rue du Bac).

It took me two trips to Paris to find this shop, not that it's hard—I just walked the wrong direction from the rue du Bac métro stop and had so much fun, I never found my way back. The shop is between the river and the métro, so you can actually walk across the bridge on rue du Bac and never go near the métro station. It's a small shop, not one I would have found on my own. I discovered it while browsing the pages of *Elle,* looking for a present to give my girlfriend (and former editor) Linda. *Elle* featured a photo of the most wonderful pair of salad servers and gave this shop as a resource for where to buy them. Although the servers cost over $100, they were so French, so chic, and so fabulous that I just knew they were perfect. Everything else in this store falls into this category. I saw another set of salad servers that I liked more, but they were pale green sharkskin and sold for over $500. Rarefied, but fabulous.

MARÉCHAL
232 rue de Rivoli, 1er (Métro: Concorde or Tuileries).

At first glance, this looks like a tourist trap selling perfume, and not a particularly memorable one at that. Still, there's a reason to stop in. Downstairs, there's a great selection of Limoges boxes. Ask for their catalog, which guarantees the French bargain price and includes mailing to the U.S.

Gail + Jack on last day in Paris
our favorite not losted ! In
same area

KITCHEN STYLE

Paris is rightfully renowned for its table arts; luckily for tourists, there are a number of kitchen supply houses within a block or two of each other, so you can see a lot without going out of your way. Price is not the object here; selection is everything. Please note that most of the kitchen shops open at 9am (sometimes earlier), so you can extend your shopping day by beginning with these resources. The "kitchen neighborhood" is a matter of a block and a cross street; you can easily start at one and walk to the others.

A. SIMON *Here   but closed*
36–38 & 48 rue Montmartre, 2e (Métro: Étienne-Marcel or Les Halles).

A major supplier of kitchen and cooking supplies for over 100 years, this store is conveniently located down the street from the Forum Les Halles mall and the great shopping street Étienne Marcel. You can buy everything from dishes to menus here; I buy white paper doilies by the gross—they have many sizes and shapes not available in the U.S.—at fair prices. Touch everything; this is a wonderland of gadgets and goodies. Remember, rue Montmartre is not in Montmartre; it is near Forum des Halles.

DEHILLERIN
18–20 rue Coquillière, 1er (Métro: Musée-du-Louvre or Les Halles).

Perhaps the most famous cookware shop in Paris, Dehillerin has been selling cookware for over 100 years. They mostly sell to the trade, but you can poke around and touch the copper, cast iron, tools, gadgets, and more. Or someone may even help you—try out your French; it goes a long way here. And they open at 8am! They're closed for lunch, so show up early.

LA CORPO
19 rue Montmartre, 1er (Métro: Étienne-Marcel or Les Halles).

This one isn't my favorite, but it, too, has a vast selection of kitchenwares, including much equipment. While you may be tempted, remember that electric gadgets are a no-no. Still there are lots of pots and pans and supplies that are very enticing.

DUTHILLEUL & MINART *Snooty - not too good*
14 rue de Turbigo, 1er (Métro: Étienne-Marcel).

This shop sells professional clothing for chefs, kitchen staff, waiters, etc. It would be a great resource for creative fashion freaks or teens. You can buy anything from kitchen clogs to aprons; a *toque* costs $12 while the *veste chef* is $30. There are various styles of aprons (which make good gifts) and many wine-related items. You'll find it right round the corner from the other kitchen shops and right at the Étienne-Marcel métro stop.

MORA
13 rue Montmartre, 1er (Métro: Étienne-Marcel or Les Halles).

Similar to A. Simon, but with more utensils (over 5,000 in stock), Morda has a salon for bakery goods that sells *fèves* in small (and large) packages. It has a huge paper goods section as well.

CANDLES

One of the first stores in Paris that ever bowled me over with just how clever the French can be was a candle shop, **Point à La Ligne.** Now that line is available at any French department store and in the U.S. Still, when you wander Paris, you will find extravagance and wit, often at an affordable price, at shops selling candles.

I now travel with my own candles, which I light in the bathroom while I soak in the tub or place by my bedside while I read. Do remember to snuff out the candle before you go to sleep! I used to buy **Rigaud** candles at my favorite duty-free shop, **Catherine,** but I now use other brands since I am always testing what's new.

Rigaud was the leading brand of scented candles when no one else was into this notion, and they are still at the top of the market in terms of status and quality. Most of the big fragrance houses (**Guerlain, Manuel Canovas, L'Occitaine, Roger & Gallet**) sell scented candles in addition to perfume or soaps. For more home scent resources, see "Smelling French Style," earlier in this chapter. The listing below specializes in novelty candles, not scented candles.

Point à la Ligne
67 ave. Victor Hugo, 16e (Métro: Victor-Hugo); 25 rue de Varenne, 7e (Métro: Rue du Bac).

Probably the most famous of the contemporary candle makers in Paris, Point à la Ligne has candle sculptures as well as ultra-skinny, enormously chic long tapers that make sensational birthday or celebration candles on a cake. In sum, they have all sorts of fabulous things. Their products can be found in all French department stores.

DELUXE LOGO STYLE
. . . .

Want a chic souvenir? Purchase something from a famous French address. There are several shops, cafes, and even tourist attractions selling attractive logo merchandise in Paris.

Salon du Thé Bernardaud
11 rue Royale, 8e (Métro: Concorde).

This is tricky because there's an entire Bernardaud china shop at this address. What I'm suggesting you

purchase are the Bernardaud logo souvenirs, in porcelain, that are sold at the front counter of the tea shop.
I have the white, gold, and celadon ashtray, 50 F.

BOUTIQUE CRILLON
Hôtel de Crillon, 10 place de la Concorde, 8e
(Métro: Concorde); 17 rue de la Paix, 2e
(Métro: Tuileries or Opéra).

The Crillon is one of the most famous hotels in Paris.
Even if you aren't staying here, you may want to
visit for tea. Or to shop. Because the hotel is part of
a chain of hotels (Concorde) that's owned by a famous French family (heard the name Taittinger before?), their gift shop sells products made by other
companies in which the Taittinger family has an interest. Accordingly, you'll find an amazing array of
French luxury goods—Annick Goutal and Baccarat,
to name just a few. They also have Crillon logo goods
that you wouldn't dare steal from your room—robes,
slippers, note cards, etc.

The Crillon actually has two boutiques: one in
the hotel and one along the rue de la Paix. The merchandise ranges from glassware and porcelain to
handbags. Some items are decorated with the hotel
crest; everything is beautiful to look at. Prices usually begin around $30, but wait: They have napkin
rings for $10. Gorgeous ones, too.

Even without its association with the Hôtel de
Crillon, this would be a good group of shops. Better yet, the gift shop located within the hotel is open
on Sunday and stays open late during the week.

BOUTIQUE DU CAFÉ DE FLORE
26 rue St-Benoît, 6e (Métro: St-Germain-des-
Prés).

The Café de Flore is one of the three famous Paris
bistros on the Left Bank (the other two are Les Deux
Magots and Brasserie Lipp), but so far the Café de
Flore is the only one that has opened its own gift
shop. The tiny store is around the corner from the

cafe and just adorable. You get a free chocolate when you wander in (you may buy a box), and you can choose from dishes, serving pieces, paper goods, and all sorts of gift items. Rumor has it that this store may close because of the value of the real estate, but you will be in the neighborhood anyway, so have a look-see.

COMPTIOR DE LA TOUR D'ARGENT
2 rue du Cardinal Lemoine, 5e (Métro: Maubert-Mutualité).

La Tour d'Argent is one of the most famous restaurants in Paris and has withstood the comings and goings of new rivals. Whether you eat there or not, you may want to shop next door where you can get a picnic to go or a gift basket to take home. There are also ashtrays, crystal, china, and more.

CHINA, CRYSTAL & SILVER

French crystal and porcelain have been the backbone of French luxe for centuries. Prices can be fair in France, but the shipping will kill you. Come with a price list from home because a sale in the U.S. may wipe out any French savings.

BACCARAT
30 bis, rue de Paradis, 10e (Métro: Château d'Eau); 11 place de la Madeleine, 8e (Métro: Concorde).

Baccarat has two headquarters—its factory in the 10e arrondissement, which has a museum and a gigantic shop (no seconds, sorry), and the boutique amid the high-rent district of the 8e arrondissement. Prices are the same at either venue.

Finding the shop at the factory can be confusing the first time you try it, since you must walk through the company's offices and head up some stairs to reach it. Once up the stairs, the shop is to your left.

It's hard to distinguish it from the museum that sprawls in front of you. In both, long tables are laid out with merchandise in rows—you may touch. You can even try on the earrings. Whether or not you can walk out with your choice is up to the gods. Baccarat is often 6 to 7 months behind in its orders, so if they don't have what you want in the shop, they will send it to you . . . someday. Prices are not negotiable. They ship anywhere in the world and will mail-order. If something breaks in your package, Baccarat will replace the item. The selection in the sublimely located rue Royale/place de la Madeleine shop is not as overwhelming, so you won't have as much fun.

BERNARDAUD

This is a great street. One-Vendor stores

11 rue Royale, 8e (Métro: Concorde).

If you're making the rounds of the hoity-toity tabletop houses, don't miss Bernardaud, which means Limoges china. Especially impressive are the newer contemporary designs, with their art deco roots. If you don't have to ship, you can save over New York prices. The tea shop is located farther back in the passage.

ROBERT HAVILAND ET C. PARLON CRISTALLERIES
ROYALES DE CHAMPAGNE

*Village Royal, 25 rue Royale, 8e
(Métro: Madeleine).*

This shop is a little bit hidden, and very, very fancy. It's best not to bring the kids. Check out the way in which the printed patterns are mixed and matched—it's the essence of French chic.

CRISTAL LALIQUE

11 rue Royale, 8e (Métro: Concorde).

One glance at Lalique's crystal door and there's no doubt that you've entered one of the wonders of the world. Get a look at the Lalique-designed Olympic

medals created for the 1992 Winter Games. The rue
Royale headquarters is sort of like a museum: People
come to stare more than they shop. The prices are
the same as at factory sources on the rue de Paradis,
by the way, so don't think you may beat the tags
here. Besides, you get to apply for détaxe, everyone
is friendly and speaks English, and they ship to the
U.S. This is an excellent case of a brand name that
has expanded like mad—there's everything from jewelry to handbags to belts to perfumes.

DAUM
4 rue de la Paix, 2e (Métro: Opéra).

There's a lot more to Daum than large-size lead crystal cars, and this two-level shop is a great place to
discover how much more. The extra room allows
them to display inventive glass art and colored-glass
pieces that will surely become collector's items one
day.

PUIFORCAT
2 ave. Montaigne, 8e (Métro: Alma-Marceau).

If you believe in studying only the best, here's where
you can get your graduate degree in fine French silver. Puiforcat was founded in 1820 and dedicated
since that date to making shoppers swoon, and the
most collectible pieces are currently from the late
1920s and 1930s.

PARADISE & MORE

The street for wholesale crystal, china, and tabletop in Paris is the rue de Paradis, where the
headquarters of many big names are located. There
are just a few catches: This is a low-rent district, but
prices are no different than in the high-rent districts.
It's a bit of a walk from the nearest métro stop in a
not-so-interesting area (but it's not dangerous), or

an $8 taxi ride from the 1er arrondissement. It's fun, true, but you might prefer a quick visit to Cristal Vendôme instead.

If you decide to head for rue de Paradis, be sure to take in the **Baccarat Museum.** Then just browse from one shop to the next. Prices are generally fixed by the factories; there is little negotiation. After a few shops, they'll all look alike to you. Many of the stores carry other European brands; all have a bridal registry.

CRISTAL VENDÔME
1 rue de Castiglione, 1er (Métro: Concorde).

Right underneath the Hôtel Inter-Continental on rue Castiglione is a factory-direct store that will even ship to the U.S. (You can phone in an order once you have bought in person, a service the factory will not offer.) Various lines are sold here, which makes the shopping easy: Baccarat, Lalique, Daum, and more. The store offers tax-free prices, which means they are the same as at the airport. I priced a Lalique necklace and found it to be almost half the U.S. price.

EDITIONS PARADIS
29 rue de Paradis, 10e (Métro: Château-d'Eau).

This is an enormous source with so much stuff that you'll be nervous if you are carrying a big floppy handbag. It's fancy, with table settings on display to give you ideas. And, of course, they carry small Limoges boxes—the perfect collectible.

LA TISANIÈRE PARADIS
21 rue de Paradis, 10e (Métro: Château-d'Eau).

A country-style resource on a street filled with more traditional showrooms, this porcelain shop has stacks of kitchenware and tabletop at prices that are fair. Some promotional items are downright cheap. Much fun.

LIMOGES-UNIC
58 rue de Paradis, 10e (Métro: Château-d'Eau).

In spite of the name, this factory does not sell Limoges exclusively. It's merely one of the bigger, better-stocked traditional stores on the rue de Paradis. Locals consider this the anchor of the neighborhood, although there are other similar shops. They will ship; of course, you may apply for the détaxe.

PROVENÇAL FABRICS

. . . .

If you aren't headed for Provence, Paris has a selection of traditional country French prints.

SOULEIADO
78 rue de Seine, 6e (Métro: Mabillon); Forum des Halles, 1er (Métro: Châtelet); 85 ave. Paul-Doumer, 16e (Métro: La Muette).

You have to be a real Pierre Deux freak to know that Pierre Deux is the name of the American franchise for these prints, but is not the name of the company in Europe. So remember the name Souleiado—which will get you happily through France.

The flagship rue de Seine shop, a great shop, is everything it should be. You will be in country French heaven. Be sure to see all parts of the shop (there are two separate rooms); the main shop winds around another showroom in the far back, where more fabrics are sold by the meter. There is a showroom for the trade next door. The Passy shop on avenue Paul-Doumer is almost as good, but is not quite as quaint. Nonetheless, it is chocka-block with the look we love—plenty of fabrics plus ready-sewn clothing and all the table-top in the world.

LES OLIVADES
*1 rue de Tournon, 6e (Métro: St-Sulpice or
Odéon); 25 rue de l'Annonciation, 16e
(Métro: La Muette).*

I have been told that Les Olivades was started in the
mid-1970s when someone in the Souleiado hierar-
chy departed and started a new firm. Indeed, Les
Olivades reminds me of the Pierre Deux/Souleiado
look, although the colors are more muted—pastels,
and the like. Les Olivades sells much the same
merchandise—fabric by the yard, placemats, tablecloths, napkins, umbrellas, travel bags, etc.

While the goods are not cheap, they are about
30% less expensive than Souleiado in France. The
Right Bank store is small and a little hard to find—
it's on a small street directly behind the rue de Passy.
The Left Bank shop is almost directly across the
street from Souleiado.

BED LINENS

The sizes of continental beds differ from their American counterparts. They're measured in metric, but
why should that stop you? Just bring your tape
measure. Or, if price is truly no object, have Porthault
custom-make your sheets.

D. PORTHAULT
*18 ave. Montaigne, 8e (Métro: Alma-Marceau);
370 rue du Faubourg St-Honoré, 8e
(Métro: Concorde).*

Porthault was making fancy bed linens with pretty
colored flowers on them long before the real world
was ready for patterned sheets or the notion that a
person could spend $1,000 on their bedclothes and
still be able to sleep at night.

There are two Porthault lines of goods for sale
in America: One is identical to what you can buy in

France and just costs more in the U.S.; the other is contracted by the Porthault family and is available only in the U.S. The French laminated products are not sold in the U.S.; the American wallpaper is not sold in France. One Porthault saleswoman swore that our pattern was not "theirs" because she was unfamiliar with the American wallpapers. The Montaigne shop does do a whopper of a sale in January, during which they unload everything at half the retail price, or less! You cannot phone in orders from the U.S.

You may think that Porthault is totally beyond you and hurry by to avoid temptation; I beg you to reconsider. There are many little accessories and gift items that are affordable, fun, and speak volumes when presented. I always travel with my Porthault shower cap because it makes me smile and beats those plastic jobs supplied by hotels. I gave my niece a traditional Porthault bib when she was born: $25. You have to know the Porthault name to appreciate items like these, but for those in the know, this could be your gift headquarters. They wrap.

There is a teeny shop on the rue du Faubourg St-Honoré, I guess it's there to be more convenient to madame on her next spree, but the shop is very tiny and doesn't have the selection or the feel of the mother store . . . or the factory shop.

If you are headed for Lille, note that discontinued prints cost a fraction of their regular price at the Porthault factory outside Lille. If you are a fan, this is a trip you will never forget. I am still drooling; thankfully I bought a lot of bibs.

DESCAMPS
44 rue du Passy, 16e (Métro: La Muette).

Descamps no longer has its own stores in the U.S., but their products are sold in higher-end American department stores. You may not find prices much better in Paris. Still, every time I visit Paris, I buy a few items (those oblong terry-cloth bath mittens) that aren't available in the U.S. I also buy my Primrose Bordier (that's the designer's name) home scent here. Check out the starfish for 48 F. It's a perfect small gift to give yourself. There are truly hundreds of Descamps shops in France; there's one in every trading area in Paris.

YVES DELORME

Le Louvre des Antiquaires, 2 place du Palais-Royal, 1er (Métro: Palais-Royal).

Yves Delorme makes linen that is sold under the Palais-Royal label in the U.S., and he has his own boutique on the street level of the Louvre des Antiquaires, along with shops in Monaco and Lyons. This is luxury linen that isn't as wildly priced as other premium French luxury linens (such as Porthault and Descamps) but is still chic and mildly (not wildly) expensive. Bed linen freaks won't care about the prices; there's a certain French charm to the total look that makes it a must-have.

OLIVIER DESFORGES

26 blvd. Raspail, 7e (Métro: Sèvres-Babylone).

This is Descamps's main competitor, with fewer stores in France and none (to my knowledge) in the U.S. Sometimes, the line has a country look to it. There are other locations in Paris; this one is a can't-miss.

CHIFF-TIR

1 rue Duphot, 1er (Métro: Madeleine).

This is a bargain basement selling mostly everyday linens. Often, you can find something unique enough that it will look right in your home. Once taken out of the context of the junky store, the item may sparkle. This is a chain, with other stores around Paris; I usually go to the one that's closest to Madeleine.

BLANCORAMA
12 rue St-Placide, 6e (Métro: Sèvres-Babylone).

This tiny shop is a regular haunt of mine because I always like to see what's in store at the discount shops that line the street. While there is bed linen in the shop, I buy bath mats here—very traditional French rugs for 50 F each.

Chapter Eleven

. . . .

PARIS SHOPPING TOURS

TOUR ONE: THE DO-IT-ALL-IN-A-DAY TOUR

This tour not only takes you by most of the best shopping in Paris but gives you a good workout as well. Since some of these stores are quite expensive, you may find yourself mostly window-shopping. If that's the case, you can complete this tour in half a day.

Begin the tour at Printemps Maison on boulevard Haussmann. They open at 9:35am. Remember to save your purchase receipts so you can claim your détaxe at the end of the shopping tour. Don't mind the perfume and makeup on the street level, just get a free spritz and take the escalator up. Shop the three floors of housewares, being careful to ignore the non-French merchandise, of which there can be a lot.

Now head over to Galeries Lafayette. Pick up the free guide to the store (at the Welcome Desk). Check out the stained-glass ceiling, the souvenirs (why not?), the tabletop and housewares area, and the designer floors. You might want to take notes on the new styles and trends you see.

Although you can spend a week at Galeries Lafayette, when you're ready to move on head for Lafayette Gourmet, which is upstairs in the Men's Store. When you're done here, you can get a quick fix at Bouchara, a fabric store, now on the far side of Galeries Lafayette main store. This is one of my favorite stores in France. All of these shops are on boulevard Haussmann, except for Prisunic, which is located in an alley behind Printemps.

Now then, there's this little tiny pedestrian street called Havre-Chaumartin. It's very, very junky looking, but who cares, right? This is a super little alley, especially if you like low-end junk. If you are the Chanel/Armani type, you may not be nearly as enthusiastic as I am. This is the street where Monoprix is, as well as several other branches of French multiples that sell copies of the latest looks at moderate prices. There's a street vendor back here some days who sells old PTT calendars, and there's the back entrance into the little mall, **Passage du Havre,** with more multiples and a big **FNAC.** In short, everything you need in life is in this little area.

I can spend the better part of a day in these resources alone, but I can also trim it down to a few quick hours and be out by lunchtime. It's your call.

If you want to do this slowly and carefully, then you will make a day of it—eating in any of the many restaurants in the department stores or at **Toastissimo** in the basement of the Passage du Havre mall. If you zip through all of this by lunch, continue on:

Hit rue Tronchet and walk toward the Seine; you are headed toward place de la Madeleine, which you will reach in a block. There are a number of fancy food shops around here; surely you have time to press your nose to the glass at **Fauchon** (26 place de la Madeleine) and **Hédiard** (no. 21).

If it's lunchtime or even a little before (beat the crowds), try the famous tearoom **Ladurée** on the rue Royale. After you pass the place de la Madeleine, the rue Tronchet becomes rue Royale. Ladurée looks like the kind of tearoom your grandmother would take you to; they have desserts galore, but also salads and omelets at moderate prices—plus a great-looking clientele.

From there, it's time to hit an American-style mall that's filled with small, fancy boutiques, **Les Trois Quartiers.** It may lack authentic French charm, but it gives you a quick look at some fast fashion. I like **Chacok, Tehen,** and even **The Body Shop.**

There's a tiny little knife of a street that runs alongside Les Trois Quartiers called rue Duphot. At no. 25, right across the street from the mall, is **Le Cedre Rouge,** a French country-style home furnishings store that's worth a peek. But wait, there's another knife-slice street, rue Vignon, which is another favorite. *Note:* There are several plus-size shops right at this corner. Walk on rue Vignon one time or cross over to the far side of the place de la Madeleine, where the famed **Lucas-Carton** restaurant is located. Look for the discount perfume shop. This shop is on the outside of a *passage*. If you walk through the *passage*, shopping as hard as you can, you'll soon reach the rue Boissy d'Anglas, another tiny Parisian street known only to locals. There are several great stores back here, among them **Territoire** (no. 30).

Shop your way to the rue du Faubourg St-Honoré, and *voilà*, you are at the door of **Hermès!** This is one of the swankiest streets in Paris; you will want to window-shop, if nothing else.

Now then, if you took the option of walking on rue Vignon, you saw plenty of cute little shops, a branch of Tarte Julie where I always eat quiche (I like the Julie quiche best). You passed by Mephisto and their famed walking shoes, the honey store, a cutie-pie kids shop, and all sorts of things before you tucked over toward Madeleine to rejoin this tour. Get macaroons at Ladurée and prowl the rue du Faubourg St-Honoré right where it begins at the corner of the rue Royale.

Phew!

TOUR TWO: SHOPPING CHAMPS TOUR

Start this tour at the top of the Champs-Elysées near L'Étoile at the new **Louis Vuitton** store and walk toward Rond Point, where the Champs-Elysées meets the avenue Montaigne.

Turn right onto the avenue Montaigne and stroll the entire length of the avenue (only 2 or 3 blocks). I like the side of the street away from the Arc de Triomphe, since it has more shops, but you should plan on prowling both sides of this street. Don't miss **Joseph, Christian Lacroix,** and **Porthault.**

When you get to the end of avenue Montaigne, you have choices: You can either double back and hit the other side of the street, ending up at Rond Point, or you can follow the signs to the *bateau mouche* and collapse on a boat tour of Paris while you wave to the Princess Diana memorial. Or, hop on the métro at Alma-Marceau, conveniently located right at the end of avenue Montaigne. Luckily, there's a cafe inside the **Joseph Store** (no. 14), so you can sit down and think it over before deciding what you want to do.

But you are the champ and you're headed back to the Champs-Elysées. You've obviously chosen the other side of the street (smart move); don't forget that downstairs at **Nina Ricci** there's a bargain basement filled with couture gowns, and don't forget all the little shops that are originals, such as the **Caron** perfume shop.

When you get back to the Champs-Elysées, you will cross it and shop the far side, ignoring places like The Disney Store and concentrating on **Virgin Megastore** (buy Johnny Hallyday here) **Monoprix,** and **FNAC** (more Johnny). You are exhausted, so after you visit **Sephora,** head right up into the lobby of the **Marriott Hotel** for tea, drinks, or a meal.

After shopping your heart out and absorbing so much visual splendor, take a peaceful walk through the green paths that lead toward the American Embassy and the place de la Concorde. Now it's time for your reward for not buying too much: Hit the gift shop at the **Hôtel de Crillon.**

If you're not staying at the Crillon (well, maybe next trip), you'll note that a few meters beyond the hotel's entrance is the Concorde métro stop. *Voilà!*

TOUR THREE: MAKE MINE A DISCOUNT TOUR

This tour uses a lot of taxis, which may seem antithetical to bargain shopping. But when you see how much time they save you and the kind of bargains you can get on designer and big-name merchandise on this tour, using this mode of transportation may strike you as positively thrifty by the time you're finished.

Begin your day with a croissant or two loaded with jam (you'll need the sugar) and a strong café au lait. Wear your most comfortable shoes and take the métro to Trocadéro. Give yourself time for a quick glance at the Eiffel Tower, but don't take too long. Remember, you're in Paris to shop!

Head for the **Dépôts-vent de Passy** and visit Catherine Baril's shop on the rue du Tour—a resale shop specializing in designer clothing with an emphasis on Chanel. You could shop the rue Passy from there, but this is the bargain tour, remember?

Take a taxi to **Réciproque**, the grandmother of Paris resale shops. Now you are French. Réciproque begins at 95 rue de la Pompe; don't miss their other shops up the street or the fact that there are clothes upstairs and downstairs in this temple to designer resale. Prices are average to high, depending on the age and condition of the garment and the designer. There's a virtual library of Sonia Rykiel on one rack.

If you can manage all of your packages, hail a taxi now. If not, head back to your hotel, unload, and grab a bite to eat.

Have a taxi take you to **Église d'Alésia-St-Pierre de Mantrouge.** Walk along the rue d'Alésia, where you will find the **Sonia Rykiel** outlet store almost immediately (no. 64). Check out the kids' clothing at **Cacharel Stock** (no. 114), **Fabrice Karel Stock** for knits (no. 105), **Stock 2** for Daniel Hechter clothing (no. 92), and a few of the other stock shops. Ignore the regularly priced stores; this is the bargain day.

After all those bargains you may need a pit stop or a trip back to your hotel to unload your packages.

For your discount afternoon you can either do some more Left Bank shopping or get out of the métro at Sèvres-Babylone. Dash into the indoor flea market at **Le Bon Marché**, the department store, to round out your bargain hunting by negotiating with a few of the 35 antiques dealers here. Or you can walk along the rue St-Placide, which is filled with even more stock shops. Be sure to check out **Mouton â Cinq Pattes** (nos. 8, 14, and 18), with three different shops selling kids', men's, and women's designer clothes at discount. Things are in bins or crammed onto racks, but there are big names and big savings to be had.

Finally, walk on the rue de Rennes toward the Commercial Centre Montparnasse, which you will pass as you head into **Inno.** This dime store, with a grocery in the basement, has afforded me some of my best bargains in Paris. Picky people with maps may wish to note that the rue de Rennes becomes the rue Depart after you've crossed the boulevard Montparnasse at the base of the Commercial Centre.

Now it's time to pop into the métro at boulevard Montparnasse and take it to Concorde. After you've alighted, walk 2 blocks along the rue de Rivoli until you get to rue Castiglione. At no. 7 is **Catherine**— my regular perfume discount shop. Well, who says a discount day can't end on a high note?

If you didn't opt to continue on the Left Bank, you can head for St-Paul and the string of discount jobbers on the rue du Vielle Temple starting right at the corner of rue Rivoli. *Bonne chance!*

TOUR FOUR: LEFT BANK IN A DAY TOUR

The best way to see the Left Bank is to live there. Failing that, try to spend the best part of a day there. Get an early start because starting at noon the Left

Bank's neighborhoods take on the hustle and bustle of any busy part of town. Early morning has a slowness to it that allows you to absorb the vibes.

Here's an optional pretour for the early birds in the group: Any early morning but Monday, start off at the street market in the rue de Buci, right behind the church St-Germain-des-Prés. Get out of the métro at St-Germain-des-Prés and hang a left on the rue de Seine. This will take you right into the thick of the street market. After you've checked out all of the wonderful fruits, vegetables, and fresh flowers, grab a table at Café de Flore. The awnings have the name clearly marked; you can't miss it. There's a kiosk just past it if you need your morning newspaper. There isn't much of a crowd for breakfast— all the better for you, my dear. You may eat outside, even if you don't see other people outside. If you are indoors, certainly sit near the glass walls— you come here to watch the parade. Since most stores won't open until 10am, and some won't open until 11, you can still sit and sip, write postcards, read the news, and watch the world go by. This is what you came to Paris to do; take your time and enjoy.

When you're finished, head back toward the rue de Seine and catch the street market at the rue de Buci, if you didn't see it before. If you've already seen it, cut onto the rue Jacob, making sure not to miss the tiny place de Furstemberg, and walk the narrow streets, full of antiques shops, behind the church. Take the rue Jacob to the rue Bonaparte, and turn right. Shop, shop, shop.

Now, take the rue Bonaparte all the way back toward the church (this is all of 2 short blocks). Before you get to Deux Magots, hang a quick right onto a street that's only half a block long. Get a good hard look at the art nouveau tile-front cafe on the corner to your right, then turn left so you can shop at the retail store alongside the Café de Flore.

You have now come full circle and are on the boulevard St-Germain. Cross the street and head downtown toward the Musée d'Orsay. But don't go that far; you're stopping at **Sonia Rykiel** (no. 175). Just beyond here, turn left onto rue des Sts-Pères and begin to work the shoe stores. Segue from rue des Sts-Pères onto the rue Dragon, which hits it at an angle, and work your way through more boutiques. Take the rue Grenelle (more Sonia) when you reach it, and you'll eventually end up on the rue de Rennes.

Walk up one side of the rue de Rennes (toward the black office building you see in the background) and down the other side. Be sure to get as far as **Geneviève Lethu** (no. 95), and then head back toward St-Germain-des-Prés.

Back on the rue des Rennes, look for the left-hand fork once you reach rue du Four; you'll see **La Bagagerie** (no. 41) as you turn. Explore all the trendiness you can stand. Then, turn right onto rue Bonaparte—a street filled with the sights you came to Paris to enjoy. At the corner of rue du Vieux Colombier, you'll see the church of St-Sulpice. Turn left. There's a little store for religious articles, and **Georges Thuiller** (8–10 place St-Sulpice), and then you'll bump into a string of designer boutiques.

Leave place St-Sulpice via the rue St-Sulpice and pass a few wonderful shops and even the new branch of London's **Muji,** which sells minimalist chic.

Eventually, you'll come to the mall **Marché St-Germain** and rue de Tournon. There's a **Souleiado** shop here. Rue de Tournon becomes the rue de Seine on the other side of the street. Take the rue de Seine toward the Seine. It dead-ends at the quai Malaquais.

Hang a quick left for a block to reach the quai Voltaire and some fancy antiques shops you missed previously. Follow the quai uptown toward the Cathédrale de Notre-Dame. The antiques stores will peter out, but the stalls along the riverfront sell wonderful, touristy jumble—postcards (old and new), books, prints, and old magazines. Stop at a few, and don't forget to make a wish as you stare into the Seine.

TOUR 5: THESE FEET WERE MEANT FOR WALKING TOUR

This tour resembles the tours above, so it's best to read the others first. The advantage of this one is that it walks you across Paris quickly, covering only the best and the brightest shops. It's a very tony tour.

Begin at the duty-free shop **Catherine,** 7 rue Castiglione, in the 1st arrondissement. This shop is very tiny and gets crowded during the day, so get here first thing in the morning. Ask them to hold your purchases for you, since you have a big day ahead and don't want to schlep too many heavy bottles. If you've bought only a few small items, consider asking them to mail them to you in the United States—you'll get a bigger duty-free discount, and the postage may not be as expensive as you think.

From the rue Castiglione, walk toward the Tuileries (half a block) and hang a left to walk along the rue de Rivoli. This gives you ample opportunity to shop at every tourist trap in Paris. When you see the gold statue of Joan of Arc in the middle of the road, right before the Hôtel Regina, turn right and walk alongside the Musée du Louvre. Cross the river (on a bridge) and turn right onto rue du Bac. Welcome to a very fancy and private part of the Left Bank.

Prowl every inch of the rue du Bac, even though it twists and turns a little bit. You will pass the Hôtel Port-Royal, where the road curves a little, but don't let that throw you. The first blocks of rue du Bac are a tad slow, with just a few antiques shops and real-people places. By the time you hit the Port-Royal, things are sizzling. But before the sizzle, there are some quiet statements of style that shouldn't be overlooked, such as **Beauvais** (no. 14), one of the oldest engraving and print shops in Paris, and **Laure Japy** (no. 34), for stylish tabletop designs. Japy doesn't open until 10:30am, so take your time and don't rush to get here. At no. 38, you'll find **Myrène**

de Trémonville, a designer who sells hipper-than-thou clothing to Henri Bendel and Barney's in the U.S.

At no. 43, I have a specialized find that may not be for everyone. **Deyrolle** (upstairs) is where you go to buy dead stuffed chickens. Don't stand there snickering. They happen to be gorgeous and fabulous (and expensive) and very country French. And, no, I have no idea how to get yours home with you. At least you won't ruffle any feathers at U.S. Customs, since the animals are quite dead. Deyrolle does close for lunch, so don't spend too much time in the previous stores if you plan to stop here.

Very shortly, you will be at the crossroads of boulevard St-Germain. To your right, on the corner, is a leather shop that opened in 1815. Called **Atelier Schilz,** it's like Hermès without the hype. They sell a gorgeous handbag for 4,450 F, which isn't cheap, but does enable you to get a détaxe refund and is less than Hermès.

Cross St-Germain and continue along the rue du Bac. Note there is a métro stop (rue du Bac) here. But as you walked crosstown, you don't need it, do you? Smart you. At this junction, the street gets even better, so if you must modify this tour, you can start here (which, of course, means you can use the métro, if you wish).

Walk along rue du Bac, enjoying every minute of it. Note that a number of these shops close for lunch, so you may want to do the same. Otherwise, keep on prowling—check out **Etamine** (no. 63), a fabulous home decor shop, and **Olivier de Sercery** (no. 96), for engraved stationery. But my favorite of them all is **Irena Grégory** (no. 130). I love it for two reasons. One, it's a great shop with cutting-edge yet classic looks that make every woman look snappy. Second, their business cards are printed on condoms. You read that right. Clothes start at $200; condoms are free.

You are still walking on the rue du Bac and having the time of your life. If you need a spiritual moment, tuck into Chapelle Nôtre-Dame de la Medaille Miraculeuse, where you can buy medallions at the gift shop and say a prayer in the chapel. This is as magical as it sounds. *Very nice*

Once back on the street, you are half a block from the big department store, **Le Bon Marché.** You can spend the rest of the day at Bon Marché, shopping its boutiques, eating lunch at **Le Grand Epicerie,** and checking out the antiques market upstairs. Just be sure to keep up your strength because you must, *must* make time afterward to hit the rue St-Placide. It's across the street from Bon Marché and to your left 1 block.

St-Placide is only a block long (for you, anyway), but it houses several discount designer shops where you may snap up a big-name designer garment for a few hundred francs. Because the rue St-Placide is very dumpy and can be depressing, you'll need a pick-me-up once you're finished. Walk 1 block along the rue de Sèvres right into the lobby of the **Hôtel Lutétia** and plop yourself down in the art deco lobby for a glass of champagne. Then you can face the métro ride back to your hotel. You're staying at the Lutétia? Clever you. *great neighborhood*

Size Conversion Chart

. . . .

Women's Clothing

Local 95 Bra Size —

American	8	10	12	14	16	18
Continental	38	40	42	44	46	48
British	10	12	14	16	18	20

Women's Shoes

American	5	6	7	8	9	10
Continental	36	37	38	39	40	41
British	4	5	6	7	8	9

Children's Clothing

American	3	4	5	6	6X
Continental	98	104	110	116	122
British	18	20	22	24	26

Children's Shoes

American	8	9	10	11	12	13	1	2	3
Continental	24	25	27	28	29	30	32	33	34
British	7	8	9	10	11	12	13	1	2

Men's Suits

American	34	36	38	40	42	44	46	48
Continental	44	46	48	50	52	54	56	58
British	34	36	38	40	42	44	46	48

Men's Shirts

American	$14\frac{1}{2}$	15	$15\frac{1}{2}$	16	$16\frac{1}{2}$	17	$17\frac{1}{2}$	18
Continental	37	38	39	41	42	43	44	45
British	$14\frac{1}{2}$	15	$15\frac{1}{2}$	16	$16\frac{1}{2}$	17	$17\frac{1}{2}$	18

Men's Shoes

American	7	8	9	10	11	12	13
Continental	$39\frac{1}{2}$	41	42	43	$44\frac{1}{2}$	46	47
British	6	7	8	9	10	11	12

INDEX

289